LAST STANDS

D1069339

"IN HIS 'notes from memory,' pieced together brilliantly in the patchwork manner of the mind, Hilary Masters has given new life to the dead, and has illuminated much about American life and the nature of memory. Masters portrays his father's foibles even-handedly, and his mother's tough, unifying spirit. The characters are portrayed with love by a man who does not need to judge them. His wisdom is pervasive."—*Seattle Times*

"HILARY MASTERS makes judgments—not as a disillusioned son of great heritage with an ax to grind, but as a poet himself trying to love a big, sad world, knowing the past is a mirror before which we are required to stand."—*Chicago Tribune*

"THE PORTRAITS are at once funny and sad—elegiac—but they are portraits in the round, of people understood and accepted, and there is even, in their strong individuality, a touch of universality. A model demonstration of the uses of memory."—*The New Yorker*

"AS IF TO EMPHASIZE this alloy of past and present, Hilary Masters has built his book so that both are intricately intertwined. An immensely artful book. The care its author has taken with his arrangements ensures the illusions of truth."—*Newsweek*

"THIS MEMOIR, free of adulation or bitterness, should be read not merely for the events it records—events such as any family knows—but for what the author has so inventively made of the slippery realm of memory."—*Village Voice*

"A MOVING, inclusive book [that ends] near the point at which it opened: the end that is the beginning of memory."—*Time*

"DEMONSTRATES THE IDEA that we are the product of all we have experienced, whether it happened yesterday or 50 years ago. Masters creates a temporarily random tapestry out of what has gone before. A lovely tapestry it is, its elements of sadness mingling with memories of the good times. *Last Stands* also illuminates how families somehow survive. For that reason, it is a book from which we can all take heart, even as we warm to the grace of its language."—*Kansas City Star*

"MASTERS HAS USED his novelist's care and skill in fashioning from all the memories a cohesive and fascinating narrative pastiche whose effect and shimmering quality entrances and lingers. His father might well have been proud of him."—*Chicago Sun Times*

"A LOVELY WORK. A quiet, evocative memoir that cuts back and forth through time, revealing the complexities and ambiguities of one family's life."—*Publishers Weekly*

"A BOOK TO BE SAVORED for its anecdotal richness, for its memory technique of crossing and crisscrossing lines of thought, for its nostalgic value in showing an America which no longer quite exists."—*Smithsonian*

"AN AFFECTING and exquisitely drawn family portrait. Masters ranges far beyond his childhood years, lyrically evoking—from a mix of memories, letters, and imagination—a hundred years of family history and Americana."—*Library Journal*

"A POETIC STUDY of the American character, encompassing the spirit of Tom Pendergast's Kansas City, a literary time in New York City, iron stubbornness forged on the Western frontier, and bucolic prairie life in central Illinois."—*Milwaukee Journal*

"LAST STANDS deserves your attention and will repay uncasual reading with many cherishable effects: the most subtle and craftily oiled shifts in time-levels outside Proust, Robbe-Grillet, Garcia Marquez, Vonnegut and Pynchon. A book of many layers, many tones."—*Cleveland Plain Dealer*

"MASTERS RECALLS these people with affection and respect. He makes a serious attempt to understand their sometimes baffling rows and reconciliations, and appreciates their comic misadventures and his own juvenile blunderings. He also writes very well indeed. An exceptionally fine memoir."—*Atlantic Monthly*

OTHER BOOKS BY HILARY MASTERS

Novels

The Harlem Valley Trio
Clemmons
Cooper
Strickland

Home Is the Exile

Manuscript for Murder

Palace of Strangers

An American Marriage

The Common Pasture

Short Fiction

Success

Hammertown Tales

Essays

In Montaigne's Tower

HILARY MASTERS

LAST STANDS

NOTES FROM MEMORY

New Introduction by Phillip Lopate

New Afterword by the Author

SOUTHERN METHODIST UNIVERSITY PRESS
DALLAS

LINDENHURST MEMORIAL LIBRARY
LINDENHURST, NEW YORK 11757

Copyright © 1982 by Hilary Masters
Introduction copyright © 2004 by Southern Methodist University Press
Afterword copyright © 2004 by Hilary Masters
First Southern Methodist University Press edition, 2004
All rights reserved

Requests for permission to reproduce material from this work should be sent to:
Rights and Permissions
Southern Methodist University Press
PO Box 750415
Dallas, Texas 75275-0415

Cover Design: David Timmons
Cover photo: Hilary Masters with a Crow Indian at the site of Custer's Last Stand.
Courtesy of the author.

Library of Congress Cataloging-in-Publication Data
Masters, Hilary.
Last stands : notes from memory / Hilary Masters ; new introduction by Phillip
Lopate ; new afterword by the author.—Southern Methodist University Press ed.
    p. cm.
ISBN 0-87074-492-5
1. Masters, Hilary. 2. Masters, Hilary—Childhood and youth. 3. Authors,
American—20th century—Family relationships. 4. Authors, American—20th
century—Biography. 5. Masters, Edgar Lee, 1868–1950—Family. 6. Fathers and
sons—United States. I. Title.

PS3563.A82Z47 2004
813'.54—dc22
[B]   2004053639

Reprinted from the 1982 edition published by David R. Godine, Publisher, Inc.

Printed in the United States of America on acid-free paper

10   9   8   7   6   5   4   3   2   1

FOR MY CHILDREN,

JOELLEN CATHERINE JOHN

———————

*I want to express my gratitude to
Drake University, Des Moines, Iowa, and to
Clark University, Worcester, Massachusetts,
for the shelter and sustenance
those excellent institutions gave me
as this book was written.*

Introduction

Memoir, as we have come to appreciate during its recent craze and subsequent backlash, is a very tricky form. The unreliability of memory, the plethora of potential detail, the temptations toward narcissism and self-righteous score-settling, the complicated double-perspective maneuverings between the I-character's callow, past consciousness and the understanding the author now possesses, the literary expectations of frank honesty served up in a sparkling prose style, all conspire against getting it right. To encounter a memoir that still holds up brilliantly, still satisfies utterly, more than twenty years after it first appeared, seems something of a miracle. Such a work is Hilary Masters's *Last Stands.* I doubt there has been a better-written memoir, page for page, in the past twenty years.

When first published in 1982, it received enthusiastic reviews, enjoyed decent sales, and then, in the manner of most books, good or bad, went out of print. Yet over the years it continued to generate an almost cultish word-of-mouth: writers would press it on each other with the recommendation, "This one is really good" or "This one I know you'll like." The literary grapevine kept it alive as a rumor of memoir excellence. Now that it has returned to print once again, we can see what it truly is, or rather has stealthily, imperturbably become, through the settlings of time and fashion: a classic American autobiography.

Let me put the stress on *American* for a moment: this family chronicle of three generations spans our national history, from Hilary's grandfather's tales about fighting the Indian Wars to his grandmother's involvement in the Pendergast Democratic machine in Kansas City, from his father's awestruck visits to the Chicago World's Fair to his mother's maneuverings to get seats on a train packed with soldiers in World War II. Masters has also pulled off a complicated chronological structure that darts from decade to decade, but with such clarity that the reader never gets lost. The advantage of this fluid, circular structure is that it invites an awareness of family patterns across generations and allows for reconsiderations on the author's part of his initial perceptions, while doing justice to all four of Masters's guardians—his grandparents and his parents, who took turns raising him.

The author's famous father, the poet Edgar Lee Masters, might be expected to draw readers' interest initially, but however much his shadow might hover over these pages, he is not allowed to dominate his son's memoir—especially since he was often absent and, even when present, absent-minded. Indeed, Edgar's writerly self-absorption is seen as setting in motion the complicated custody of young Hilary:

It had been fifteen years and many books since *Spoon River Anthology,* and perhaps he was beginning to wonder if his creative powers had all been expended in that one book, or if the collection of epitaphs had been a one-shot, lucky hit, as some critics and a few poets had begun to suggest. I can imagine him taking an oath to give himself, at sixty, five or ten years in which he would work very hard to prove them wrong, to prove himself once again. Thus a plan was devised. My mother's parents would keep me in Kansas City during the school year, and in the summer I would come East to join my parents. The arrangement gave me the best of two different worlds, for a time; no one told me it was unusual.

Characteristically, the narrator neither complains nor expresses resentment, in the current victimized-memoirist fashion, at what amounted to being abandoned by his parents. Hilary describes his upbringing under the care of these doting grandparents as fairly happy, with Mark Twain-like strands of a normal American midwestern boyhood for that era, balanced by exciting summer visits to his bohemian parents in the East. It is only gradually that the idyllic note darkens, the plan falls apart, and young Hilary begins to question, with a tone of mild remonstrance, his mother's complicity in sidestepping the maternal role:

"Come and get your kid, is what he wrote me," my mother will say when we discuss this time of our lives. Her tone is accusatory and meant to make me an ally in an old contest. "Come and get your kid," she repeats, mimicking his harsh rhythm. But, in truth, when my grandfather sold the house on Roberts Street and moved to the large, rambling place on Troost, I was fourteen years of age, he was eighty-two, and my grandmother, disabled and destroyed, only ten years younger. Perhaps it was time for me to be got.

Hilary's mother, Ellen, is in many ways the dynamic force in this memoir: an attractive, restless, resourceful, ambitious woman, she seems forever split between her dreams of work or self-actualization and her sense of duty toward husband, parents, and only child. Ellen also has an unforgiving side and fingers her collection of grievances, as do all four of them in their way: Edgar's age-old gripes are described as "an amphora of sour wine," the grandfather cannot accept his daughter's intellectual ambitions as anything but silly and "schoolmarm," the grandmother sulks in "prima donna" silence, convinced that she married beneath herself. The Coynes and the Masterses would have fit right into O'Neill's *Long Day's Journey into Night,* displaying a genius for brooding grudges.

It is Hilary's job to take it all in, to see each one's point of view— and to forgive. He is the go-between, or, as he himself puts it, "So I was the thin wire through which my grandparents and my father and mother were able to talk to each other, like a country party line. . . ." In the process, Masters holds back his protagonist-self from being a main actor, keeps him almost a minor character in his own memoir. (Natalia Ginzburg employed a similar strategy in her *Family Sayings*.) This restraint is not just a way of avoiding egotism; it is a by-product of the effort to distribute his compassion evenly among the four sacred monsters who impressed their powerful natures on his character. This moral discipline of empathy, this evenhanded compassion, which yet does not flinch from recording truthfully the flaws of his family members and himself, is the moral triumph of the book.

For example, consider one of the most compelling episodes: Ellen is trying to get Edgar and Hilary on the train so that she can resettle the three of them in North Carolina, where she has found a teaching position for herself. Edgar begins to dig in his heels in the Pennsylvania Station waiting room, not wanting to leave his beloved New York City; nor does he relish the shame of being financially dependent on his wife. One can see both of their points of view. Meanwhile, young Hilary is buckling under the weight of his father's aged, debilitated body and dying of embarrassment. Ellen begins yelling at her husband: "You foolish, silly man! What do you mean, you won't go?" Edgar quickly gets up and moves toward the train. Masters observes with equanimity: "Her public outburst had been guaranteed to stimulate this response, sting that part of his nature that always hoped to avoid a public scene whatever the cost. She was from a different background where there was no such false decorum, no holding back." The poet's futile insistence that he was not going to leave the station is one of those "last stands" referred to in the book's title. Another is the soldier-grandfather's decision to take his own life rather than dwindle away. The memoir's circular structure reinforces a dirgelike revisiting of losses. Funerals play a big part in the memoir's arrangement, as rest stops in the narrative, places to take stock. In his boyhood, Masters notes, he was already a connoisseur of funeral services and their amenities, their cakes and flower arrangements, the brevity or long-windedness of the priests. As an adult, he comes to see the real source of his family's grievance: their inability to find "some cure for the terminal condition of life."

This book's enduring achievement resides on a double triumph: the first, as I have already mentioned, is moral, its compassionate psychological grasp; the second is literary, stylistic. These two are naturally intertwined. Sentence by sentence, Masters's informally elegant prose, with its worldly, ironic perspective, allows us to view with sympathy and humor the follies, betrayals, and self-betrayals of those he describes, including himself.

Every page brings its own wonderfully succinct metaphors and epigrams, such as "the bony turnstile of my grandmother's embrace." Masters's earlier training as a novelist shows in the deft way he tucks reflections into a dialogue tag or salts away insights in passing. For all his temporal meanderings, the author keeps a firm hand on the narrative rudder and steers via nervous, quickening tensions. Nor is the narrative allowed to bog down in summary: the basic progression is from one vivid scene to the next. Novelistic, too, is the way the main characters are delineated, with their full idiosyncrasies and fixed ideas.

If Hilary's mother, Ellen, is the dynamo who sets the others in motion, it is finally the celebrated poet-father who inspires his most complex portraiture. Whatever resentment Hilary may have felt from having to go through life as the author-son of a famous writer, he waited until he was in his midforties to undertake this memoir, and the payoffs in wisdom and perspective are palpable. This is no Pappy Dearest. If anything, it seems at times a heartbreaking tale of thwarted love between father and son. "I was an easy prey to his embrace, and suffered the scrape of his grizzled cheek as he kissed me," he writes. E. L. M., for his part, having given away his boy to his wife's parents' care, keeps second-guessing his decision. In one of the most poignant passages in the book, Masters quotes a letter his father sent him, saying: "Perhaps, and this hurts, I should have given up writing, and devoted my time to you. That might have been a contribution to America better than I have made by isolating myself to do it. Who knows?" One summer, when the poet looked forward to his son's company, the grandparents asserted their rights, and Hilary's mother decided to side with her father over her husband. By the time Ellen could connive, years later, to have them living all under the same roof, it was too late for easy communication: she had "put my father and me together in a way that was new to us, a day-to-day relationship that was strange to us; our syllabus of conversations only covered short courses, not an extended conversation."

For all his affection, Masters refuses to sentimentalize his father or cushion the truth about his vanity and other weaknesses, including a bit of anti-Semitic raving that shows the old man was not immune from the ugly prejudices of his day. In many ways, the lawyer-turned-poet remained a provincial autodidact who could not rise above his narrow intellectual beginnings. Masters is also too honest to argue for the later writings by his father. He pronounces most of them "unreadable" and characterizes the long narrative poems as "studded with the facts and dates from his prodigious reading so that the poems resembled barn sidings in the Harlem Valley, unpainted and toasted by the sun and marked randomly by the nail heads that had once fastened tarpaper to their bleached sides."

There is a special pang in this portrait of the aged writer who has outlived his talent or contemporary relevance, continuing to toil out of some wild hope that he may yet burst into poetic flame again and avenge himself on all those who had put him on the shelf. "He worked so hard," says his wife. The cruel truth, we realize, is that endless toil is necessary but not sufficient for literary greatness. Yet when he sends his son a poem, "About Hilary," it shocks us with its redemptive, noble sincerity. Edgar's literary gift, like his paternal love for his son, was intermittent but undeniable. It is Hilary Masters's special gift to be able to render in tough, delicate, precise prose all the intermittent shadings of human connection, all the mysterious ambivalence and warmth of family ties.

PHILLIP LOPATE
2004

LAST STANDS

1

We follow the flag-covered casket. The honor guard steps before us in cadence, as the wheels of the wagon spin the light, and the red, white, and blue colors of the flag charge the quiet morning. The undertaker and his assistant walk through the grave plots beside the drive, out of step and detached though yet a part of the event like villagers who follow the route of a parade. It is already warm. I can feel the perspiration on my mother's arm as we walk together; already, heat currents rise from the Potomac River to distort the classic lines of the Lincoln Memorial. The geometric panorama of Washington wavers like a quilt on a laundry line. It is June, 1954.

'It has a splendid view of the city,' my grandfather told me about a year before. 'And it's right by a tree so they can't plant anyone beside me.' He had slapped his leg with one hand; it was the sound of a dry leaf scraping pavement.

'You have a long time to worry about such things,' I replied. We sat on a bench on the grounds of the Soldiers Home in Washington. Lincoln had lived in the small house behind us when Lee and Jackson had threatened the Capitol after the second battle at Bull Run.

'Why, boy, I'm ninety-four years old. Do you know how old that is?' he asked me. His eyes were clear, cornflower blue, and his hands were steady. 'I wake up every morning and say to myself, "Today might be the day." But it doesn't happen. It doesn't happen.' He shook his head in wonder and leaned over to spit carefully between his feet. Then, with the same precision, he crossed his legs, one hand wedged between the thighs.

'Don't talk like that,' I said.

'Why, hell's fire,' he continued. 'What am I supposed to do anyway? I've read all the Zane Grey they have in this place three or four times.' He laughed, head tilted back on a thin, brittle neck. Some younger residents of the Home, perhaps World War I veterans, played golf on the greens below us. 'Look at them,' my grandfather said scornfully, though it was not clear whether his attitude was directed toward the players, their game, or their war.

How like an old cavalryman to talk of the view of the city, though it would be a prospect from his own gravesite. Scott's view of Mexico City. Napoleon outside Moscow. Sherman before Atlanta and Grant surveying Richmond. These were tableaux put into my imagination by the bedtime stories my grandfather had told me in Kansas City. In my mind, I could see all those conquerors stand in their stirrups, give a ghostly command, and the great host of their combined armies would suddenly rise from their saddles to look upon the city that was about to be taken.

In my grandfather's case, the view had been of Indian villages in Montana and Wyoming in the 1880s, and most of his duties with the cavalry were to maintain order in Yellowstone Park, under the jurisdiction of the army, by order of President Grant. Rustlers and stage robbers had been the objects of his patrols and not the pitiful remnants of the Sioux and Cheyenne. But the views were still important: the views of Jackson's Hole and the Tetons, or of the old Indian camps. Or the view of the Little Big Horn, where he and some of his platoon would ride from Fort Custer to pick over the site, for holiday and to bury pieces of bone and harness and indulge in the traditional recreation of soldiers visiting an old battlefield: to refight the engagement and win the day.

[4]

When he picked this site in Arlington, he must have stood where this fresh earth has been turned back—perhaps leaned against the small locust that grows nearby and looked across the river at the Capitol. A city, a land to be taken.

THOMAS F

COYNE

Pennsylvania

Sgt

Trp M 1 Regt Cav

July 4 1860

June 6 1954

Pennsylvania, not Ireland. Perhaps the army accepted no immigrants into its ranks in those days and so he put down *Pennsylvania* on his enlistment papers. More likely, there had been a space on those forms for 'last permanent address' and the young man who had somehow found his way to San Francisco from the steel mills in Pittsburgh had put down Pennsylvania. The address followed him through all his transient life—not Galway, not Ireland—to be recorded finally on this stone tablet set into this Virginia hillside.

'We'd ride the horses right into the sea to calm and cool them.' His back room on the second floor of the house in Kansas City was a cozy crucible of aromas and far from the Presidio in San Francisco in more ways than one. Patent medicines, balms, ointments, and surgical dressings were ranked on the bureau top in the order of their application. The smells of camphor, wintergreen, witch hazel, and quinine predominated.

'Why'd you do that, Gee Gee?' The name was pronounced with a hard *g* and no one could remember how I came by it. 'How come you rode the horses into the ocean?' I toyed with the heavy Colt .44 revolver as I sat beside him on the bed.

'As I said, to calm them down.' Like an aged, wounded gladiator, he bent over one upraised leg, a large bandage roll in one hand. He had just trimmed his toenails, an operation as precise as it was delicately performed—the small finger of the hand with the scissors raised like a guidon. 'We would exercise them there on the beach, put them through their drill, and then wheel right and charge the breakers, the surf. It gave them courage, prepared them for battle.' Carefully, he wrapped the leg from foot to mid-calf with the long bandage. The entire limb had already been prepared with a coating of analgesic balm.

'Did'ja ever shoot any Indians with this, Gee Gee?' I asked, lifting the heavy pistol with both hands. I knew the answer but it was part of the evening ritual. It came with the leg wrappings, the eye washes and chest plasters.

'No Indians,' he replied, neatly securing the wrapping on one leg and then starting on the other. 'But many another poor sonuvabitch. Did I ever tell you of the time I had to go into Jackson's Hole after two desperadoes who had held up the Cheyenne stage?' He had but it didn't matter. 'Me and Jim Reilly, sergeants both, we were the only ones that would go into Jackson's Hole in those days. Two crazy galoots, I tell you. It was October, I remember.' The familiar details unrolled as he wound the bandage around his leg. It looked like a puttee. His voice carried softly on a dry lilt.

He and his companion had captured the two men and started back to the fort. The territory was wild and the temper of the Indians uncertain, so the prisoners had been put on their honor and left unshackled. 'Oh, it was cold,' he continued, neatly folding the dressing into a right angle at the heel and starting the smooth spiral up the calf of the left. 'It was December by now, almost Christmas I recall. We ate the elk meat these bandits had been selling. *Tom, Tom,* I heard her clearly calling my name. *Tom, get up. It's time to get up for school.* It was my mother's voice calling me. So, I woke up. I had fallen asleep by the fire, Reilly and me were taking turns keeping guard, and here was this *perdido* coming at me with a knife the size of a butcher's —he must have stashed it in his boot.'

'Whad'ja do then?' I asked, holding my breath. I knew the answer.

'Why, I pulled that revolver that you got there and shot the sonuvabitch right through the heart.' The evening mummification of his legs completed, he pulled the legs of the long underwear he wore, winter and summer, down over the wrappings. He took great care of his extremities. The hands were lotioned, the nails checked and trimmed; ears were swabbed with cottonseed probes soaked in alcohol, and the hairs in the nostrils cut back. The vein across the bridge of the nose was smoothed with a bit of petroleum jelly; then the whole head was held under a heavy towel tented over the bathroom washbasin where a pool of water only a few degrees below boiling point had been waiting. Snorts and bellows sounded beneath the towel, after which the steamed face was rinsed in ice water, prepared in a tin pan set upon the window ledge. 'Learned that from the Blackfoot,' he gasped.

But it was the feet that received the most thorough attention. Every night they were soaked, washed, scrubbed, and bathed in different salts, anointed with various unguents, trimmed and polished; inspected and finally wrapped in linen bandages to preserve and protect them against whatever diseases might be so foolish as to attack during the night. It must have been part of the old army concern, a ritual that had practical origins, for a cavalryman understood that if his horse gave out, his feet would have to be in good shape.

'That harms the hammer,' he told me. I had cocked the revolver and pulled the trigger with the gun pointed out the back window of his room. It was pointed toward Kansas, the same direction he always fired the weapon every New Year's Eve, emptying the whole cylinder of bullets thunderously and high into the night air while he stood by the back door. *Snack!* The sound of the firing mechanism was splendid and precise.

'Jesus H. Christ!' His curse accompanied a rip and tear. He had just pulled the large adhesive plaster off of his left side. It was his protection against pleurisy, and apparently needed to be redeployed against the ailment's encirclement. The top part of his underwear had been unbuttoned and pulled halfway down, off his shoulders. It was the only part of his body, excepting his feet and legs, that I was ever to see bare.

Now that the defense of the chest cavity had been made, there might be time for some manual of arms with the saber. The long curved sword in its metal scabbard leaned in a corner of his bedroom closet. In another corner was the straight machete he had brought back from Cuba with its curious message inscribed in Spanish. On the shelf above, in an old Knox hat box, the Colt revolver was kept fully loaded. The saber came out of the scabbard with the dry scrape of metal on metal.

'Here's the position for "parade rest." ' The trim figure in gray underwear became taut, a look of command ignited the blue eyes. 'PA-a-rade . . . REST.' The sword flashed in the bedroom, snapped smartly and suddenly to the correct angle by the right leg. 'Now then, Hilary, you want to watch carefully for the salute. The sword is not to lay against the shoulder—you're not hefting a sack of potatoes. It's here in the hand, where you grip it, there's the control to it—not on the shoulder. Now watch. Pre—senUNT . . . h'ARMS!'

The brass basket guard whipped before his face, and the long naked blade pointed to the ceiling in an unwavering perpendicular. It could have punctured the roof of the house and did so sometimes, in my imagination, going through with the sound of a penknife poking through a matchbox. From behind the handle, the blue eyes stared straight ahead with a disciplined focus that approached the look of the blind; that is, it had a far-sightedness that seemed to burn through the dun-colored wallpaper of his room, through the night air and across the state of Kansas to look upon some distant parade ground.

'Or—DER . . . h'ARMS!' The commands were feathery, light whiskers of the full-broomed authority that must have swept across Fort Custer and Fort Yellowstone. Some years later, I was

to listen to old soldiers, a few of them generals who would pre-
cede my grandfather to this hillside in Arlington, hear them
speak of the Sgt. Tom Coyne who had guided them through the
rigors and routines of soldiering on the frontier when they had
been young officers fresh from West Point. They still spoke of
him, nearly fifty years later, with awe, and a little fear maybe;
not that his exploits were very extraordinary—though he apparently had a reputation for riding horses into the ground—
but because of the startling, unexplained fierceness that could fire
his manner. He was neither large nor physically very strong,
but there was something about his posture, his swagger, thrust
of chin, and a frost on the cornflower eyes that suggested he
would be willing to go to the end, to the death, over the smallest
point, even the slightest difference of opinion. The most formidable opponent, especially one with reason, would usually back
down.

'Pa—ah—RADE . . . REST!'

The use of the sword on horseback, particularly how to parry
pike thrusts, usually came next. The right arm sweeps back,
swinging from the shoulder, so that the saber knocks aside the
spear pointed up from below; then, the sword whips up in a
gleaming arc over the horseman to slice point first through the
head and body of the hapless footsoldier. The height of the
ceiling, the room's furnishings, prohibited the use of the saber
in this free-wheeling exercise, so a long pair of barber's shears,
lately employed to trim hairs within the nostrils, was substi-
tuted.

'Hu . . . ZAH!' my grandfather would cry as the scissors
flashed down and his eyes aimed along the length of their blades.
I could see the luckless pikeman split apart like an apple.

'But what if he ran, Gee Gee?'

'What? What? What if who ran?'

'The man on foot. The man with the spear. Why would he
just stand there and let himself be stabbed? Why wouldn't he
run?'

'Run?' His cheeks puffed out, filled with the incredibility of the idea. 'Run? Why, he's to stand there, in place,' he commands. 'He's to stand there like a soldier. He's supposed to . . . shush . . . shush . . . quick, quick—' He gestures for me to give him the pistol and he throws it under the quilt. There are steps coming up the stairs.

The sudden contrast of my grandmother's appearance, even as she came into the room with milk and cookies, like a healing figure moving over a field where armies had only just clashed, was never to become familiar to me, remains unresolved: to see them together was to view the enigma of their marriage.

'The boy should be in bed, Tom,' she admonished with her mellow voice. 'The boy has school tomorrow and must not be kept awake with your wild stories of derring-do.' A flicker of anxiety in her voice, perhaps—she had been entrusted with my care and health since I was a year old. 'I'm the one who must wake to calm his nightmares.'

'Yes, yes. All right. He'll be along.' My grandfather sheathes the saber and returns it to the closet. My grandmother is taller and heavier than he and far more impressive-looking, particularly with him standing there only in his long underwear and smelling of various liniments. However, she was not overweight, but carried on her tall frame a well-fleshed fullness that perfectly fitted the corsets and all the other elaborate paraphernalia of that day. Her large brown eyes seemed to turn upon me, to bathe me in affection and amazement, far different from the twin jets of ice that directed my grandfather's vision. If the same elements had ever existed within Tom Coyne's wiry framework, they had been burned to ash long ago by his furious spirit. 'Yes, he'll be along,' he repeated.

She took the cookies and milk into the bedroom that we shared until I started high school. My grandfather came toward the bed, rattling in his closed fist the handful of brass cartridges he had shaken from the pistol earlier. He reloaded the weapon. The bullets slipped into the cylinder like thumbs into a machined fist, the port was closed, then he lifted the revolver back up into the hat box.

'Good-night, Gee Gee.' I tried to kiss him.

'Get on with you,' he said.

*   *   *

My view of Kansas City was initially proscribed by the house on Roberts Street that my grandfather had built. My mother was born in it, in the bedroom that I shared with my grandmother. It was not a large house, but it was solidly put together of stone, cement, and stucco, and demonstrated my grandfather's empirical successes in heavy construction as well as his conceptual deficiencies. He had supervised its reconstruction on one of his trips home from Central America where he had been building railroads. He claimed to have built the first rail link to the middle continent and he may well have had some hand in its construction, for he studied civil engineering while in the army, by correspondence school, as part of his attempt to enter West Point.

Underneath the dining room were oversized keystones bolted to the house's framework, no doubt similar in size to those that strengthened train trestles across Andean gorges. The walls were a couple of feet thick, helping to insulate the interior; they could also have guaranteed some defense against the heaviest artillery. At the same time, though, a large plate-glass window breached the front room wall that faced the street, and a similar cut-glass panel in the front door; all this long before the picture window concept, for my grandfather read almost continuously and good light was required. Imbedded in the heavy walls of plaster and stone were heavy-gauge wire and the copper pipes of a model plumbing system; a furnace roared in the basement winter and summer to fire a boiler salvaged from one of Kansas City's old hotels. As a victim of both malaria and yellow fever, Gee Gee only felt comfortable in near-tropical conditions and the water for his facials and other nightly ablutions had to be the correct temperature, a few points below boiling.

This passion for modernity was selective. We never had a telephone until my mother, home on a visit, met him eye to eye, her green ones as cool as his of blue, and forced him to install an instrument. 'What do you want us to do?' I remember her saying. 'Stand on the roof with signal flags?' However, the phone was removed a few years later, when she began to spend most of her time in New York City.

My grandmother used an old-fashioned icebox (ice delivered on Tuesdays, Thursdays, and Saturdays by Mr. Paloucci) long after friends and relatives had traded in their original refrigerators, the ones with the round coil on top, for the newer, streamlined models. Once again, my mother was the agent of change: during a trip to bring me to New York City for the summer with her and my father, she forced my grandmother to go to Montgomery Ward's one afternoon and buy an electric model. My grandmother did, not without some apprehension of my grandfather's reaction nor a little regret. 'But,' she told my mother, 'I like Mr. Paloucci. I will miss talking to him.'

Electric light bulbs might be an improvement over candles and lamps and the merits of indoor plumbing over trench latrines had been proved, but my grandfather never approved the exchange of a perfectly useful icebox for the refrigerator; as for messages—'We have the finest postal system in the world,' he would say. And if they were so important they could not wait delivery by mail, they could be taken on foot.

The Moynihans, his future bride's family, must have been as unprepared for Tom Coyne when he arrived in Kansas City in 1885 as the world had been. It was eleven years after he had sailed from Ireland, five of those years spent with the cavalry in the West. He would have been twenty-five years of age.

'How did you get to San Francisco, Gee Gee?' I asked one night. After years of bedtime stories, I had become aware of a large gap in the narrative between the time he left Ireland at the age of fourteen, with his brothers and one sister, and when he en-

listed in the army in California. These six years were blank
pages in his informal memoirs.

'I worked in the steel mills in Pittsburgh, Pennsylvania,'
he told me as he trimmed the toenails of one foot. 'I was not
much older than you are.'

'But how did you get across the country then? How did you
get to California from Pennsylvania?' Saturday afternoon movies
at the Chief Theatre had depicted such journeys in covered
wagons guided by Richard Dix or Randolph Scott.

'I took a train,' my grandfather said. Snip went the scissors
and the hazard was removed. It was all he ever said of this empty
parcel of his life.

*　　　*　　　*

'Pre . . . sunt . . . h'arms!'

The young soldiers who compose the honor guard are veterans of the Korean War and their pressed tunics show many
colorful decorations. To bury old soldiers like my grandfather
is cushy duty awarded such valor.

> *Sisters Residence*
> *U.S. Soldiers Home Hospital*
> *Washington 13, D.C.*
> *4–1–53*

Dear Hilary

   I am still alive & thats about all I am not able to get around any
more my legs are getting weary bad heart I dont know what to
say to you

   Good by be a good boy

>   *Gee Gee*

He wrote this letter a year before his death, but it did not
alarm me since the members of my family were always making
such farewells—it's a minor art developed by the Irish. So, when
the call came, I was taken by surprise.

'It doesn't matter,' my mother whispers to me. We are in the small chapel set up in the basement of one of the large hospital buildings. A priest had darted out from the vestry to run through the mass, assisted by a couple of shaky veterans of the siege of Santiago. The chaplain performs like a one-man band, touching all the points of bell, book, and candle as his brown shoes squeak beneath his rumpled cassock. I am incensed.

'But he didn't believe in any of this stuff. He hated the Church, would have nothing to do with it.'

'It doesn't matter,' my mother whispers back. She's raised one hand, a tired gesture—tired of answering gratuitous arguments. 'It doesn't matter to him. What matters is that he gets buried in Arlington. When I got here, they were questioning that because of what he did. So, we do it this way. It's a short-cut.'

'FIRE!' The volley seems puny and I wonder if the six rifles are loaded with reduced charges, perhaps some economy measure enforced by the government. Another shortcut like the one between Pennsylvania and California.

There was a shortcut also between my grandparents' house on Roberts Street and Independence Avenue. It went through several backyards and finally ran beside Perky Brothers Storage. There it traversed the top of a narrow cement wall that enclosed the warehouse's loading area, a wall about fourteen feet high above the paved floor below. This path was about nine inches wide and bordered the lawn of the house next door to Perky's, but make a false step one way and you would fall into the concrete canyon, a drop as high as the Hoover Dam, it seemed.

None of us who used the shortcut would ever step onto the lawn. It was our unsworn but no less solemn article of faith that the crossing must be step by step along the nine-inch-wide cement ribbon. Not even at night, on the way home from the Chief Theatre, would foot be set upon the adjoining lawn. Not even when alone. It was a test of purity. Of valor.

'READY . . . h'ARMS . . .'

It is the summer of 1942; I am fourteen. My mother sends me to the corner to catch a taxi and I take the shortcut for the last time. We cannot call a taxi since Gee Gee had had the phone removed many years back and besides, we can't even get inside the house on Roberts Street now—this house where my mother was born and where I had grown up—because my grandfather had already rented it out. The tenants refused to let us come inside so we stood on the cement porch in the heavy heat of summer, my mother arguing with the people inside, through the screen door. My grandparents had moved to a large, rambling place on Troost Avenue, a house with alcoves and long, dark hallways and many rooms, which my grandfather intended to rent. It was to be the last rickety outpost in a wilderness that finally overcame him.

This move also signaled the end of my residency with my grandparents, so my mother had come to retrieve me. Before our train left from Union Station, she had decided to make a last desperate salvage of Roberts Street in hopes of finding something Gee Gee may not have thrown on the bonfire he had kept burning in the backyard for several days. It had been his own scorched-earth tactic and it had consumed everything: letters, pictures, my mother's diploma from the University of Chicago, plans for railroad trestles, mountain cuts. The saber and Colt were disposed of some other way.

'Run to the corner and get a cab.' My mother's eyes flashed like the green jewels of a deity being handled by tourists. The tenants even claimed anything left behind to be theirs now. I could look through the screen door and see rooms where I had moved and played all my life. The black and white Navajo rug was still on the living room floor. 'Go, quickly.'

I run up the block, cut through the baseball lot, slip beside a garage and step carefully onto the corner of the Perky Brothers warehouse wall. One, two, three steps. Another and I'm far out on the lip of the concrete ravine, too far to turn back casually without looking like a coward. The young man is standing, waiting for me, halfway across the narrow strip. Some of my playmates—we had grown up together—stood around on the adjoining driveway of the house next door, sheep-killing grins on their faces. They had warned me earlier in the day, when my mother and I had arrived on Roberts Street, that he was looking for me, and now their sidewise looks suggest they had told him that I was back in the neighborhood as well. They look at the ground, kick their toes, and wait for the slaughter they have arranged.

It is my last day in Kansas City, I say to myself. My last day. If I can just get past him—he seems to grow older and bigger by the minute—and up to the corner and the taxi stand at Jim's Hamburgers, I shall be away from him and Kansas City for good. Safe. To the left, the windowless, brick facade of Perky Brothers warehouse rises like an ancient fortress surrounded by a deep concrete moat. He must sense my desperate stratagem, for his expression undergoes a frightening change. Anger curdles the acne scars so they clot in bluish clusters over the skim-milk surface of his skin. He stands easily on top of the cement strip and pulls from his back pocket a long, black-handled pocket knife. It flips open—the size of a small sword.

All that spring and summer, until Gee Gee's sudden transfer to Troost Avenue, I had spent my time across the street with a family that had just moved to our neighborhood from Texas. Linda Mae was a girl about my age, certainly no older than fifteen; slender, pale, and with a languid quality that struck me as the exact nobility shown by Madeleine Carroll in *The Prisoner of Zenda*. Her face, her meager form and bland personality, suggested a sketch left behind by an artist so discouraged by the original concept that he never finished the canvas. Yet, nearly every afternoon I would kneel beside her as she lay on the glider of their front porch, my adoration as vibrant as the song of the cicadas in the elms that turned Roberts Street into a chapel. I read her poetry. Elizabeth Barrett Browning, Omar Khayyám, James Russell Lowell, and William Cullen Bryant. Once I tried some *Morte d'Arthur,* thinking she might recognize herself, but we went back to 'Thanatopsis.'

The anemia I interpreted as the manner of a Guinever was more likely due to the nightly portion of her life that I did not share. As this family's furniture and belongings were unloaded from trucks with Texas license plates, young men arrived in two and threes, or larger groups, to lounge on the front porch of the house across the street, its lawn and curb. They were strangers to me and my playmates, much older than we were, and gave the impression of being out of high school and already working. Most important, all but a few arrived in cars: Model A's or Chevy coupes with softly throbbing radios and tassled fringe tickling the rear windows. They spent a lot of time polishing their cars parked before Linda Mae's house, endlessly adjusting, resetting, tuning the cars—all part of a process I recognized as I watched from across the street, ostensibly flying my model airplane, for I had read about similar rituals in *Morte d'Arthur.* Indeed, perhaps deep within the pale gelatine of Linda Mae's consciousness, those passages I had read to her had evoked some recognition.

True to Art, the number of suitors diminished over the spring, the contests for Linda Mae's favor being fought somewhere other than Roberts Street, and only one attendant remained, this same one who now awaited me halfway down the narrow walkway by Perky Brothers Storage. The long black knife, perhaps the instrument of his mastery over Linda Mae, now flashes in the sunlight as he cleans his fingernails with all the feigned nonchalance of a bum at a banquet. It is my last day in Kansas City, I say to myself. If I can just get by him, make this shortcut, I shall be free.

His Model A was also black, but with orange wire wheels, and it would turn onto Roberts Street at the top of the block every evening to coast silently down the hills and come to rest against the curb. I stood on top of my terrace across the street, slowly winding the rubber-band motor of my airplane, and kept watch.

From the top of the radio aerial dangled the fur trophy of an animal, no doubt killed and skinned by this very black-handled knife that threatened me now. The elbow of his left arm would rest on the car door, but he did not move. He never got out of the car, nor even turned off the motor nor even honked the horn. There was no need. Linda Mae would walk out of her house, down the walk, and into the black car as if in a trance, as if summoned by some awful spell, her face blank but strangely luminous. As the car pulled away, I would catch sight of her pale hair through the tawdry crochet that screened the rear window. Once or twice, I thought she looked back toward me.

Late at night, the syrupy sounds of orchestra music would wake me. From my front bedroom window, I could make out the dark shape of the car before her house and the dim light of its radio dial would pull me unwillingly back into sleep like the oncoming light of some unreachable star.

But the summer days were mine. Or more exactly, the afternoons, since Linda Mae always slept late. After lunch, book in hand, I would cross the street to find her stretched out on the glider at the end of the porch that was screened by bamboo shades. Sometimes a cool cloth would lie across her narrow brow, but her face would always seem drawn, minimal features even more reduced during the night. She usually wore a peasant blouse that came low across her collarbones, a skirt, and sandals upon her crossed feet, the toenails of which were a different color every day, all shades of red, green, purple, silver, and even black. Painting toenails was one of the more important morning rituals.

' "How do I love thee? Let me count the ways," ' I'd begin, kneeling on the floor, book open. If it were raining, or for other reasons I can't remember, the scene would take place in her living room, Linda Mae lying on a violet-nap sofa and I sitting beside her on the floor, my book on an ottoman of maroon imitation leather. She would sigh and adjust the cloth over her

face though; never shift her position but remain as still as the
alabaster effigy on top of a medieval tomb, like those I had seen
at the Nelson Art Gallery, except for the toenails, of course.
Sometimes, I think she must have gone to sleep as I read, for her
breathing became deep and regular, her frail body seemed to
melt into the fabric of the couch, or become so light as to slip off
the glazed oilcloth cover of the glider. To recuperate from her
ravishments required deep, transcendent meditation; this I
understood somehow, while at the same time the imagined details
of her enslavement sometimes threw me to the cold floor of the
locked bathroom where I would wrestle my own erotic fury;
afterward, ashamed that I had used her in such fashion.

So I would read her Omar Khayyám through the afternoon,
through the summer-afternoon routines of Roberts Street. The
clip-clop of Mr. Paloucci's horse-drawn ice wagon, no longer
stopping at our house these days, but two houses down the
street. Later, the huckster's truck would grind up the hill to
come to a stop before my grandparents' house. It creaked and
wheezed, and the metal scales jounced on their springs, the
whole rig sounding like a clipper ship going gently aground.
Still later I would hear my friends, the same ones who now
await my disfigurement or death beside Perky Brothers; I would
hear them ask for me and hear them laugh when my grandmother
tells them where I am. Their remarks are scornful but their feelings are hurt and they ride away quickly on their bicycles down
Roberts Street as if away from the scene of a crime, something
offensive. Perhaps it was I who had betrayed them.

'Read thet whun agin.' So she hadn't been asleep after all.

'Which one?' I asked quickly.

'Thet whun,' Linda Mae repeated, lifting a translucent hand
into the air, one finger up as if to point toward Assumption.
Which one, which line had sparked this response, this dazed
and feverish request? Which line of iambic pentameter had
brought her to the surface from the dreadful enchantment?

If thou must love me, let it be for nought
Except for love's sake only.

Or was it, 'Betwixt the stars and the unaccomplished fate'?
Or 'Who can fear/Too many stars, though each in heaven shall
roll.' Of course, it did not matter, for whatever I read, the effect
would be the same—a gradual re-immersion into that deep
coma of her possession. Moreover, it was the form that mattered
to Linda Mae, not so much the content; so that her requests for
a poem, always unspecified, were merely a queenly effort to
observe the protocol, the inborn gesture of a patroness.

Sometimes she would raise a small mirror in her thin hand, a
round mirror encased in heavy blue celluloid with the all-too-
pretty image of a screen actor named Dennis Morgan pasted
on the back. As I read to her, the glass would be held above her
face as if to inspect the development of the nose, the thin mouth
and small chin, or the shadowed cavities of the eyes as they slowly
reappeared in the filtered light of the porch or living room,
to be effaced once more at night. Once or twice, a line of poetry
yet sifting on my tongue, I would catch a face in this mirror:
the eyes turned up and the mouth line tremulous, the nostrils
sweetly flared. It was my face.

*   *   *

'Or . . . DER . . . h'ARMS!'

My mother stands with her back to the view of the Lincoln
Memorial. She seems very calm, almost relaxed, her arms at her
sides as if they have just put down a heavy burden, as indeed
she has, though it occurs to me that she who had tried to put together a home for all of us was now without one and now she,
herself, would begin to move through rooms in other households.

Not even the flag is to be hers, for when a soldier presents her
with the red, white, and blue folded tricorn that had draped Gee
Gee's coffin, she simply inclines her head toward me and I receive it. The last sounds of the bugle have become absorbed by
the damp metropolitan hum that floats across the Potomac. The

honor guard steps off. The undertakers dawdle by the open grave. My mother and I walk down the hill toward the taxi.

She had arrived from Philadelphia before I had and had been directed to the desk of a young medical officer. A shavetail, she told me, using the old slang for second lieutenant. He seemed nervous and asked her a lot of questions about Gee Gee, about the family, its history; the interview got off to a bad start.

'What's all this about?' she finally demanded.

'Well—' The little squirt almost laughed, she told me. 'We can't understand why he wanted to do it.'

'Do what?'

'Commit suicide. He was perfectly normal in all of his tests.'

I smiled. 'You should have told him that he had read all of the Zane Greys they had—three or four times over.'

'Ha!' Her burst startled the cabbie. We were following the hearse out to Arlington. 'I wish I could. But you see, suicide. They were beginning to make funny sounds about his being buried here. No mass, no burial in Arlington maybe. Anyway, what was it their business?'

But it had been made their business. Between the time he had been found in the lavatory, slashed wrists bleeding into a basin of warm water, in the best manner of a Roman senator, and the time he had died of pneumonia from loss of blood, the army had managed to give him several psychiatric tests. It was like a court-martial, almost, an investigation of his attempt to step away from fate on his own feet—he had not stood there and taken it like a good soldier, and that had to be investigated. 'None of their Goddamn business.' My mother seethed in the taxi seat beside me. Her anger gave off its own heat. Not even when the tests proved him stable, when he had been acquitted as it were, and the young doctors had admitted their confusion—not even that had been enough to soothe her. 'So you see, Hilary, none of it matters. This matters.' She points ahead through the windshield at the hearse in front. The cemetery is just ahead.

Unfortunately, what mattered in Kansas City that summer's

day in 1942 was that I was wearing a new pair of brown leather shoes my mother had bought for my last trip East and they were stiff and unmanageable and not the legendary sneakers with the wings embossed on the round ankle patches that had made my speed on the bases the boast of Roberts Street. If only I had on those sneakers, I thought, I could whip around him, keeping my feet on the cement strip, and be gone. I take two more steps, and the distance between us is now about nine feet, not close enough for conversation and too far for a rush. My shoes slide treacherously on the concrete surface. My friends—and in my desperation I still think of them as friends—continue to smile, though their expressions have cooled; they show a little uncertainty now. The knife glints in the sun. They had not known he had this knife on him, I say to myself, or they wouldn't have tipped him off.

If I can just get by him, I think, somehow run between him and my friends, while still keeping a foot on the narrow strip of cement, still being right with the code. . . .

'What's up?' I ask. About three feet separate us now. We face each other like aerialists on a high wire who have mixed our signals. He says nothing, continues to work on his nails with the long, pointed blade, and smiles. It is the official, formal smile of an executioner. 'What's going on?' I ask the boys to the right, standing easily on the lawn. Some have the good grace to look away.

'I'm going to cut off your puny dick.' His voice is flat and very serious.

My sense of injustice outraces my fear, for if I had besmeared his honor, as instinctively I knew I had, it was not that member, alas, that had made the offense. Moreover, my fear is swallowed mixed with pride, for I think, *It isn't puny,* at least I didn't think so.

'Why?' Already eunuched, my voice has risen into a soprano range.

'She's told me what you've done with her,' he replies, and

strangely it is his voice that sounds hurt, on the verge of tears. 'Don't try to lie out of it. Linda Mae's told me what you've done with her.'

What had I done? What had she told him, what half-formed but hotly forced idea had risen in the haze of her mind to seize her imagination unawares? Had she played upon his jealousy, fashioning me as a competitor, I who had only read her some poems? My friends are solemn, their faces bleached with the suspicion that they have lightheartedly arranged an event that will have serious consequences. They did not know about the knife, I tell myself again; they wouldn't have told him I was back in the neighborhood if they had known about the knife. On the other hand, something forestalls my telling this jury that my only offense, my only activity with Linda Mae was to read her poetry in the afternoon. Let them think otherwise. The perjury emboldens me to take a step closer.

'I'm going to cut you to pieces, Masters,' he says. His Adam's apple works up and down angrily on the string of his neck and the knife swings up in an arc and pauses high above his head, high above Kansas City—I can see its blade tilt slowly and point straight down at me. Behind him towers the monolithic, window-less wall of the Perky Brothers warehouse. With my eyes on that steel blade, 'Thanatopsis' comes to my mind. For whatever rea-son—and I only now may understand why—Linda Mae often re-quested: 'Thou shalt lie down/With patriarchs of the infant world—with kings.'

No, not for anything was I going to end up in the 'mighty sepulchre' of Perky Brothers warehouse; not for anything would my remains, however nobly dressed and attended, be deposited inside them in some dim chamber; no matter how decorated with heraldic devices or how many times visited by the pale pietà of Linda Mae on leave from her convent down on Armour Boule-vard. No, sir, not for her, not for the honor of Roberts Street; not for anything. The blade is coming down.

'Run!' one of my friends shouts.

I run: off the cement strip and across the driveway and lawn toward Independence Avenue, just making the traffic light at the corner. My pursuer is held back by a continuous band of moving automobiles and street cars. I get to the other side of the broad avenue and jump into an empty taxicab by Jim's Hamburgers. I give the man the address, lock the doors, and roll up the rear windows. The cab turns and passes my adversary, his face blue with anger, but the knife put away, a fist in one pants pocket. I wave.

My mother has begun to walk up Roberts Street to search for me, so we ride back to the house and pick up our luggage from the porch. The tenants have closed the front door, and we leave like unwanted relatives. However, the cab must proceed to the corner of Benton Boulevard and Independence Avenue, where it stops for a red light. There is a rapping at the window on my side.

He has waited for me, all of his frustration and anger erupted in his mottled face. His eyes are clouded marbles.

'I'm going to get you, Masters,' he snarls. 'No matter where you go, how far you go, I'll get you.'

So my mother and I are in this other taxi now, but the windows are open and we are returning from the ceremony in Arlington. No one waits to threaten me at an intersection. The only thing that matters, she has just said, is the practical application of life, of getting on with it. Let's get on with it, was the saying on Roberts Street. Codes, degrees, principles—all had to be shaped to be got on with.

'You can imagine that little shavetail telling me about putting your grandfather through their baloney tests,' she is saying. ' "He showed no signs of mental disorder," he is saying to me. Ha! So I say to him—' She pauses to girdle herself with her arms, a re-enactment of that part of the interview no doubt. 'I say, "Well, did he say anything about it? What did he say?" "Well," this little quack laughs, "he said that he cut himself while he was shaving. Imagine, cutting both wrists while he was shaving." ' My mother laughs herself, her tongue held between her teeth as if to stopper a grander amusement.

'And what did you say to that?' I ask.

' "That's probably how it happened," I said to him. "That's the way it happened." '

2

'But how did Gee Gee get from Pennsylvania to California,' I ask my mother. 'He said he took a train.'

We are also on a train, going East once more, but it is 1950 and this time we have come from Illinois and the little town of Petersburg where my father has been buried next to his beloved grandparents.

'Your grandfather might have taken a train,' my mother replies. She looks about the empty club car. It is late and the steward waits patiently for us to retire. Her widow's black becomes the graying hair, her alabaster complexion; sets off the brilliant eyes. 'There were trains by then that crossed the country. But I've often thought he worked on them rather than rode them. The Irish built a lot of railroads across the continent. He always had something to do with railroads, you know, except for his army days. I've often thought your grandfather could have become a very good civil engineer but that he wasted his talents and energies.' She finished the last of her drink and rattled the ice cubes in the glass. Without meaning to do so, her gesture summons the attendant.

'No, I won't have another,' she says. 'You do if you wish. Anyway, Grace has not finished hers.' She looks at the drink belonging to the friend whom she had asked to accompany her on this journey. I nod to the waiter. 'Gee Gee built railroads all over

South America and Mexico,' she continues. She is only fifty years of age but seems much older in the cool light of the Pennsylvania Railroad club car. 'For example, he was the chief engineer in charge of construction of the Quito and Guayaquil railroad in Ecuador—you remember those photographs on the wall in Kansas City of the railroad track going around that mountainside?'

'The Devil's Nose,' I recall. The photographs hung on the wall at the foot of the stairs and were among the items Gee Gee burned eight years ago, when he left Roberts Street.

'Yes, that's right, the Devil's Nose.' My mother's voice seems to wax and wane over the steady rush of the train's passage. 'He had to leave that job and come back to Kansas City. I was about two or three years old at the time. But he had to come back and take care of your grandmother and me because Grandfather Moynihan had fallen down the elevator shaft in the old post office building.'

'Who had fallen down what?' My mother's companion has just returned. She settles into the art-deco-style chair next to my mother, a comfortably upholstered lady with a generous expression.

'Oh, my dear.' My mother laughs. 'There was always something happening to us. No, my grandfather, this was my mother's father, stepped into the elevator one day—they had no safety devices then—and it wasn't there. He dropped five floors.'

'I thought it was only three,' I say.

'No, it was five,' my mother corrects me. The green eyes spear my error. 'Fortunately, he landed on his head.' We all laugh. 'Oh, we can be tough when we have to be,' she says to her friend. Her jaw is thrust out, the lip line firm. 'When we have to be,' she promises, 'we can be very tough.'

A startling transformation begins around the eyes, as if the openings around them are made of cloth that starts to turn in on itself and crumple up the rest of the face; the tough expression

[27]

tears apart with soft, choking sounds. She looks at me quickly, as if for permission, and then permits her companion to cushion and comfort her.

This friend is about ten years older than my mother and had known my father for many years, from the time he arrived in New York from Chicago. I wonder if she had had an affair with him and I conjure a situation, widow and former mistress comforting each other. The curved rear window of the club car scans a dark panorama that is sucked into nothingness at tremendous speed. Rails shoot erratically into the void and disappear. A crossing strikes past. A small town goes by like a stage set out of control and the lights of a solitary farm flash and drop silently behind us. We must be in Ohio by now.

Several mornings ago my roommate had put me on the train in Providence after my mother had called. I had to change trains in New York City, transferring to Pennsylvania Station for the second train for Philadelphia, and there I read my father's obituary in the morning editions as I ate breakfast. The articles were fairly accurate, the outline of his life and career; most of the facts were there. One detail, that he died in a nursing home in Philadelphia, bothered me. The sound of it offended my inflated sensitivity, though I knew it was the only way my mother could assure him the care and medical attention required. He was bedridden the last year and a half of his life, his urine drawn off through a catheter. Get on with it.

'Hiya, Pop.'

'Hello there, Mr. It.' A large, pink Buddha rose up against the white background of the cranked-up hospital bed. 'How's school?'

'Fine.' I kissed him. His cheek was prickly and smelled of witch hazel. Beneath the pajama top his torso and shoulders remained solid, of great size, suggesting their previous strength. As a boy I would be both thrilled and terrified to be hugged and crushed in those arms during a roughhouse. 'How are you doing?'

'Better. Much better,' he replied sternly. Masters, the lawyer, advising a client, briefing a jury. 'I'm going to get out of here pretty soon. How long are you home for?'

'Oh, for Thanksgiving.'

'Well, be good to your mother. She's a fine woman.' Masters, the aged Odysseus counseling Telemachus on the treatment of Penelope.

His room had been the sunporch of a substantial suburban house that had been transformed into a nursing home. The walls around his bed were mostly window panes that opened to a clear November light so pervasive that there were no shadows. There were plants and flowers; books, magazines, and correspondence. A small portable typewriter perched on top of a stack of books. My mother used it to type the letters he dictated, the few poems he tried to revise. And there was the smell, the same odor I encountered when I visited my grandfather at the Soldiers Home in Washington. Part antiseptic, part waste; wax polish over decay.

'Say, Pop, did you get those poems I sent you?'

'Yes.' He looked away, the moonlike head glowing. The eyes softened behind the spectacles. Masters, the poet, rising from a bath of aesthetic values. 'There's no song to them. Poetry must sing, boy. It has got to sing.'

'That's right,' I agreed, thinking I had been unable to hear much music in any of his poems. I'd have to read them again. There is the trickle of running water. On the floor beneath the bed is a gallon jug similar to the ones in which cider is sold at roadside stands and, in fact, the liquid that dribbles into this jar through a slender rubber hose is the color of cider. The hose disappears beneath the bed's counterpane. It will bind him to this bed for the rest of his life.

'Isn't that the cat's pajamas,' he said and laughed. His laughter was dry, a crackling scrape of old corn husks, as yellowed stumps of teeth appeared in a jack-o'-lantern expression.

'Excuse me, ladies.' The train steward stands over us. 'But I'd like to close up now.'

'All right. Of course,' my mother says. 'Let's go to the state-
room—well, you know what I mean.' She shrugs and stands up.
'I don't feel quite like going to sleep yet. We can talk more.'
Her eyes plead almost coquettishly.

'That will be perfect,' replies Grace.

We walk single file through the swaying carriages of the train,
wrestle through the connecting doors and across the steel foyers
that jounce above the couplings. The two women go before me,
giggling like schoolgirls in a funhouse. The berths are prepared
in their double compartment and I sit down on one. My mother
takes one of the chairs, kicking off her shoes to massage one foot
against the other. Grace has opened her traveling bag and pulls
out a beautiful silver flask that, to me, suggests a crisp afternoon
in the Yale Bowl. Maybe even Scott Fitzgerald had been part of
that crowd.

'Gerry'—she refers to her husband—'Gerry said I'd better bring
this because there was no telling how dry it might get out here.'
Her laugh is as deep as her bosom. 'Let's have a nightcap.'

'Oh, good,' my mother says gaily. Her eyes flash happily. It is
a party, a deferment of the moment when she will have to lie
down in this berth and turn out the light. 'Now then—' She takes
the flask from her friend and sips. 'Oh my, that's good. What is
that?'

'That's Scotch, Ellen,' Grace says, supporting her bosom as she
laughs.

'That's very smooth.' My mother passes the flask on to me. 'It
went well, didn't it?' she asks us again.

My father had planned his funeral also. He had asked to be
buried in Petersburg next to his grandparents. No religious
service, no prayers, but rather a program of his favorite music.
He chose two of his poems to be read, one at the funeral home
and the other at graveside. When my mother called to tell me
he had died, she also went over the list of records required. Did
I have the *New World Symphony* by Dvořák? Yes, I had an old
recording, a heavy album of shellac records. She had the Bee-

thoven, the Sibelius, the Saint-Saëns. What about the Chopin? He especially liked to listen to José What's-His-Name. Iturbi. Yes, José Iturbi; did I have any of his records playing Chopin? No, but maybe we could find a record of that in Illinois. Are you sure we'll be able to find one? Her anxiety to obey these final instructions to the last detail momentarily consumes her grief. Yes, I'm sure we can find one. I was to fly out from Philadelphia, in advance, to arrange such details.

'What about Ethel Merman singing "Doin' What Comes Natur'lly" from *Annie Get Your Gun*?' She does not acknowledge the question, does not hear it, or perhaps her attention is focused on some other aspect of the funeral arrangement. It is two o'clock in the morning and the lights of downtown Providence glow below my windows. A light March drizzle has varnished the streets. There is no sound on the other end of the line, and then she begins to read me the obituary notice she had just approved for the *New York Times*.

Or perhaps I never said it but only thought it. Someone gave us the album of the Irving Berlin musical and my father would play it or have it played over and over again, laughing at the innuendos and country vernacular in the lyrics. 'That's good, that's good!' He'd grin, and suck on his pipe. He spent most of those days reading in a metal lawn chair that was placed in the bedroom of a small apartment that came with my mother's job as a teacher in a junior college outside of Philadelphia. It was an easy chair for him to sit in, to rise from; moreover, it was practical, having the strength and resilience to withstand the shock when he sat down, as no other chair could. His legs had become so weak that he would almost fall into the chair's seat, his body's heavy bulk smacking against the back, and the whole rig would bounce and wobble like a huge toy set in motion.

'Put on some *Annie*,' he'd ask my mother when she returned from her classes, and she would put the records on a small phonograph. Sometimes they would sing a line or two of the lyrics together as they had their drink before dinner or while she fixed that dinner on a complicated arrangement of electric hot plates. The apartment had no real kitchen since it was part of an old Dutch farmhouse the school owned, using it to house three members of its faculty, one to each floor. My mother turned and stirred within a serpentine nest of electric extension cords, balancing pressure cookers and frying pans and a set of saucepans that threatened to fold up like Boy Scout drinking cups. But she created an astounding menu of roasts, stews, fricassees, and accompanying sauces on the precarious arrangement.

'Doin' what comes natch-er-ly,' Pop would croon as my mother ran cold water over a pressure cooker in the bathroom sink. 'By God, that's rich.'

Or what about the 'Washington Post March'? That record should be on the list also; one particular recording, a heavy, thick disc with only one side inscribed. It was in their apartment in the Hotel Chelsea, kept along with other records in the cabinet of the square, wind-up Victrola. It would be the first record I played when I came to New York in the summers. Over the hash of the train's swift progress eastward, away from Illinois and my father's burial, I can hear the tinny trumpets and muddled tubas of the Sousa march, distant and miniaturized as if heard through the wrong end of the speaker.

Despite the air conditioning of the railroad car I grow warm remembering the heat of the New York summers and how that Victrola smelled. The needles were made of wood or steel and had to be changed frequently. The smell of the Victrola, the aromas of mahogany, felt, metal, and oil were intensified by the summer heat, and I imagined the dark cool chamber inside the machine where the music would be deafening.

Such heat required siestas. After lunch, my parents would retire to the bedroom, and close the door; I would be put on the sofa in the living room. I slept here at night also. There were books with pictures to look at in the half-light of the shaded room, a toy car to play with or sometimes a comic book to read, but usually I lay in my underpants and sweated and waited for the end of the rest period. Somehow, I knew when it was time to get up, and the siesta's end would be proclaimed by the 'Washington Post March.'

Hup-two-three-four, hup-two-three-four, around the room, past the fireplace, into the alcove made by the bay window and around the large desk covered with papers, pencils, and pens; *left-right, left-right, hup-two-three-four,* along the wall of books, *left-turn-*MARR-*ch* to the sofa and then on to the same route once more. *Left-right, left-right.*

'By God, there goes Mr. Ittie.' My father stood in the doorway of the bedroom. He'd be barefoot and shirtless. 'Go to it, Mr. It,' he'd cheer as I marched around the room to the sound of the 'Washington Post March' in my underpants, hands stiff at my sides, and feet smacking the floor. I pivoted as smartly as I knew how around the floor lamp.

Then there was a piece of music called the 'Mr. Ittie March,' but no one can remember how it goes.

'How does it go?' my mother asks. A crossing bell ding-dongs by the train window as if tossed into space.

'How does what go?' I ask her. I return the flask to Grace, who takes a second gulp of the whiskey, then screws on the cap.

'You know,' she replies a bit impatiently. 'That part of the *New World Symphony* he loved so.'

'The "Goin' Home" part?' She nods. I start to hum the refrain. '*Going home, going home, I am going home/Going home, going home,* something, something, dah-dum . . .'

We run out of words but continue the melody. Grace's rich contralto, somehow appropriate to her build, softens my mother's strident soprano. The three of us sing together but when we start the crescendo of the song's bridge my mother's voice falters and drops away. She looks very old all of a sudden, and her lips swell up as if bruised. She takes a deep breath and smiles at her friend.

'Well, I think I can go to sleep now,' she says.

In my own compartment, I lie down in the small berth. On

the other side of the window, the darkened landscape moves on an endless belt, the worn, poorly lit backdrop of a penny arcade. Going from one place to another. Going from Providence to Philadelphia. Then going from Chicago to Springfield and then to Petersburg. Going from one place to another.

Going from Kansas City to New York almost every summer and then back again to my grandparents in Kansas City for school. Sometimes going from Kansas City to Columbia County, New York, and then back again. Going from Kansas City to New York and then to New Hampshire and then back to New York. Going to North Carolina and then back to New York and then to Philadelphia. Going from Philadelphia to Providence, then back to Springfield, to Petersburg. Going from one place to another.

Memory switches the different lines onto a single track so arrivals and departures are scheduled differently from the way they actually took place. We spent only one summer together at the Hotel Chelsea, though I think of it, even speak of it sometimes, as though it had been an annual occurrence. Prior to 1935, my mother, father, and I would get together in rented farmhouses in Columbia County, New York, or nearby Colebrook, Connecticut. Once even down in the Ozarks. Today, my mother refers to this time as the 'little family' period, and it was little enough. After 1935 we never got together as a family until I had graduated from high school. That one summer in 1935, the three of us compressed within the walls of that small hotel-apartment, has been parceled out by my memory into other summers.

September 1, 1935

Dear Mr. Ittie: We had a wonderful summer in the Hotel Chelsea —good rooms, a bath and everything, with Capt. Louis, Slim, Eddie, Sydney to take care of us; and Belinda, a good maid, at the last. Just think of it. You have been well all summer, good sleep and good eats—and no accident. And you have seen New York City

from end to end. I planned to have you have a wonderful summer,
and you have had it. Now school begins, and you'll have to work.
I do too, for I have loafed nearly all summer. That's the way it
goes; fun and work. Remember the fun and pitch into the work.
You are going to do fine at school everyday; brush your teeth
night and morning, keep your clothes clean—sleep lots. Next
summer we'll have joy again.

Your loving Poppie,
E. L. M.

My father claimed he stayed at the Hotel Chelsea because the management never complained when he missed the spittoon. Every morning for nearly fifteen years, he would work on poems and prose at a desk placed in the bay window of his two-room suite, smoking his pipe or chewing a cud of Ivanhoe, and, if he were chewing, he'd lean back occasionally to let fly a thick, rich spume in the direction of the spittoon by the table's leg. Sometimes he would hit it.

My mother never liked the Chelsea. It was a minor novelist, according to her, who recommended the place to my father one night at the Players Club, and my parents moved there about 1930 from an apartment on West 16th Street. My mother can call up an affectionate supply of details about their first apartment, so I suspect her dislike of the Chelsea was not because the rooms were any smaller or that it looked a little seedy, an opinion strengthened by a plague of bedbugs that swept the establishment around 1937, but because she had recognized the two rooms with bath and maid service were essentially bachelor's quarters.

Nor was it large enough for a family, and at sixty years of age, income diminished, my father must have regarded my existence with some ambivalent feelings. The wires and poems he wrote to friends and relatives announcing my birth were couched in a Homeric idiom, pretentious language that might suggest his joy in the event was a little forced, not completely spontaneous.

Also, I think he felt a desperate need for several years of tranquillity, uninterrupted by the clamor of raising a second family in the confines of a New York apartment. It had been fifteen years and many books since *Spoon River Anthology,* and perhaps he was beginning to wonder if his creative powers had all been expended in that one book, or if the collection of epitaphs had been a one-shot, lucky hit, as some critics and a few poets had begun to suggest. I can imagine him taking an oath to give himself, at sixty, five or ten years in which he would work very hard to prove them wrong, to prove himself once again.

Thus a plan was devised. My mother's parents would keep me in Kansas City during the school year, and in the summer I would come East to join my parents. The arrangement gave me the best of two different worlds, for a time; moreover, no one told me it was unusual.

The pull-out couch where I slept and took my naps at the Chelsea was located across the room from the desk in the bay window. Ailanthus trees growing up from the backyards between 23rd and 22nd streets screened these windows, but the strong morning sun of summer always forced through the leaves to illuminate my father at work, a nimbus around the thinning hair of the head's dome. My eyes would open to this image every morning of that summer of 1935. He would be freshly shaved and pink and smelling of witch hazel, and though the windows behind him would be open and the curtains billowed with a steady river breeze, it would already be quite warm; he would wear only the tops of old-fashioned BVDs and a pair of trousers. His eyes were dark, forbidding, and seemed to look right through the paper he wrote upon, pierce the mahogany table, the floor, right on down through the hotel and into somewhere deep in the ground. I would lie there, breathing as quietly as possible, and watch him. Usually, when he paused to relight his pipe or take aim at the cuspidor, he would notice me. His smile was dimpled, like that of an elderly cherub, and the eyes would lighten.

'Morning, Mr. It.'

There was an informality about life at the Chelsea that was in agreeable contrast to the army-like routines observed in Kansas City. It was like camping out; our days were improvised. The heat of summer dictated casual dress, particularly inside the rooms, where I went about in underwear and bare feet. My father would wear pants but not always a shirt and my mother padded about in some light apparel or in a kimono the color of which I cannot remember—its brilliance blinds memory. Nor was there any regular schedule for meals as was maintained in Kansas City by my grandfather's discipline. At the Chelsea, we seemed to eat when we got hungry and not always at the same place, nor, amazing to me, did we always eat together.

I'm vague about breakfasts at the Chelsea; probably my mother fixed something on the weird set of appliances, wedding gifts no doubt, that were shelved in the small pantry-closet outside the bathroom. These contrivances of chromed tin and exposed coils had hinges that seemed to fold several ways simultaneously; the handles kept dropping off. However, they were durable and traveled with her all the way to the kitchen she improvised in the hallway of that Dutch farmhouse near Philadelphia.

I sometimes ate lunch at the drugstore that was next door to the hotel and which could be entered through the lobby. One of my parents would give me some change and I'd take the clanking elevator by myself, Sydney at the controls, down to the lobby and slip into the cool, powdery atmosphere of medicaments and rubber goods for a tuna on toast and a chocolate malt at the counter. When I grew older, I ventured farther and discovered the Automat down the street toward Seventh Avenue.

My father also liked to eat at the Automat; the menu sometimes featured fried corn meal mush with butter and syrup, one of his favorite dishes. Though eating in restaurants and soda fountains was exotic compared to my grandmother's home cooking, I was not so much attracted to the Automat by its food as I was by the mechanical ingeniousness of its service.

Coins slipped into slots to bring spurts of milk, coffee, or hot chocolate from the polished heads of lions. Faces appeared, disappeared behind small glass panels as in scary movies where the eyes of a portrait would suddenly move. The compartments made a peculiar click-clack as their small doors would snap shut; metal columns within would revolve like artillery shells spinning into the breech of a cannon, then gradually return racks filled with beef pot pies or sliced turkey sandwiches.

Some days at the Automat, I'd play a sort of lottery, making bets with myself as to which compartments—say, pies over custards—would close up and gyrate first. Another fantasy featured a customer who would drop his money, raise up the glass panel, and reach in for a ham and cheese on rye. But he would be too slow; and CLICK-CLACK, his hand would reappear on a bed of lettuce in the salad section.

The women who ran the change booths in the Automat were even more fascinating. Dimes and nickels and quarters seemed to bleed from their fingertips in a continuous stream. The coins spilled, rolled, and slithered into the polished depressions of their pink marble counters, always to the correct amount and with no hesitation. More astonishing, they never seemed to count. I spent a lot of time watching them make change, and it was with some amazement when I discovered these fabulous women existed not just on 23rd Street, but were spilling silver in restaurants all over New York City. What if someone like Edward G. Robinson sauntered in and casually slipped a 'C note' across the marble counter? Or maybe even a five-hundred-dollar bill! The cascade of coins would spill out onto 23rd Street, block traffic on Seventh Avenue.

The Hotel Chelsea used to have its own restaurant; it adjoined the lobby on the other side from the drugstore, and we would sometimes eat supper there. Usually I played the juke box while my parents had a drink at the bar, now that Prohibition was over, then we'd all sit down in a booth lit by a small lamp on the wall. On special occasions, my father would slap on an old

Panama straw hat and my mother would pull on some stockings and we'd walk down 23rd Street toward Eighth Avenue and around the corner to a restaurant called Pappa's. Other times, we'd take a taxi to Lüchow's. Pappa's Restaurant (for a long time I thought my father had something to do with the place) offered seafood, and live lobsters crawled over crushed ice and each other in the front window. If someone had bought a poem and there was a check in the day's mail, my father would order a couple for supper. The lobster claws were prized back in Kansas City, and brought good trades in marbles and customized yo-yos on Roberts Street.

There were the usual museum and park tours parents employ to amuse youngsters in New York City, including the old Aquarium at the Battery and trips to the Bronx Zoo to watch a magnificent gorilla named Gargantua. I caught his heavy-browed stare more than once and wondered if his contemplation comprehended me. I still see him today, when I take my own son to the Museum of Natural History, for he was stuffed and made part of an exhibit when he died. The stare in the glass eyes is no less enigmatic.

But most of my entertainments were centered around the Hotel Chelsea and were usually self-generated. As the summer passed and I grew more adventurous, I played outside my parents' rooms in the halls and elevator, then the lobby, and finally out on 23rd Street to talk and pitch pennies with Capt. Louis. I moved on from paper clips, scissors, stamp pads, paste pots, and the other things on my father's desk to the books in his library. Those with pictures came first, and most interesting of these were drawings of naked men and women that illustrated editions of *The Iliad* and *The Inferno*. A book of Peter Arno's cartoons featured small boys coming upon naked, full-breasted women in bathtubs, beds, or what looked like the foyers of apartments, even elevators. Such confrontations had never been contemplated in Kansas City and were something to ponder on the pull-out couch at night.

The winter before, during a case of measles, I had read about King Arthur and his knights, so I came to New York in 1935 with a design in mind. Using the scissors, clips, paste, some brown wrapping paper, I fashioned a suit of armor. The helm was a paper bag. I rode the elevator thus fully panoplied, a drapery rod for a lance, and the round top of a fruit basket as a shield. Sydney would begin to giggle as we'd come to a floor, before he'd open the doors.

'Well, Sydney, what do we have here?' the new passenger would ask.

'Something special,' he'd say with a little pride. 'Yessir, something special.'

'And how doth this fair knight call himself?' the passenger might ask. The clientele of the Chelsea were a fairly literate group of people and knew the proper way to talk to a knight at arms. However, they always laughed when they heard my name: 'The Brown Knight!' Well, I had read of a Green Knight, a Black Knight, a Red Knight. Why not brown? It went with the armor.

My father claimed he brought Thomas Wolfe to live at the Chelsea and, after his death, located some manuscripts the novelist had left with the bartender at the hotel restaurant. The bartender remembered that Wolfe had given him a package before the Baltimore trip, and it was still in the back of the bar. My father turned the manuscript over to Wolfe's publisher. John Sloan had the large studio apartment on the top floor and I have a vague recollection of playing cars around Dreiser's feet. To mention any more of my father's friends and acquaintances who lived or visited him at the Chelsea would be only name dropping, for they meant nothing to me. Actually, I found the other tenants more interesting.

On the floor beneath Sloan's penthouse studio lived an old lady who was rumored to be the widow of the hotel's architect. She never used the elevator, which suggests that she knew something about the building no one else did; on the other hand, she may have just enjoyed the exercise, a vertical jogging up and down the stairs, three times a day to take her meals. I literally ran into her one day during a patrol I was making of the top floors, and without exchanging a word, we both started running down the stairs. I don't remember that we ever spoke, but she was impossible to beat going down the stairs, and it would take me at least one floor to overtake her going up. Sometimes I would lie in wait for her on a landing, listening to the whispery scamper coming closer on the marble treads, my body tense and ready to spring like a greyhound, but it was no use. She almost always won.

Several floors above, in an apartment identical to my parents', lived an old man with an enormous collection of used books. We became very good friends, for he never questioned my legitimacy at The Round Table, and he gave me a beautiful edition of Malory's *Morte d'Arthur*. He also gave me a watch fob which, alas, did not bring as many aggies in Kansas City as a lobster claw. From floor to ceiling and wall to wall, his suite of rooms was packed with old volumes, magazines, and moldy editions. When I visited him I would walk into a canyon of books, a maze of titles that reminded me of the illustrations in my father's *Inferno* where the damned wandered endlessly.

One day this old gentleman and I shared the elevator. No matter how hot it got, he dressed correctly—spats, vest, cravat, and high, luminous celluloid collars. The collars were new to me, and I wondered how he could stand them; and, in fact, his neck usually looked red and sore. He permitted my inspection patiently, as he did this afternoon, looking at the back of Sydney's head. As I watched, a small bug—perhaps one of the pilgrims that were about to colonize the place—crawled up the glacial surface of the collar, surefooted and obviously at home, paused at the top, and then dropped down the other side, out of sight.

I moved out of the Chelsea and into the world on roller skates that I learned to use in the hotel lobby. No one complained when I knocked over one of the brass spittoons by the revolving door. The sidewalk's rough sizing sent unpleasant vibrations through the feet, so I discovered what every New York City kid knows: the best place to roller-skate is on the velvety macadam of the street, preferably in the middle. The weekends were the best time, for I could skate down 23rd Street from the hotel to the Flatiron Building and back and encounter very few cars, no trucks. I skated almost everywhere in Manhattan. Klein's On The Square was a favorite spot because of the wooden floors and the small ramps that connected floor levels for the use of wardrobe carts. With a little speed I could shoot the ramps like ski jumpers in the newsreels.

I skated on the Staten Island ferry several times, discovering the trick of skating in the opposite direction to the boat's way, which seemed to stop time and history. I am unable to duplicate the trick on this train going East from Illinois. Central Park, Bronx Zoo, Fifth Avenue, Broadway, Madison Square Park: my skate wheels drummed the pavements. Even in the Museum of Natural History.

If it rained on Sunday, or if I didn't want to skate, my father would give me a nickel and I'd ride the Seventh Avenue subway all day long. The subways smelled different then, and I liked the smell, for it reminded me of the cool musty aroma of the basement in my grandparents' house, where I often would play on rainy days. After several round trips, it would be time for supper, and I'd get off at 23rd Street and Seventh Avenue where the journey had begun. Saturday afternoon movies were a dime in Kansas City then, but here there was a whole day of adventure for only a nickel. The place was fantastic.

More fantasy. My father swam at the YMCA across from the Chelsea nearly every day and he took me along this summer of 1935. Once my seven-year-old prudishness got over seeing men swimming naked, my imagination began to cook in the steamy atmosphere of the place. It was like being in an illustration in one of my father's library books. Moreover, there was a picture in my classroom at Scarritt School in Missouri that enforced this feeling of *déjà vu,* for the painting, David's Socrates drinking the hemlock, was reenacted beside the pool of the 23rd Street YMCA. My father became the philosopher—sans cup and beard, but his figure took the same pose in the obscure light; the same broad shoulders, the same thickened torso, and even down to the detail of a towel draped negligently across naked thighs. When he made a point in conversation, he even raised long, bare arms the same way as the figure in the picture. I began to suspect that the man I left Kansas City to visit was one of those half mortals I had read about in *The Age of Fable*.

That one summer of 1935, the Hotel Chelsea became my other home, and though I returned to it other times only to stay a few nights with my father in intervals between summer camp and school, it became as familiar to me as my grandparents' house; 23rd Street between Eighth and Fifth avenues became as much my territory as was the intersection of Independence Avenue and Benton Boulevard in Kansas City. It was the last summer we would share such intimacy, but its memory was spread over subsequent summers. The next summer, there were problems that kept me in Kansas City.

> *Chelsea Hotel*
> *New York, N.Y.*
> *August 24, 1936*

Dear Mr. Ittie: My beloved boy Hilary:
The neckties came this morning and I was so touched that I could hardly look at them. I put them away, and maybe tomorrow I'll wear one of them.

For a long time to come you must understand how this separation from you has hurt and grieved me. Your schooling there in Kansas City where you started, as compared with opportunities here, gives you an American breeding. Then that yard and that house instead of hotel rooms; then my own work, trying to get out of me all that I have planned to write, of which I have doubts as to its value. Perhaps, and this hurts, I should have given up writing, and devoted my time to you. That might have been a

*contribution to America better than I have made by isolating
myself to do it. Who knows? At any rate I would have had the
happiness of being with you every day—that surely would have
been real. All my life has been loneliness: and since you came into
the world it has been loneliness with you as much when I am
separated with such painful and doubtful frequencies. And now
in these days that loneliness is less endurable than ever. Meanwhile, I hope I have laid up for you something of an income;
and I feel you will never feel ashamed that you were my son.*

*I am sending de $5 for spending money. I forgot to say above
that your grandfather and grandmother have always been in my
mind when I contemplated taking you away. A few years ago
they would not have tolerated it, and what they would do now
I don't know. If I could have bought a place in the country
here in the East I would have done so.*

Your loving pa,
E. L. M.

The train is slowing down. The lights of a city scribble the
blackboard of my compartment's window. We are coming into
Columbus, Ohio, slowing down; then the train stops and is silent.
There is not a sound on the deserted platform beneath my window. It must be well past midnight. No passengers seem to get
on; none get off. Two trainmen walk past hurriedly toward the
front of the train, saying nothing to each other, but their round
caps bob and wag sociably. They are like two members of a fra-
ternal order, late for the ceremony. *Left-right, left-right—hup-
two-three-four.* The 'Washington Post March.' The 'Mr. Ittie
March.' A silent command sends the train on its way, down the
track as if on oiled runners; the empty station platform is pulled
past, inside out, into the dark.

3

When I get to Petersburg, flying ahead of my mother and Grace and the train that carries my father's remains, it is to find no record of Chopin played by José Iturbi or anyone else. It is not easy finding a phonograph and speaker that can be set up in the funeral home.

Petersburg has not changed. It is the same small town built around a courthouse square that I had visited as a boy one summer. There had been a town celebration and my father had been invited to sit on the platform with the mayor and other dignitaries. Someone, perhaps my mother, put me in a car that was part of the parade and I waved to my father as we drove by the reviewing stand.

'My goodness, do you remember that?' my mother asks. 'You must have been only three or four years old.'

'I also remember all the birdhouses you had in your workshop in the backyard, Uncle Will.' My father's uncle, Wilbur D. Masters of Petersburg, Illinois. We are sitting in the parlor of his house. He is a spry ninety-one years of age, and his daughter, Cousin Edith, is about to retire as principal of the high school. That's where I have borrowed the phonograph and speaker. Aunt Norma has just served us slabs of angel food cake with coconut frosting to go with the coffee. It is a country concept that high caloric consumption relieves the pains and stress of grief.

'That was the summer we spent in the Ozarks,' my mother tells the group. She takes a bite of cake as everyone waits for her to continue. 'Lee was working on a novel, and he wanted some atmosphere, some place where the customs might still be the same as they were in the time of Lincoln and Douglas. My father had a large ranch in the Ozarks when I was a child and I remembered the people down there almost still spoke with Elizabethan accents. So we all went . . .'

I look around the small, dark room. She has them completely under control; all the Petersburg Masterses, family friends, Grace —about eighteen people all together; by no means her largest audience, but then she never required a multitude. She speaks cleanly with attention to detail, names, and locations, and with a narrative force that is a gift from her own father. Even though the subject was Lee Masters, a person most of the people in the room had known long before she had, she holds their attention, because she had known him better.

Bolts of protocol enfold the country village and hang the atmosphere with a portentous urgency as pervasive as if loops of black and purple velvet tied up the storefronts around the square. My father would not have wanted all this ceremony nor does my mother. 'A family funeral,' she keeps repeating.

My half brother has arrived. His two sisters are expected in Petersburg by nightfall and one of them, so goes the rumor, will accompany their mother, whom my father divorced twenty-eight years ago. An invitation for us to dine at a cousin's house at Springfield awaited us, but would it be all right if a particular relative were also invited? The messengers came and went. 'Just a family funeral,' my mother keeps insisting, then under her breath to Grace and me, 'Tiresome . . . tiresome people.'

My eyes catch on the sharp bric-a-brac set in the subdued light of this Midwestern parlor. Family photographs, a figurine, a valued piece of china and fresh flowers. Cousin Edith's diploma and awards are framed and on the mantel are plaster mementos of holiday excursions. Aunt Norma was an advocate of temper-

ance, so my father never stayed here when he visited Petersburg but usually at the home of Judge Blane, a boyhood chum.
In fact, my mother is staying with the Blanes now, though the
judge died several years ago; but I am staying somewhere else.
My mother's narrative continues impeccable, uninterrupted.

'There she goes again,' my father would say, looking across
the room and winking at me. She would be delivering a redress
of all the wrongs done to them by his family, her family, and the
world in general. 'Talk, talk, talk.' His paunch jiggled with
amusement. Just then she came into the bedroom where he and
I sat—she had been fixing supper out in the hallway—and tripped
over the heavy cane left carelessly aslant on the bed's footboard.
The sudden fury in her eyes accounted the number of times
she had tripped over it before, the number of times she had
asked him not to leave it there.

'Yes, talk,' she said through clenched teeth. She picked the
cane up in both hands. 'Where would you be, where would any
of you be without my talk? *Where?*' she yelled and brought the
cane down full force across the end of the bed. Whack! It split
down its length.

'That was where the "Mr. Ittie March" came from,' my
mother says, looking at me across the Petersburg front room.
Then turning back to the others. 'That summer in the Ozarks,
near Galena, were two brothers, Homer and Wilbur Leverett.
They played—well, it's called folk music these days—I think
Homer played the fiddle and Wilbur the guitar. Every evening
Lee and Hilary used to walk down to the Leverett house and the
Leverett boys would get out their instruments and play way after
dark. Lee loved that sort of music, you know.' The group nodded,
forks delicately tapped the cake plates, and cups were eased onto
saucers.

'Oh, yes, he was very fond of that music and what it represented. That's why he took Theodore Dreiser to hear old Hannah Armstrong's son play the fiddle; you remember that piece

[47]

he wrote on that,' she says to Grace, probably the only person in the room who might have read the article. '*Esquire* magazine published it. Anyway, the Leverett boys. I took pictures of Lee and Hilary sitting with them as they played and one of them was used in a poster for the Ozark fair that summer. . . . Oh, *that's* how it happened,' she reminds herself and me. 'They were going to play in some sort of competition and Wilbur needed a new guitar so your father bought him one and the two boys composed this tune they called the "Mr. Ittie March" in gratitude. Lee called Hilary "Mr. It," ' she explains to the group.

'How did it go?' Uncle Will asks. A childhood ailment, scarlet fever perhaps, had impaired his voice so that he spoke in a feathery whisper that complemented his ninety-one years. 'Let's hear the tune.'

'How did it go, Hilary?' my mother asks.

'I don't remember,' I tell them.

'Ellen, there's some people from *Life* magazine that want to talk to you.' It's Sam Blane, the son of the late Judge Blane. Sam met me at the plane in Springfield and he has been helping us with the funeral arrangements. He's also a lawyer and, in fact, is about to run for the same judgeship his father held. 'Do you want to see them now or shall I tell them to come back?'

As if Sam Blane's interruption were a cue, the group in the parlor rises, collects cake plates and cups, and passes from the room to leave my mother and me alone. Some tarry a bit in the kitchen to leave by the back door or to tiptoe down the hallway of the tiny house and out the front. Grace has also been asked to stay for the interview.

'Thank you very much,' my mother is saying to the reporter's professional condolence. 'But we must all be grateful that he did not suffer. He really just . . . went to sleep.' She nods at me, nods at Grace, and then nods at the journalist. The skin around her eyes had begun to turn inward, her mouth swells. I look out the window but Seventh Street is quiet; I had half expected to see large limousines pulling to the curb with other members of the family: children, wives and mistresses, grandchildren and old business associates, all trooping into this slight frame house for coffee and cake.

But the village has done a good job keeping us apart as much as possible, putting us up in different parts of Petersburg or nearby Springfield, so that the atmosphere is not unlike one of those Shakespearean battlefields, busy with couriers arriving and departing to report locations and broken allegiances and generally give a handy exposition to clarify the awkward confusion.

'No, I won't permit that,' my mother says to the magazine reporter. 'I must think of the other members of the family. They want to take a picture of him in the coffin,' she says in a tone that seeks support, but with another breath she continues. 'No, I'm sorry but I can't permit that. This is just a family funeral and if you wish to take pictures, you may, but we're not going to make a . . . those people in New York—' She turns to Grace, who had already heard—several times on the train—what was to come. 'Those Poetry Society people wanted me to cart him into New York just so they could put him on display for their benefit. You should have heard the way Padraic Colum talked to me about how all of Lee's old friends would be so disappointed. Well,' her voice leveled, took aim, 'where were all those old friends when he needed them?'

The man from *Life* magazine had no answer nor was it his assignment to get this particular story of abandonment, as interpreted by my mother, but only to take some pictures of a poet's burial in a cemetery that also kept some of his poems' subjects. He rose and took his leave respectfully.

'I was right, wasn't I?' my mother asks Grace.

'Perfectly right,' her friend assures her.

'Just a family funeral, that's all,' my mother repeats almost dreamily.

[49]

'You're absolutely right, Ellen,' her friend says.

But how many families are attending this funeral? The bitter estrangements caused by my father's divorce twenty-eight years ago had become part of the town's lore and gossip. His version of the event, poured out for my mother and dutifully passed on to me, was an amphora of sour wine, thick with old matter and murky motivations. There had been the property lost, houses in Chicago and Michigan, his library confiscated, the treachery of Clarence Darrow, who had involved himself in the dispute with a portfolio of confidences my father had entrusted with him when they had been law partners. These details and others were set down again and again with no variation or dimension, like the sentences of an uninspired manuscript from an off-morning's work; in fact, they had probably intruded and spoiled many a good morning's work.

'Here, look at these,' Uncle Will says in his falsetto whisper. We are upstairs in the small room from which he puts out a worldwide correspondence on an old portable typewriter. Several years ago, Cousin Edith sent over a couple of girls from the high school secretarial course and they taught Uncle Will how to type. There are several wire baskets stacked near the typewriter with IN and OUT signs on them, and the OUT contains a dozen or more fat envelopes with the same gummed sticker pasted in the upper left hand corner of each.

Wilbur D. Masters
Seventh Street
Petersburg, Illinois
USA

'This is a fella I write to in Ireland,' he says, holding up a blue envelope. 'He's a Catholic priest,' the old man says, with a twinkle in his eye that suggests something daring in such correspondence.

There's the rest of it. From the other side, there must have been a sense of betrayal too, for my father had not been the most faithful of husbands, by his own testament in autobiography and poems; and the number of reconciliations before the final divorce suggests a lack of resolution, if not cruelty, on his part: the unauthentic acts of a man with no commitment. And then there was his betrayal of the region when he left Chicago and Illinois and the Midwest and took up residence in New York City. And then, *then*, a few years later to marry a woman almost thirty years his junior who was reported to be an Irish Roman Catholic!

'What do you write about to him? To the priest?' I ask Uncle Will.

'Oh, all sorts of things. Farming. State of the world. All sorts of things. Here's one—' He picks up another envelope. 'Australia.' He shows me the stamp. 'That's a kangaroo.'

So the petit bourgeois prejudices of the first family were seared by the possibility of the Papacy getting a toehold in the second. It was a laughable excitation, though no less real for those haunted by such inquisitions, for an actual search for the truth would have shown just the opposite to be true. My mother was even more of an agnostic than my father, having been raised in the anticlerical atmosphere generated by my grandfather, whose hatred of the Church and all organized religion sometimes reached maniacal proportions. One time, in Kansas City, my grandfather planned to shoot the local parish priest. The man had submitted, rather audaciously, a 'bill' for candles burned and prayers said to assure my grandmother's recovery from a traffic accident. Down came the Colt from the hatbox, its cylinder rotated and checked as he swore with a dry fury.

'Goddamn sonuvabitch. I'll shoot that sonuvabitch!' Gee Gee said. Then the final indictment against the holy father: 'He's not even a citizen, doesn't even have his papers—that son-uv-a-bitch!'

'Oh, my God, Tom. Put it away, put it away.' My grandmother was on her knees before him, in her nightgown, her left shoulder and arm in a cast. A month before she had been knocked down by a truck while crossing a street downtown.

'Out of my way, woman. Out of my way!' Gee Gee snarled, the pistol pointed at the ceiling. I stood outside in the hallway and watched. Should I go with him, to protect his flank, fight the rear guard?

'Don't distress us, Tom,' my grandmother pleaded. Her long gray hair was undone and fell to the floor. 'Oh, my God, what misery, what misery,' she sobbed. 'Think of the boy.' This final appeal worked. He looked at me over his shoulder and the ice in the blue eyes melted. 'Pshaw,' he said disgustedly and threw the heavy revolver on the bed, where it chimed the metal springs. My grandmother slowly got to her feet and Gee Gee swaggered to the window, hands clenched behind his back, to stare out at the backyard and the alley, a hero imprisoned by women and children.

Uncle Will turns back to his typing desk and looks for more letters that might interest me. He is a frail old man, neck fluted and shoulders sharp beneath his suit coat. He is the same age as my grandfather and they even bear a physical resemblance. He had been a good companion to my father in his boyhood, more of a brother than an uncle; a gentle, quizzical pal for fishing and hiking or for locating those islands of a dream that surface on the prairie on summer afternoons.

The age differences also must have been very bothersome to many people. My mother was thirty years younger than my father; he was nearly her father's age. Moreover, it must have been very difficult for my half brother to be the son, the only son for nearly thirty years—he is the same age as my mother—and then to have another boy child appear, another male who would carry on the name. To be the last of something can be an honor as jealously guarded as to be the first. So we are here together in Petersburg for the last time, some of us looking for places to stay, others seeking order in a sequence misaligned by human passions, and yet others with more ordinary quests: a Chopin waltz, Number Nine in A.

February 3, 1936

Dear Mr. Ittie: I love de.

*Today is your birthday, you are eight and I send you a check
for $8 to pay you for being eight, and being such a fine boy all
around. When I was eight I lived in Petersburg. My pa had a
law office on the west side of the square. You must have seen the
building. I used in those days to sit in the window of that office
and watch the circus parades. I used to see William H. Herndon
there talking to my pa. I used to go down with them to the
courthouse, where they talked about Lincoln and law cases. On
the way I saw my pa play jokes on Mentor Graham, an old man
then towards eighty. What a time that is ago.*

*About the time that I was eight my Aunt Anna came back
from Philadelphia where she had seen the Centennial Exposition,
and visited with Aunt Minerva who lived there. I sat with my
Grandpa Masters and Aunt Anna while she told him about
Philadelphia and the Exposition. He had just recently been to
Tennessee, Overton County, where he was born. They sat before
the fireplace, blazing with logs, all in the comfortable living
room of the Masters farm house. My but I was happy! Everything was so comfortable there, and such good pancakes and
ham and hominy and gravy. Such good cheer and fun! Snow
outside and sleighing, and neighbors coming in to talk to
grandpa about cattle and corn. Uncle Will was then 17 and
grandpa was 65. He seemed like a very old man; but he wasn't
so very old. He lived 28 years after those days. It all seems like a
dream, I see that fireplace, I see my grandpa sitting there. His
head was white as snow and had been white for years before
that. Aunt Anna was then about 28; and didn't get married for
a year or two after that. She married a pink bearded man who
was a church member. He got money from grandpa and blew
up. Aunt Anna died of a broken heart, leaving a lot of children.
Now after so long a time, Mignon Callish, a granddaughter
of Aunt Anna, is an actress in Hollywood. So things go from the*

farm and the past to the city and today. It is funny.

When you are as old as I am it will be 1995—think of that. I'll
be dead a long time then, and all the world will be changed.
I hope you will carry on happy memories of today, and all the
way. God knows what will happen! Anything can happen, and
we have to take it. I pray the gods for good luck for you—Tyche
[sic] the god of chance and fortune—to Hermes the guide—to
them all.

Your loving pa,
ELM

The funeral home in Petersburg is an imposing mansion with
a high mansard roof that sits on one of the hills overlooking the
village square. It had been built by a wealthy man during my
father's boyhood, and had been the object of his wonder as well
as the subject for many of his poems. He had used bits and pieces
of it, parts of its builder's history, in a number of the *Spoon
River* epitaphs and now, almost as if to achieve a final possession of the place, he had ordained that his funeral take
place in the high-ceilinged ostentatiousness of its Victorian
living room. I remember him talking of its stairway, the
banister of carved, polished wood, and as I enter the place, after
leaving Uncle Will's, I have a sudden urge to try it out. Had Lee
Masters, Squire Davis Masters's grandson whose father was the
Copperhead lawyer—had he hung around outside the front door,
to glimpse that beam of oak that angled down from the darkness
like a shaft made of amber? Had he waited, the house still but
for the sound of servants in the distant kitchen, then rushed
through the open door, up the carpeted stairs, one leg over the
rail, and swooped down the banister, heart and stomach changing
round, to fly weightless from the newel back through the open
door, over the porch and down the lawn—scot-free! He had done
it. I know he had.

'We're in here, Hilary.' It is Sam Blane's voice from the
kitchen. He and a young man who had volunteered to play the

records, a nephew of the undertaker's so perhaps not so much a volunteer, are looking over the apparatus that has been borrowed from the school. On the white enameled top of the kitchen table is a small phonograph turntable of the sort that plays through the amplifier of a radio. The arm must be placed and lifted manually. Two wires hang loose from the phonograph and, after trying several combinations, we hook them to the correct terminals in the radio. Two more wires lead to the large speaker that is propped against the kitchen door jamb and faces the front of the house.

'You're going to be like one of those disc jockeys, Benny,' Sam Blane jokes with the boy, who blushes everywhere but his ears. I lay out the heavy albums on the table, remove the record of *The Swan* by Saint-Saëns from its dust jacket and place it on the turntable. Piatigorsky's elegant bowing caresses the walls of this old mansion while I go over the program, arranging the records in the order they are to be played.

'First comes the Beethoven *Seventh,* but only the third movement. Then the second movement of the Franck. Then this record that's playing now, the Saint-Saëns. Then . . . then there was to be another record here but we don't have the right one so skip this.' Chopin is scratched. 'The Dvořák movement comes next, and then after the poem, put on the Sibelius, the entire symphony. That will be the last and will be played as people leave for the cemetery. The recessional.'

He nods and seems to understand the sequence. Some of the albums contain six heavy shellac records, and the spines of the covers are broken, the envelopes torn and patched. Around us are large square cabinets, glass-paned and as high as the ceiling of this spacious kitchen. A step ladder must be required to reach the top shelves. A modern refrigerator hums against the oak chair rail and the original plumbing of the boat-sized sink is exposed, put on display. Henry Adams could have written an essay on the plumbing beneath that sink. The undertaker and his family also live in this house, so there are pans and dishes and

[55]

utensils set into a red plastic drying rack that takes up a corner
of the white porcelain drainboard. Supper dishes; I guess they
had just eaten at this table. This evidence of family activity, of
life, seems out of place, or an oversight, in the preparations for
tomorrow's funeral. The family is probably upstairs somewhere
but it is as if they have ceased to exist, vanished to leave these
supper dishes drying on the drainboard and some images of sons
and daughters, smiling, capped and gowned, on the front hall
table.

I walk into the front of the house to listen to the volume level
of the music. Sam Blane comes with me and we go over the seat-
ing arrangements in the small parlor across the hall from the
main front room. Rows of folding chairs have been set up here;
not many, because only the family and some friends of the family
have been invited to this ceremony. There is movement behind
us, a cushioned slur of wheels on deep carpet, but I do not turn
around. My mother will sit here and I beside her. The Petersburg Masterses over there. My half brother and his wife behind
them. Sam Blane nods with each direction—he already knows
the arrangement—but he listens patiently. Then Marcia Schmid
and her husband. Better leave room for her daughter, though
no one knows if she's here; the intelligence network has broken
down. Nor has there been any information as to whether my
other half sister will attend the ceremony, though it's reported
she is in town. Well, on the other side, let's put the Springfield
Masterses, some other distant cousins here, and then those friends
that have been invited will be placed between the different
groups of family. Truly, positions of friendship.

But, at last, I must turn around. The undertaker has been attending me silently, patiently waiting for me to turn around as
he knew I would have to do in order to fulfill one of my obliga-
tions. Over his shoulder, I see the dark mahogany mantel, supported by Ionic columns in the same wood, and to the left, in a
bank of flowers so prolific in color as to challenge credulity, the
long metal case of the coffin rests on its coiled carriage. It re-

sembles a projectile, a peculiar missile because of its rectangular shape, as if it were a prototype developed before the efficacy of round barrels had been proved. It waits fully armed and ready to be fired by a method that will never be conceived.

'Will you view?' the undertaker asks gently. What for? I want to ask, to see if anything has changed since Philadelphia? To see if something has been jostled or turned around or has even disappeared during the train trip? Before I took the plane, I had briefly looked at his corpse, a perfunctory glance only to satisfy my mother's anxiety. Had she done the right thing? Did he look all right?

'Of course,' I reply.

But nothing has changed. The same gray suit with the small gravy stain near the fourth button of the vest. It has been nearly cleaned away; a slight amoebic outline remains, only apparent to someone who knows where to look for it. The large hands are folded upon one another, the nails of the long square fingers manicured. He always took special care of his fingernails. One hand might lift, fingers curled, as the nails scratched the pink skin of the bald head. The curvature of the skull would be illuminated and warmed by the reading lamp above his chair in the dining room.

It would be after dinner, a meal eaten with silent tension but still eaten. Pot roast and noodles and gravy and green beans. Ice cream for dessert. A silent evening. He had been reading, drawing on the pipeful of Prince Albert; my mother had been grading papers and reviewing the next day's class work. Then she picked up the shattered cane and began to bind it, carefully wrapping cellophane tape around its length. My father had put aside the copy of *Faust* and quietly observed her through a cloud of tobacco smoke. The hand is raised. Fingers curled, nails scratched the scalp, the hand brought down, and the fingernails studied judiciously. He looked across the room again, over his glasses, at my mother, who continued to repair the cane.

'By God, kid,' he said, 'that was a mighty swat.' The belly quivered, jiggled as the cackle started and then she began to laugh also, soundlessly at first but after a breath, with sharp, explosive sounds. They laughed together.

'Everything's fine,' I tell the undertaker.

*　　　*　　　*

Life magazine never published any of the pictures taken that day, presumably because no coffin shot had been permitted, but I have seen some of them. Many were stereotyped scenes arranged by an artful photographer: a barefoot boy on a country road with a fishing pole over one shoulder, or low perspectives of Oakhill Cemetery with the chiseled epitaphs looming in the moonlight. But there is one picture of my mother and me. We are either walking to our place at the gravesite or leaving it. It must have been chilly because we wore heavy coats; hers black, black hat and veil. My overcoat is a light-colored camelhair in the exaggerated style of that time. The width of the shoulders makes my neck seem even thinner and the thin face paler. The head seems too small for the coated body, like a paper doll. Moreover, the photographer had used a wide-angle lens for this picture, and it distorts our figures to give a peculiar motion to our promenade. I have a hand under her arm, and our right feet are both extended in mid-step; our bodies lean into the center of the picture. We are like dancers completing the fast-paced figure of a reel.

The slower distortions of memory are no less focused than those pictures. As members of the funeral are conducted to their assigned seats I pass into the kitchen to make a final review of the musical selections for the undertaker's nephew. When I return, the seat next to my mother—meant to be mine—has been taken by the widow of my father's brother. The two men had become bitter enemies in the last years of their lives. All during the ceremony this woman leans toward my mother when a *Life* magazine camera is pointed in their direction. I take a chair that is near the kitchen door.

The music begins and the mourners compose themselves to

listen, some staring at the flower-banked casket, others idly looking about the room. Some of the family members seem impatient; perhaps the selection of music is not to their taste. In fact, I sense something is wrong with the music myself. The record continues to scratch out Beethoven's *Seventh Symphony* but it is no longer the third movement—it is the second movement. The boy in the kitchen is not playing the records sequentially but is playing the flip sides as well, so the third and the second movements are intermixed. He plays the whole program in this manner, dutifully setting the phonograph needle into the grooves on each side of the selected records. The Dvořák *New World* is the most interesting. The composer's version of the old spiritual 'Goin' Home' is segued with the variations on 'Three Blind Mice' in the third movement. *Three blind mice, three blind mice.* The jaunty nursery melody dances about the funeral parlor, simultaneously inappropriate and wonderful. But it doesn't matter. I am the only one in the room who hears the difference, the only one who knows the program.

Then a man stands and walks to the small reading stand by the doorway. He bears a remarkable resemblance to Abraham Lincoln. I look at him closely. He's not as tall as Lincoln, but his face and shape of head are as exact as the image on the penny. In fact, he plays Abraham Lincoln in the summer pageant presented at the New Salem restoration nearby. He's also a state legislator and has volunteered his legislator-actor's voice to read the poem 'Silence.' This is all my father wished to have read over him. My half brother, an elder of the Presbyterian Church, had hoped my mother would permit a minister to conduct a brief service.

'No.' She pulled her arms up tight under her bosom. 'This is not my funeral or your funeral,' she spoke firmly. 'It is Lee's funeral. This is what he wanted.'

Some of the family are quietly crying. The lines of the poem are very fine and speak to each of us with sweet directness. Hearing these words and rhythms, I stare into the polished side of the coffin. The casket assumes a bulk, a mass it had not had before; the metal softens and becomes permeable. My mother's face is rice-powder white, the eyes dark and attentive and without a tear. The woman next to her no longer weaves back and forth. The photographers have left the home, to take up positions along the route. Sam Blane stands by the door, hands clasped before him. He seems more stricken with grief than anyone in the room.

> . . . And the silence of the gods who understand each
> other without speech.
> There is the silence of defeat.
> There is the silence of those unjustly punished;
> And the silence of the dying whose hand
> Suddenly grips yours.
> There is the silence between father and son,
> When the father cannot explain his life,
> Even though he be misunderstood for it.
>
> There is the silence that comes between
> husband and wife.
> There is the silence of those who have failed;
> And the vast silence that covers
> Broken nations and vanquished leaders.
> There is the silence of Lincoln,
> Thinking of the poverty of his youth.
> And the silence of Napoleon
> After Waterloo.
> And the silence of Jeanne d'Arc
> Saying amid the flames, 'Blessed Jesus'—
> Revealing in two words all sorrow, all hope.
> And there is the silence of age,
> Too full of wisdom for the tongue to utter it
> In words intelligible to those who have not lived
> The great range of life.

[60]

And there is the silence of the dead.
If we who are in life cannot speak
Of profound experiences,
Why do you marvel that the dead
Do not tell you of death?
Their silence shall be interpreted
As we approach them.

Abraham Lincoln's double pronounces the final lines of the poem. The room draws in on itself. Some pull back their shoulders, a gesture to support their sorrow or to endure the final moments of this unorthodox ceremony, it is not clear which. The stillness stretches to the breaking point. Slowly, I nudge the swinging door open with my foot and peek into the kitchen. The young man sits dutifully by the table, a distance in his face and large red hands slack in his lap. I cannot know if it is the poem that has so mesmerized him or some more ordinary preoccupation. I hate to disturb him but do so with a wave of a finger. He swallows and lifts the needle onto the record that has been silently revolving on the turntable. The brassy booms of Sibelius take the day.

When I stand, others follow my example until, with the guidance of the undertaker's staff, the funeral party is ushered outside. Family members file past the coffin. My half brother is weeping openly and I turn away and do not look. And then my mother and I are alone in the two large empty rooms. I take her arm and we go to the bier. She becomes very heavy on my arm. Her tears fall like drops of mercury. I have never heard her weep so profoundly and the depth of her grief embarrasses me though we are alone. Her knees seem about to buckle and I use all my strength to support her. The wild sounds of Sibelius swirl around us and my father's fixed expression is pink and fresh. At eighty-two, he looks too young to be there.

I often wonder how long that young man sat in the kitchen, playing those records. Did he play the symphony to the end, flipping the records to alternate the movements so that their sequence was not what Sibelius had intended? Yet he may have achieved the right order. The sounds of French horns, trombones, and cymbals caromed through the open doorway of the large mansion and followed us down the driveway. The tall, formal house stands upon the hill, all of its elegance and pride restored. The doors are open, some of last fall's leaves blow across the spare March lawn. The music contines to play. Out of sequence, it still plays.

4

'The barracks were there and here was the parade ground,' my grandfather says. We stand on a desolate plain in Montana and it is late summer, 1932. My grandmother has refused to walk up the hill to the site of Fort Custer but remains in the front seat of the Buick that Gee Gee has pulled to the side of the road below us. She wears the same peach organdy dress, gloves and hat to match, that she put on when we left Kansas City two weeks before, as if she had planned to address chapters of the Daughters of Isabella along the way.

My mother approaches my grandfather and me, bulky Kodak held before her as if she were a dowser, to take our picture as we stand beside the marker erected by the D.A.R. Fort Custer was one of several armed encampments hastily put up in the Northwest by the Hayes Administration in 1877, a year after the disaster suffered by the Seventh Cavalry a few miles away. My grandfather had been assigned to this fort around 1881, when he was twenty years old, but the Sioux had been vanquished by then.

'I spent some of the happiest days of my life here,' Gee Gee says. There is nothing on this sighing prairie to catch a memory; not a tree, bush, or rock but only this square block of granite rooted in this dry highland near the Little Big Horn River. Lacy rounds of tumbleweed roll across the plain and out of sight.

An old photograph of the place corrects the picture I have of it as I stand beside Gee Gee, my face bowed before the sun and my mother's camera. She peers into the viewfinder, focuses, and snaps the shutter. My idea of a fort comes from picture books and Saturday afternoon matinees at the Chief; it is a four-sided construction of logs upended, and with ends shaved razor sharp like so many pencils lined up and with battlements and square lookout towers at the corners. In one side, there would be a huge door that could always be swung shut and the bar fixed into place—just in time.

Not so. The actual Fort Custer, according to this photograph that I have seen recently, was a wide-open cluster of frame buildings joined together single file by the gothic carpentry of that ebullient period. The center of the establishment was several stories high and capped by a mansard roof. All that was missing was a railroad line laid down beside the buildings to make the whole affair look like one of those railroad stations knocked together quickly by an ambitious, greedy board of directors. And so it was, of course.

Lined up before this Victorian grandeur in the old photo was the regiment of the First Cavalry. Hundreds of troopers astride their horses, some of them ghostly mounts because the animals had swung or dropped their heads to smear their images on the glass plate. That itinerant photographer must have sold a lot of pictures though only the officers and staff in the front row could be distinguished. My grandfather is probably in that picture somewhere, a blur on horseback.

'One more,' my mother tells us. 'We'll take one more. Hilary, don't look down, look into the camera. Pa, move closer to Hilary. There.' She snaps the shutter and turns back to the car as she winds the film forward and folds up the camera's bellows. We stand for a moment more on what had been the parade ground and, in fact, Gee Gee is dressed as if he were to start a patrol.

A broad-brimmed felt hat is pulled low across his brow. Mother-of-pearl links are in his cuffs and rubber bands bind up the shirtsleeves. A tie is knotted into the exact angle of the stiff collar. He wears both suspenders and belt, a pair of brown leather gloves, but no coat—his only concession to the August heat. However, I know that next to his skin is the all-encompassing long underwear, worn summer and winter, because we have shared rooms across the country in a series of hotels, auto courts, and cabins that have dismayed my grandmother more and more the farther we have come from Kansas City. Pink purse clutched to her royal bosom, she would enter a musty lobby or a cramped room fuzzy with flies, her manner that of a minor duchess commanded to tour the hinterlands. 'We are going to see where *he* was a hero,' she had told my mother when we returned from the East.

The corn had been ready to pick in Colebrook, Connecticut, when my mother and I left for Kansas City and this trip west. My father had rented a small tenant farmhouse on the New York line, near Harlemville where he had taken a place two summers before. He had planned another summer's idyll for the three of us, but my grandfather had ordered us to return midseason. Gee Gee had bought a large Buick four-door sedan, had even taken a couple of driving lessons, and was determined to drive us to Yellowstone Park and the surrounding territory. I can imagine my mother trying to please both her father and her husband, and the keystone of that plea might have been the fact of my grandfather's age, then around seventy-two; that he had only a few more years to share with me. Of course, he was to live for another quarter of a century and survive my father by several years.

K. C. Missouri
7–8–32

Mr. Hilary Thomas Masters
Winsted, Conn.

My Dear Hilary,
    I received your nice letter & notice by your picture that you are getting fat. You will need that fat for if you are going on

the Yellowstone trip with me you will lose some of that surplus
flesh. I think we will be on that trip alone for Grandma is about
bluffed out now. When I talk about sleeping under the pines, she
says she can't stand it. She imagines she is going to stop at the
finest hotels. It can't be did. We will have to sleep in the open,
make our coffee & biscuits in the morning, kill our own meat
& catch our own fish. This wouldn't suit Grandma. She don't
like to dress in overalls & rough it. She is talking gallstones and
every imaginary ails now in order to get out of it. I imagine your
father and mother will side with her so I will have to depend on
you to accompany me. Don't forget the rod and gun. That's all we
want. We will hike out on Aug. 5, 4 AM, and have about twenty
days sport. You will always remember it. Everything at home
OK. Kids would all like to see you back.

> *Hoping everybody's OK*
> *I am yours*
> *Gee Gee*

Such letters must have disturbed the quiet of those Connecticut summer evenings flecked with fireflies. No tales of distant Homeric doings read by a kerosene lamp in a farm kitchen
could compete with the promise of live Indians. My father's
small garden, planted by the house before we joined him, was no
match for the wonders of Yellowstone Park.

'But he can't even drive,' my father said. They would be sitting on the small porch of the farmhouse. It would be twilight,
and I played with pots and pans around their feet, already making a campsite. 'How can he do it? It won't be safe.'

'He's taken lessons,' my mother soothed him. 'Also, I could
take some lessons when we get back, before we go. I could do
some of the driving.'

'I don't like it,' my father would say. 'What about all this?
What will I do here now?' He gestured toward the darkening
landscape. 'I drove a car once. I owned several cars in Chicago.
Then I had an accident and I never drove again.'

[66]

'Well'—my mother probably laughed—'there are a lot of people who drive automobiles that don't have accidents.'

'Yes,' his voice hissed with exasperation.

'Look,' my mother's voice lowered. I imagine she moved closer to him on the old sofa. 'We've had a good summer together. We've had good times, haven't we? You'll be able to get more work done alone. It will be for just this one time.'

'Yes, all right. All right. Well, Mr. It,' the voice raised and forced, 'you're going to look at some live bear and real Indians.' Then to my mother, 'Make sure you take a lot of pictures and send them to me.'

One more picture. A long time exposure with many blurred faces, many details lost but the outline distinct. The first street directory in Kansas City that lists Thomas Coyne is for the year 1885. This was the year that Mstr. Sgt. Thomas F. Coyne left the army, his discharge papers signed by a Col. Wainwright, father of the general who was to become the Hero of Bataan in World War II.

> *Thomas Coyne, laborer. Boards at 77 Ewing,*
> *Kansas City, Kansas.*

In that same year, he became a citizen of the United States, receiving his papers from a civil court in Kansas City. He was an Irish immigrant, with no one to recommend him, but his army service satisfied the five-year residency of record required by the naturalization act. Duty with the cavalry in the Indian Wars had been an admission to citizenship: a member of one alien class pursuing another in the same hostile territory.

'It was his own people that killed Sitting Bull,' he tells me in the bedroom one night as I play with the old pistol. 'And it was Indian scouts who murdered Crazy Horse, too. Ah, Hilary,' his voice fails, 'you don't know.'

Nor do I know how my grandparents met, nor does my mother know, though there must have been some family stories about their courtship and marriage, stories put aside, perhaps, and forgotten in my mother's second-generation rush from Kansas City to New York by way of the University of Chicago. Going from one place, but not irreversibly; here she now sits in the backseat of this huge Buick sedan as my grandfather steers it through the pre-dawn darkness of Kansas City, my grandmother beside him, gloved and veiled. It really is four o'clock in the morning, August 5, 1932, and we are starting off on the 1500-mile trip to Yellowstone Park. He grips the large, wooden steering wheel firmly, shoulders squared, and his right hand struggles and pushes at the gear shift on the floor as if forcing the wrong sword into the wrong scabbard. There is a grinding, jolting clash of metal: 'Goddamned sonuvabitch,' he mutters and my mother holds her breath, but she is here with me, away from her husband so that I might have this opportunity, this once-in-a-lifetime experience. She has not taken driving lessons.

In that same directory for 1885, my grandmother's father has two addresses.

John Moynihan, Constable.
1 Law Building, and 1936 Euclid.

In addition to serving warrants and subpoenas, Moynihan was also the superintendent of the county workhouse, a limestone structure with turrets and crenellated battlements; its inmates were Negroes who had become drunk or disorderly or had otherwise offended society by their presence. It might be said that John Moynihan served the same role, or even sentence, that his future son-in-law had already served on the Western frontier. So when Tom Coyne arrived in Kansas City in 1885, John Moynihan, the father of three handsome and talented daughters, occupied a prominent position in the community, a tall, exemplary figure to be emulated by all young Irish-Americans. Five years earlier, in the directory for 1880—when Gee Gee was just joining the cavalry—Moynihan was listed merely as the night-watchman at the workhouse, and with an address in the Bottoms, near the stockyards.

Kansas City in 1885 was a boom town. It surpassed Chicago as a railroad center, and its meat packers, dating back to the recent days of the Santa Fe Trail, still thrived. Grain was stored and traded. There were bridges being built across the Missouri and Kaw rivers, municipal buildings and boulevards to be designed and erected. Fountains and more fountains. Land bought and divided and sold again, and divided again to be sold once more. The population tripled between 1880 and 1890 to over 160,000, and fortunes were being made. It would have been a very attractive place for a young man just out of cavalry, especially a young man who had studied civil engineering through an army-sponsored correspondence course. Tom Coyne seemed to be drawn to heavy construction and management; perhaps this partiality was developed on the frontier where one of the duties of the cavalry was to patrol the lines laid down by the railroad companies, protecting the interests of an expanding economy.

So he started as a laborer, and then, according to the directory of 1887, Tom Coyne became the driver for a transfer company, his way with horses evidently a factor. The Moynihans still lived at the Euclid address, but in the meantime the Third Regiment of the Missouri National Guard had organized in 1886 and John Moynihan was made a sergeant of its commissary. Shortly thereafter he was elected to the rank of captain and would be known as 'Capt. John' until he died in 1918—even his obituary is so headed.

We have stopped. The car's lack of motion has raised my sweaty moonful face over the front seat. My grandfather is outside, in front of the car. Perhaps I had been awakened by the jolt when the Buick's right front fender hit the abutment of a small bridge. We're near Fort Riley, Kansas, and the eastern sky grows light as my mother and grandmother speak softly to each other, while my grandfather inspects the damage, a hand raised against the headlights. He garlands the front end of the automobile with a seamless bolt of oaths.

'A fine thing. A fine thing,' my grandmother says, pinning and repinning her hat. 'On the road a couple of hours and he rams us into a bridge.'

'Is there much damage?' my mother asks. Perhaps she's thinking we would have to turn around.

'We'll know if he takes out his gun and puts it out of its misery,' my grandmother replies. Then, as Gee Gee gets back into the car, her voice lifts, becomes jaunty. 'Are we all right, Tom?'

'Yes, yes,' he snaps and turns on the motor. 'Goddamn steering wheel. There must be something wrong with it. You could clearly see I was steering it correctly but it turned right into the Goddamn bridge.' He masters the reverse gear, backs the car away, and starts and jerks into forward motion.

'Well, then,' my grandmother says, adjusting her veil. 'Perhaps the bump has done it some good.'

He drove the car with the same lack of reverence with which he had handled horses, the identical determination to make it do his bidding contrary to its mechanical limitations. He never learned to operate the automobile and, in the course of the trip, fashioned gear ratios unthought of by the engineers at General Motors. His reputation as a horseman for wearing horses out, and even shooting them dead if they proved balky, seems to have been a general attitude of the Old West: a total disregard for all forms of life.

' "Coyne, take this message to Fort Yellowstone and if your horse drops dead—run the rest of the way." Those were my orders,' he told me one time in his bedroom.

'What'd you do, Gee Gee?'

'Just as ordered. And that's what happened. I let that horse go full out until he went to his knees. Then I ran on foot the rest of the way.'

'Did you shoot the horse?'

'Had to, to put him out of his misery. But when I was trying to destroy the saddle, trying to chop it up with that saber there, I noticed blood coming out of my sleeve, and I couldn't hold the sword in my right hand.'

'What happened?'

He got up and stood over the hot-air register to warm the seat of his long underwear. The winters in Kansas City were cold and damp.

'Well, I guess some galoot of an Indian had taken a shot at me and I was riding so hard I never noticed it.' He held up his right arm and pulled back the sleeve of the underwear. 'The bullet had gone in here at my wrist and come out my elbow. I never felt a thing. When I got to Fort Yellowstone there was this young shavetail just out of the Point who was serving as the medic and he sewed me up. That's why, Hilary, I can raise this hand back only this far.' He demonstrated.

Laborer, drover, and also a fireman for a time, probably the driver of a horse-drawn steamer: I imagine this cocky bantam figure moving about Kansas City in the 1880s. His sandy hair was meticulously parted down the center of his skull and the heavy handlebar moustache had been combed and brushed. The falcon eyes would be fixed for the slightest movement that could advance him. My mother remembers something about his doing the account books for John Moynihan at the workhouse, but the details are vague and when this took place she does not know. No one knows exactly when he swaggered into the steady, substantial path of the Moynihan family, but in 1893, the year of the Columbia Exposition in Chicago, their trails clearly joined.

The duties of the Third Regiment of Missouri were mostly ceremonial. The outfit had marched in the cortège of General Sherman's funeral in St. Louis in 1891 but they saw more action on the dance floors of fancy dress balls. In 1893 the Third was given duty at the fair in Chicago to represent the state during different ceremonies, and Capt. John Moynihan went along as head of the commissary. There was another pseudo-military group organized and sent to the fair, the Columbia Guards, and these were volunteers composed of former cavalrymen who would act as guides and give demonstrations of horse maneuvers. They wore special uniforms and were provided with superb mounts. Tom Coyne signed up.

At thirty-three years of age, in an era when life expectancy was not much more, Tom Coyne was yet far from the place he must have dreamed for himself, a citizen now but still a drifter with no fortune, no position, no home, no authentic place in that society. He would volunteer for such glamorous duty if only to change his luck, to return to the stability and camaraderie of a military organization, though it might be only a charade of the genuine. Why didn't he stay in the army, a life and vocation for which he was obviously suited? Advancement from the ranks in the army of that day was difficult if not almost impossible, and to become a commissioned officer without a West Point degree was very rare. As a master sergeant, Tom Coyne had gone as high as he could go in the general ranks before he took the West Point examination offered to noncommissioned officers. He failed algebra.

Advancement in the civilian life of Kansas City seemed closed off as well. Perhaps he had already worked for John Moynihan, but there was no excitement, no future as an accountant for a minor public official. He may have proposed already to one of the Moynihan girls—the eldest, Katherine—and been turned down. One of the reasons for his suit's failure was a winter sleigh ride during which he drove the horses at such a breakneck pace that the sleigh overturned, throwing Katherine Moynihan into a deep snowbank. Aunt Kit blamed that furious courtship for the deafness that kept her from the concert stage as a violinist.

However, I would suppose the reason for his rejection had more to do with the Moynihans' sense of their own position in Kansas City, a place only just won and therefore strictly posted against trespassers. John Moynihan had invested in the land speculations that swept the city during the 1880s, so that besides his political and social titles he had received another degree hallowed by an emergent middle class: a man of property. The Moynihan girls attended the old Greenwood School in Westport, an institution noted for its cultural refinements, and prominent people and politicians such as Mayor Davenport often dined with the family. Who, then, was this wiry horse driver Coyne, this ex-army man at a time when the army was known to be a refuge for paroled criminals and failures? How presumptuous of him even to attend the family musicales: Katherine on the violin, Nona at the piano as they accompanied the lush contralto of their dark-eyed sister, Mollie: 'O Promise Me.' His brusque manners and rough clothes, even the sort of shoes he wore, and his swinging gait more appropriate to a man much taller and therefore egotistical—on him, all were objects of their amusement.

There's another side and it is not incompatible. Tom Coyne might have volunteered for the Columbia Guards merely to follow John Moynihan to Chicago and stay in touch with the family. There are stories of Moynihan staying too long at the fair and Mollie, the middle daughter, was sent to Chicago to bring him home. She stayed with her mother's people and it is likely she and Tom Coyne saw each other. More than likely. He must have made an entirely different impression in his operatic guard's uniform as he sat a good horse; this was not the same bandy-legged Irish immigrant she had known in Kansas City, but, for a girl of twenty, a romantic figure.

'*Look out* . . . , *look out* . . . *that car!*' my mother screams and her arm cuts across the front seat. She points at the automobile that comes down the canyon road toward us, head on.

'That sonuvabitch,' Gee Gee swears through clenched teeth. He grips the steering wheel, courageous to the end. 'He's on the wrong side of the road—that sonuvabitch!'

'*You're* on the wrong side of the road!' my mother shouts. 'Turn right. Turn right! Here he comes. *Oh God!* We're lost!'

Gee Gee swings the wheel and we narrowly miss the other car.

But the sudden maneuver has put us on the shoulder of the mountain highway. The wheels scramble and spin on the crumbling earth. There is no fence, no tree or rock to spoil the magnificent panorama or to hamper the drop down into a gorge several thousand feet below.

'Look at that lovely view,' my grandmother observes as the car rocks and moves crablike on the edge of the canyon. 'Look down there,' she tells my mother, who does not look but falls back into the seat beside me to press her face into the embroidery of a souvenir pillow. It says GREETINGS FROM CHEYENNE, WYOMING.

'Go. Get up,' my grandfather commands the Buick. 'Get on there. Hi-yah!' Slowly, one by one, the rear tires find solid purchase and the heavy car gradually pulls itself back onto the highway pavement.

Once we had left the straight, uncomplicated route of the Lincoln Highway, my grandfather's impatience with the Buick increased, while his ignorance of its operation, after a thousand miles, remained unchanged. On the narrow, winding roads over the Rocky Mountains, this ignorance and temper were continually tested. Every hairpin curve picked at my mother's nerves. This was 1932, it should be remembered; such transcontinental pleasure trips by automobile were not common, and the roads and facilities along the way were primitive. Moreover, my grandfather seemed to take special delight in choosing the most archaic of these, sometimes locking the Buick's big handbrake before a forlorn encampment of matchbox cabins surrounded by white rubber tires thrown to the ground in a pattern of desultory rescue. He led us into a series of tourist homes, the smells of GOOD HOME COOKING in each one becoming more and more mineral as if their kitchens had been built along some fault in the earth that deepened the farther west we went.

My grandfather had left memories here a half century before: the aspirations of a young man of twenty that had been sifted in this formidable wilderness and perhaps all the more wonder-

ful to dream them in this rocky place. Sometimes we return
to such sources, old neighborhoods and reunions, as much to see
where the wrong path was taken as to renew acquaintance with
the past, where there had been a choice, where there is always a
choice, a different stream to follow that might lead to the fabulous lode—even now.

The journey was more for the benefit of my grandmother and
mother than it was for me, though I was used as the excuse, the
bait. It was a way for Gee Gee to prove his worth to the Moynihan family, his way to win an argument with the dead and dis-
interested. My grandmother's lilting sarcasm had truth to it:
he wanted to show them where he had been a hero.

Yellowstone Park had been administered by the army then,
and the cavalry patrolled its extraordinary domain to keep
order, to regulate the lumber interests, and to defend the rare
tourist of the 1880s from hungry Indian and bear. Jackson's
Hole was a hideout for bandits and cutthroats, and the Pinker-
ton detectives would not go there, but Sgt. Tom Coyne became
famous for riding into its depths alone to bring a stage robber
or rustler to justice. He was remembered, his name was on file in
the administration building of Yellowstone Park; and he supplied a recent picture, one he must have brought with him
for the purpose. It was thumbtacked to the backboard of a display case in the tourist information center.

Thomas F. Coyne
One of the first rangers of Yellowstone
Park as a Sgt. in the U. S. Cavalry.

There, he could step back and say to my grandmother and
mother—there. They were both smiling and nodding, especially
happy perhaps to be out of the Buick and on firm ground. Their
smiling and nodding sense of security was to be brief. The next
morning he led an amiable bear into their tiny tourist cabin
near Old Faithful. Fortunately, the animal could be lured out

with some stale doughnuts. The women noted the petrified forests and boiling geysers, the waterfalls and deep woods. He revealed the whole enchanted landscape of his youth for their forbearing inspection; a purse-clutched biding of time until they could return to sidewalks and good linen. So I became his only witness, but the deer and bear cubs that ambled from the forest stole my attention. No one wanted to see his credentials. We got back into the Buick, turned right, and headed for the site of Fort Custer and the old battleground nearby.

* * *

'By God, Hilary, sometimes I wish I had been with the Seventh Cavalry in '76.'

'Why do you say that, Gee Gee?' It is 1946; I am in the navy, stationed in Washington, and I visit him periodically at the Soldiers Home where he spent his last years. He met me at the top of the stairs of his hospital ward on the second floor, a blue bathrobe over his pants and underwear top and the old felt hat set squarely across his brow.

'They keep things scrupulously clean here,' he said, as he ushered me downstairs and out of the cough-laden atmosphere. 'But we can talk outside.' The spring air is fragrant with the heavy sweetness of the warming Potomac tidewater, and the grounds are in bloom. Fair weather has also produced the year's first golfers on the course below. 'Look up at the name on that building,' he said. 'What's the name of that building?'

'Legard.'

'There, you see? Legard. I knew Legard down on the Panama. He was a fine surgeon. I tried to get your grandmother to let him remove that goiter that destroyed her but she wouldn't. Anyways, I knew him and George Goethals and also Gorgas. Col. Gorgas and Legard put me in charge of a whole department in Cuba to clean up the yellow fever mosquitoes. And here I am now in a hospital named after him. It was another world. Then the other day'—he lifted the stained hat and reset it in the exact same line across his brow—'the other day I see this picture of

[76]

young Wainwright in the newspapers. For Christ's sake, he's an old man! I remember him as a little baby, crawling around Fort Custer!'

'But he's just got out of a Japanese prison camp, Gee Gee.'

'Why, pshaw.' He resembled a good-humored peasant who is the butt of a joke. 'I'm all mixed up, Hilary. I have to keep track of too many lives—and they're all mine. If I had been with that idiot at the Little Big Horn, I wouldn't have to worry about any of this now.'

'Well, you wouldn't have to worry about me,' I answered. It had been a snap shot and caught him unawares as his mind hurtled over old frustrations.

'Why, you young galoot.' He sounded as if he spoke under water but he slapped at my shoulder. We sat on a bench beneath budding cherry trees, the hospital buildings behind us. He stood up, a hand motioned for me to follow. He used the same heels-out swagger I could remember following down Roberts Street at the end of the day. My grandmother would say it tired her just to watch him walk.

'Did I ever tell you,' he had turned to me, 'how I got down to South America?'

'You mean with the Columbia Guards? The revolution in Bolivia, wasn't it?'

'It wasn't Bolivia. It was Uruguay.' He stopped by a water fountain, leaned over, one hand over his groin, and took small sips as if the water were rationed. 'This fella came up to the Chicago fair and said his country was in this revolution. He wanted to enlist us, we having been crack cavalrymen, to come down and train the government's troops.' He patted his lips dry. Above the upper lip was the silvery shadow of a small moustache.

'Yes, you've told me about that,' I replied. A couple of veterans below lined up their putts on the green.

Capt. John or his daughter Mollie, or perhaps both, had turned down Tom Coyne. The South American agent appeared at the right moment; the ex-soldier decided to make use of the only skill his adopted country had taught him, apparently would permit him to use. Something else. Perhaps he also hoped that his identity would take root and grow in the humid anonymity of the tropics or, at least, that documents in Spanish and Portuguese would record him as a citizen of the United States, a professional, rather than an Irish immigrant and knockabout.

So Tom Coyne and other members of the Columbia Guards joined the revolution and were embarked on a small freighter from New Orleans for the trip across the Gulf. Halfway across, the propeller fell off the ship and the vessel floated helplessly in the Gulf currents Moreover, it was New Year's, so passing ships answered their rockets and distress flares with similar signals, but in celebration, and continued without stopping. Apparently, there was no wireless aboard the small ship. Eventually they were towed to Tampico where they learned the revolution was over and their side had lost. Tom Coyne disappeared into the Yucatan jungle, to reappear in Kansas City a few years later a wealthy man, like a character in some serialized romance. He was as reticent about this part of his life as he was about his earlier passage to California.

Or maybe there was little to remember, scant material for a sequential narrative. His correspondence course in civil engineering became more important than his military background. From 1894 to 1898, he worked his way through Mexico and Central America on railroads as laborer, crew boss, engineer, and conductor. He was the chief construction engineer for the Quito-Guayaquil railroad in Ecuador, laying track and building trestles across the Andes. But this came later, as did his years on the Panama Canal. In the meantime, he learned to speak Spanish fluently, survived malaria and yellow fever, and was wanted for murder in several Mexican states, though this was a technicality, he would explain, since he had only been defending railroad property or gold shipments. In 1898, America declared war on Spain, but Tom Coyne returned to Kansas City with no interest in the fight and a scorn for those who volunteered to enforce

Manifest Destiny, a scorn so virtuous that it still poured down upon the old veterans on the golf course at the Soldiers Home. He had done his tour of that duty.

'Look at 'em.' He would point to some players, preparing to tee off. 'Not one of 'em did any real fighting. They all marched around in Florida with wooden guns. I tell you who won that war.' The blue eyes lightened. 'It was a Negra regiment that was ordered to take San Juan Hill. And they took it, at terrible cost. Don't forget that.'

The Kansas City directory of 1898 lists John Moynihan living at 1121 Pearl Street with 'daughters, Molly, clerk, and Nona, teacher.' Capt. John was one of many land speculators who had held mortgages on small margins to suffer financial disaster when the real estate market collapsed in the 1890s. 'I'm a ruined man,' he was supposed to have said one evening after supper. Whatever happened to Capt. John has been painted over by family pride but his downfall must have had several dimensions, because his wife left both him and their daughters to return to her own family in Chicago, where she died in 1900. He was not re-elected to his post as constable nor do the records of the Third Regiment carry his name after 1896. The new address on Pearl was a modest bungalow. Mollie had left her teacher's training to clerk in a dry goods store and Nona had become a teacher, so it appears the two daughters were supporting the father. Katherine had left home.

It was into this somber parlor on Pearl Street that Tom Coyne walked with his letters of credit and a chamois bag of gold coins that bore the images of Inca kings. There had been a lot of changes. He and Mollie were married in August of 1898, and he bought the property on Roberts Street and rebuilt the house to his own specifications in time for my mother to be born in the upstairs front bedroom the following May. Then, as if for relief from these civil chores, he turned around and headed back into the steamy environment of South America where he was more at home. Before he returned he bought several more pieces of property, also houses; he took no mortgages but paid cash in full.

'One time I went to sign up for work on the Panama Canal. This was around 1910 and I was running a railroad down from Guatemala.' I had heard this story many times in the bedroom on Roberts Street but listened to it once again as I followed the golfers' game. 'The army was giving out contracts for freight, so I get down to Colón but there's this long line in front of the quartermaster headquarters.' He pulled the robe about his legs in a womanly way and carefully sat down on a bench. I joined him.

'There were men coming back from the office saying everything had already been signed up. But I stayed in line anyhow. Then I get into the building. Then I get into the room. And then I am standing before this table where a major is looking over some papers. He never looked up at me. But by God, who do you suppose he was?' His eyes fixed upon me. The tension in his frail body welded him to the metal bench.

'It was the officer that had sewn you up when that Indian shot you,' I replied. A large commercial airliner passed low overhead, its four engines throttled back for a landing. The blades of the propellers could almost be counted.

'By God, that's right,' Gee Gee replied with astonishment, not because I knew the answer but because of the answer itself. The coincidence still surprised him, still ticked his wonder. 'Thirty years before, almost. He was just out of West Point and had fixed me up that time I ran into Fort Yellowstone.

' "I'm sorry, sir," he says to me in Panama, without looking up, "but we are all signed up."

' "I don't suppose you remember me, sir," I say right back. And then, Hilary, he looks up at me for the first time.

' "I am sorry, sir," he says, "but I do not remember you."

' "Then, sir," I say back to him, "perhaps you will remember this," ' and my grandfather held out his right arm, pulled the bathrobe sleeve up, and bent his right hand back as far as the old scar would permit.

' "My God," the galoot says, "it's Coyne!" '

'And you got the job,' I said. A fresh quartet of golfers are on the tee. They wear bright-colored caps.

'Eh?'

'I said, You got the job?'

'Oh sure.' He looked down at his crossed feet as if to inspect the high-topped shoes, neatly laced and polished. 'I got the job. We had men then. There were heroes in those days, and I knew some of them. All gone. And here I am. Why is that?'

My mother wants to take more pictures at the battlefield. She has opened the back of the camera and has inserted a fresh roll of film, sets the flap in the empty spool, shuts the case, and slowly winds the film while observing its advance through the tiny red eye in the camera's body. She does all this crouched on the floor of the Buick's backseat. The shades on the car's rear windows have been lowered to minimize the risk of the film's exposure to light; she has read all the directions and follows them to the letter, not wishing to make any mistakes. The pictures are to be sent back to my father.

We have stopped at a small cabin by the road where an Indian sells beaded belts, purses, and jewelry in addition to postcards of the battlefield nearby. He is a very handsome man, a paradigm appropriated by magazine illustrators and motion pictures. There is a picture of me standing beside this man. I am looking down at my feet again, away from the sun and the camera's lens. The Indian is very tall, with two long braids over his chest. He wears a beaded vest, pants, and moccasins, and his right hand rests upon my head. I have a toy pistol and holster strapped around my chest.

My grandmother has walked into the small cabin to look at the display, but my grandfather has become unusually shy and will not pose with me and the Indian when my mother suggests it. He has lifted up one side of the Buick's hood and stares into the oily darkness, pulls out the crankcase dip stick and slides it back into its holder, never looking at it. Later, when my mother, grandmother, and I are all inside the cabin, a peculiar mumble begins outside the door. My grandfather and the Indian are talking in a strange language, accompanied by precise hand gestures. They both seem to be crying.

'What did you say to him?' my mother asks as we drive toward the Custer battlefield.

'He's a Crow,' my grandfather replies, his chin level with the top of the steering wheel. 'We talked about the crops. About the weather. His wife died last year. TB.'

The rolling hills enfold us, desolate and dry. My grandmother pulls up the slack in her long gloves as my grandfather keeps the Buick in second gear. Again, this is 1932 and there are no tourists, no guards or information booths, very few signs; so this morning there are just the four of us in this tall-bodied, green Buick with wooden-spoked wheels that mill the road dust. It is quiet within the car and my grandfather steers without a mistake, following an old route taken sixty years before.

'Well, I guess you've heard all my stories,' Gee Gee said. He shivered slightly in the changing breeze from Maryland.

'Yes, but I always like to hear them again,' I told him. It was getting late in the afternoon, probably a Saturday afternoon.

'It all seems like a dream to me, Hilary,' he said as he pulled the brown envelope from his bathrobe pocket. It bore a government postal frank. 'Take this for instance.' He pulls out the stiff, green pension check. 'Every month this comes to me for the time I spent on the Panama Canal, but when it comes I look at the name and the address and I think it must be for someone else. I sometimes think of returning it.' He laughed suddenly, slyly. 'Don't worry. I won't send it back. You young galoot. What do you do with all the money I give you? I suppose you spend it on some girl?'

'No, I'm saving it for college,' I said and looked away. He gave me the check, already endorsed.

'Be careful of women and liquor, Hilary,' he continued. 'Look what happened to Franklin Roosevelt. Save your money. Look what happened to me; think of the fortunes I had and lost because I was foolish. Anything can happen. Why, some night, one of these fifth columnists might sneak in and blow up the Panama Canal and that would be the end of these checks. Where would you be then? Well, go along with you.' He stood up. His arms motioned me forward as if I were a squad to be advanced. 'Go on. Get out of here.'

There is a picture of my grandmother beside the Buick. It is not remembered if my mother took this picture at the Little Big Horn battleground or someplace else, but my grandmother wears a straw hat and veil, a long full dress, what used to be known as an 'afternoon dress,' and the usual purse grasped by both hands below the gown's sash. Her arms form two sides of a narrow, inverted triangle, and her legs, the feet crossed, repeat the design; both patterns like trusses meant to contain her soft, ample proportions as she leans against the angular, hard shape of the automobile. Her stature and manner suggest that she is the one who controls the large vehicle and not the slight, wiry man who had set the handbrake and led my mother and me up the small hill randomly picketed by gravestones.

It is likely that my grandmother did get out of the car finally. Perhaps it was cooler to stand beside it than to remain seated on the overstuffed velour upholstery; to lean against the dark green car in a pose to suggest she held all her softness together to keep it from spilling over the Montana prairie, and to peer from beneath the straw hat's brim up the rise of the hill and watch us move among the rude markers set here to indicate where the different officers of Custer's command had fallen. It was at that moment, perhaps, that she decided to give up.

If she had bargained herself to provide a home for her father and restore a family's pride, then she may have decided she had had enough, for Capt. John had been dead fourteen years and her only child—the conception of a child was, I think, a shattering experience for both my mother's parents, never to be repeated—her only child had left Kansas City, married now and with a child of her own. There had been years of housekeeping or trying to keep a house together; trying to keep the Haviland china and the crystal and the vases hand painted with the heavy blooms of peonies; but they had disappeared one by one, left behind in this house or thrown away in another one in Kansas City, or used by some housegirl in the Ozarks to dip water or feed table scraps to hounds.

So too had the furniture gone: the sideboards and dining tables and the chiffoniers, burned or thrown out as soon as a chair or a bureau showed failure at a joint, a rupture of mortise, or, in the case of a crib or child's rocker, when the specifications were no longer applicable. She had watched it all go, each item punished, it seemed, executed for its betrayal of the person who had sat upon it or tried to open it during the one moment of its frailty. I wonder if it ever occurred to her that my grandfather's dispersal of all her fine things, his scorn for the genteel collections and artifacts of her family's rise, things that only attracted dust and kept the rooms from being scrupulously clean, had been set up by that family's earlier scorn for him. Not to be recognized at the right time for one's rightful accomplishments, for one's worth, can precipitate a greed for such recognition, a compulsion to make up for that slight though it can never be made up.

His appearance on the hill above her, almost skipping about the graves of the slain cavalrymen, also must have urged her to withdraw. It was no contest, never had been. His energy, his sudden enthusiasms and dreams pursued at a gallop had exhausted her, and the puritanical logic that barracked all of his emotions, all of his human relationships, had driven her spirit deeper into the sentimental rooms of her placid nature, rooms carelessly, yet forgivingly furnished in the half-light of her compassion. She could withdraw quietly, unnoticed. Her social works with the Church, her recent involvement with Tom Pendergast's Democratic Party would be used to escape from a house she could no longer keep and that no longer kept anything that belonged to her. Her time in life and the time of her life inhibited her mind from thinking any other way. True, her own mother had left her father, had left them all for whatever reason she would not think about now, but the example was there for her to follow.

There was no reason for her to keep up a home, prepare meals for someone who would rather fry his own bacon, boil his oatmeal, and toast bread on the end of a fork held over the gas grate. As for linens, the clean bedclothes that were to be changed on Wednesdays and Saturdays, the long muslin leg wrappings redolent of liniments and the shirts with cuffs and collars to be starched to the stiffness of celluloid—well, there were laundries to do that now. He offended her. He exhausted and offended her, and to stand in the dusty coulees of Montana and watch him move happily over this site of an old savagery, this desolate arena of a barbarism that she could not, would not imagine, and for him to sport in it as if he had taken part and wished to bring it all back to satisfy some awful thirst, to seek a refreshment on this dry plain that would revivify the clash and roar and screams of that battle, bring them all back as a drop of water will sometimes make a stain that has all but disappeared reappear on cloth, to do that so he could deliver one clean, brutal thrust, appalled her. No, she would not leave, not physically, but there was nothing, no one to keep her.

'Here's where they found him.' My mother stands over a square tablet stuck crookedly in the ground.

'Crazy Horse swept up over that rise,' my grandfather shows us, 'at the head of his men. He caught Custer completely by surprise. By God, he was as great as Marshal Ney.'

'Custer?' asks my mother.

'No, Crazy Horse.' Gee Gee kicks at the dry soil. 'The Sioux were the finest lighthorse cavalrymen the world has ever known. Custer! Why, pshaw,' he spits to one side. 'That dumb sonuvabitch. Divided his command. Ignored his scouts' reports. He was going for glory. He wanted to be President. The Democrats were meeting in St. Louis at the very time he rode in here. He hoped for a great victory so he would be nominated.' He lifts and resets the felt hat, the brim so low over his eyes that his mouth is in shadow. He looks over the folds of landscape, locates something.

'On Sundays,' he continues, 'after we'd groomed the horses, cleaned the barracks, and stood for review, some of us would ride out here from the fort—we'd come right down through that gully over there.' He points. 'Sometimes we'd find something, a piece of leather, an empty cartridge, such stuff. We'd bury it around here. Well,' he looks away, 'there wasn't much else to do out here on a Sunday.'

'Did you find any bones, Gee Gee?' I ask.

'No. No bones.' His laugh is light as if absorbed by the dry soil he stands upon. 'No bones. They found him sitting up right there.' He motions to the marker at my mother's feet. 'They set him there naked, facing west with all of his officers stretched out around him on the compass points. But he wasn't scalped, the only one they didn't scalp, nor was he otherwise tampered with.' He clears his throat and looks away again.

'Why not?' my mother asks. 'Why didn't they scalp him? Did they respect him too much?'

'Respect him?' My grandfather snorts. 'That sonuvabitch? I guess not likely. Nobody knows for sure why he wasn't scalped. I talked to some Blackfeet once who said that he shot himself. The Indians believed that anyone who committed suicide had put a hex on his body. They wouldn't touch such a body, not scalp it or mutilate it so as not to let the evil spirits escape on to them. But, we'll never know for sure. It might be the only clean thing he ever did. One thing is certain, if they had had sabers with them, some of them might have been able to cut their way out. The brass in Washington had come up with a new policy just before that took the saber away from the cavalry except for ceremonial occasions. So all the Seventh Cavalry had with them were their sidearms and those old carbines that froze up after a couple of rounds. The Sioux had brand-new Win-

chester repeaters they'd got from traders. Also, arrows and spears.
Why, it was hardly any fight at all. But if the cavalry had had
sabers, they could have made a run for it and maybe cut their
way out. After the massacre, that order was turned around.'

He had moved about the hillside as he spoke, moved among
the crude markers. I watch him closely, expecting that he will
turn up something with the round toe of his high-topped shoes,
a souvenir I can take back to Kansas City. Sweat stains parallel
the white suspenders over his shoulders. He pulls the leather
gloves snug and swings up to the top of the hill, the same strategic
promontory that Custer and his men were denied. His feet are
apart and his hands grip his waist, elbows out. It is a pose to be
taken on the world's highest peaks; perhaps he had stood this
way on top of the Andes, but this pimple on the Montana prairie
is only a hundred feet or so above sea level. It is high enough,
reaches an altitude of his being that can never be topped. My
mother responds quickly to the moment.

'Here, let me take a picture,' she says, coming forward with
the camera, bent over and trying to fit his image into the tiny,
jiggling viewfinder.

'Put that thing away,' he commands with a wave of a hand.
'We've had enough pictures.'

'Just one here, Pa,' she implores. 'Especially one here.'

'I said put that thing away,' he repeats. His eyes are losing
their color, and the cheekbones sharpen beneath his skin. He
gestures down the hill toward my grandmother, who stands by
the car. 'Take a picture of her, why don't you.' His mouth shapes
a silent laugh, a mask. 'There she stands,' he says, a gloved
hand up. 'There she stands. Waiting. Always waiting and waiting. Never . . .' His voice stops abruptly, and he pulls at a
gold chain looped around the right suspender before it drops
into the pants pocket on the same side, one link dangling a small
gold coin—the last of the South American plunder. He has lifted
out the slim Hamilton watch with the engraved platinum face.

'It's time to go,' he says as if the hands of the watch carried the message. 'It's time we got back to Kansas City. There's nothing more to see here.'

I am running down the hillside through the memorials of that awful conflict. My grandmother smiles and her face dimples; the lines cleave her cheeks like the divisions in ripe peaches. Her large brown eyes swim in their own rich liquefaction and their light pulls me on faster and faster.

'Grandma, Grandma,' I yell as her arms go out to me and I leap upon the soft couch of her body to be borne on the rise of her breath above this dry and ancient landscape. I can smell her flesh, warmed and moist, a residue of Evening in Paris upon it as there is scent of lavender sachet still caught in the slippery folds of her organdy dress, so slippery that I must cling to her with both arms so that I do not slide off her bosom, my knees, my legs now apart, now pinched; a frantic scrambling, swimming motion upon that high, silky sierra. My hands knot themselves behind her neck and my mouth tastes the pulse that beats there involuntarily, a tremulous shifting of blood as delicate, as precarious, as my perch above the earth.

'Grandma, Grandma.' My arms ache, and the sweat-slick weave of my fingers begins to come undone. 'We are going back to Kansas City. I am going back to your house.'

And then her arms enfold me, her arms move away from her sides, lift and support me as I climb upon her but from no necessity, no obligation to hold me save for the dumb, unknowing turn of her heart, the selfless surrender that would bring her to destruction but for now presses me to her forever. 'Grandma's boy,' she says.

5

Yesterday, my mother pulled into the driveway of our house in this Midwestern city where I have a teaching position. She is seventy-seven, heavy with those years and the anxieties that push her two thousand miles across the continent to correct a date or locate a misplaced document that will establish, once and for all, the true version of my father's existence. Since she learned to drive a car, after the Yellowstone trip, she has taken the same route many times: to Petersburg, Illinois, where he is buried, to Garnett, Kansas, where he was born, to Chicago where there are some yet alive who knew him as a young man, and back to New York where they had married and lived. She worries the continuity of his life like a collector of rare stuff, smoothing a fold or turning over a fault, so that his life and her life with him assume the character of an historical novel, but like any piece of prose, something to be endlessly corrected.

My father stayed on in Colebrook, Connecticut, when we returned to Kansas City from the Yellowstone trip. I picture him on the small porch of that rented farmhouse, the smoke from his pipe curling in the moonlight, the crickets for company. Every day he would work at the kitchen table, tap-tapping the keys of a thin black portable typewriter or covering pages of manuscript with neat, nearly indecipherable script. His productivity rivaled the sun's and, in fact, he seemed to be engaged in a race with the sun, like one of those ancient Greek heroes he would tell me about, always chasing but never catching up. The year before he had published two books, his biography of Lincoln and *Godbey,* six thousand lines of rhymed allegory that were mostly doggerel. That summer of 1932 he had written *Tale of Chicago,* his version of the great fire and its results, not a very good book, but it would be published the next year and bring in some money. And there were always the long, narrative poems to be laid down, to be studded with the facts and dates and references from his prodigious reading so that the poems resembled barn sidings in the Harlem Valley, unpainted and toasted by the sun and marked randomly by the nail heads that had once fastened tarpaper to their bleached sides.

Later in the day, Hartigan might drop by in his Model A convertible. The local handyman taxied summer people around, made trips to the store or post office, or met trains at Millerton or Copake Falls. Some afternoons, Pop might climb into the front seat beside Hartigan for a drive to Hillsdale, just across the New York line, to visit with friends such as Arthur Ficke or John Cowper Powys or Edna Millay up in Austerlitz.

'By God,' he would groan between teeth clenched on the pipe's bit as the little car would wobble and bang over the dirt roads. 'Watch out. Oh-oh.' One hand held the straw Panama to his head while the other gripped the windshield post as if to hold himself on the earth's surface. 'Whew!' The car had stopped before the Powyses' cottage in Harlemville, a small house that seemed to be secured to the hillside by clematis vines. As he stepped down from the running board, he would begin to smile, the rimless glasses signal his good humor and anticipation of the talk and banter that was to come. Or if Hartigan had stopped before Ficke's house, there would be homemade applejack to be shared along with the day's mail. There may have been a postcard from Wyoming or Montana, or even a packet of Kodak pictures to pass around. 'Look at Mr. It standing beside that Indian,' he would say.

But it is the picture of him on that old sofa on the front porch of that farmhouse that is the clearest; even taken by moonlight, it has more definition than any other. He wears no shirt, though the evening would be cool, and the sleeveless top of the summer BVDs shows his arms milk-white. They seem to bend awkwardly, unnaturally at the elbow as he lights and relights the old brier. The corn is etched on the fields across the road and an owl cries behind the porch steps. It was only ten years ago that he had left Chicago for the East, divorced his first wife and separated himself from his children, ten years ago that he had given up the practice of law to come to New York City and work full time at being a poet. The pipe has gone out once again and is put aside.

Thirty years before that, he had made another arrival, at the Polk Street Station in Chicago just as the Columbia Exposition was being built. It was a hot July afternoon when he stepped off the train in 1892, a round-faced, dark-eyed rube wearing his hair long over a starched collar and carrying a satchel of books that included Anthon's *Homer, Mademoiselle de Maupin,* and an Italian grammar. There were also poems, many poems, packed among the underwear and shirts along with the same portfolio for success all country boys lug into the city, bound in ambition and edited by dreams. His plan was to be a poet, a successful poet in comfortable surroundings: 'settled,' as he was to describe his fancy—'settled with a wife, with my books around me and long peaceful evenings when I could turn a poem.'

These genteel conditions were to be realized, almost modeled after illustrations by Charles Dana Gibson, and there are reports of these long evenings, perhaps all too long for some of that first family, when the poet stood by the living room mantel, books shelved on either side, to read elegant lengths of verse full of classical allusions. They had been turned out in an upstairs study as his wife played waltzes on the piano below for his inspiration. The children were not permitted to dance to the music or otherwise cause a disturbance.

'He worked so hard,' my mother is saying. 'Worked so hard.'

We sit in the backyard of this small bungalow that we've rented for the year in Des Moines. The grassplot is enclosed by a steel mesh fence, as are the eight or nine yards that adjoin this one, but there are never any people in these other backyards, though the grass and hedges are neatly trimmed. It is a mystery to us when this yard work is done, perhaps at night, in secret and quickly.

'Those people in . . .' My mother continues a familiar litany that neither my wife nor I fully attend for we know its shape and content. Only the place names change, are in fact interchangeable: Lewistown, Petersburg, Springfield, Chicago, Garnett, New York, the Hotel Chelsea: an atlas of betrayal. Surely, to be wronged in so many places, to be deceived so many times in his life and even after death, my father must have been a total innocent. Moreover, my wife is a little annoyed, her eyes ride dangerously high in their sockets, because my mother had given us no forecast of her arrival, no phone call or note, but appeared in our driveway yesterday like the solution to a Zen problem. She is here.

The summer of 1932 he would be sixty-four years of age and the violet distance of that Connecticut twilight would be foreshortened by fireflies and shadows. He could remember his grandmother on her deathbed, talking of Andy Jackson, of how she had heard him speak one time. His father and grandfather had known Lincoln, had hired Abe as a lawyer. The pulse of fireflies casts other shadows more familiar to him. William Jennings Bryan. Vachel Lindsay. Altgeld. Teddy Roosevelt. Here, gone. There, gone.

His own image, caught in various attitudes, would also be traced in silhouette. The successful lawyer. The secret poet. The Calumet Club member. The family man. The early pal of Sandburg. The womanizer. The political dilettante. The partner of Darrow. The man of property. The defender of union causes. The outsider at Chicago literary salons. The corporation lawyer. The *paterfamilias* of a society household. The writer of verse dramas never performed. The steady customer at the Everleigh Club. A match is struck and the pipe is sucked: the world-famous author of *Spoon River Anthology*.

In a few years he would write his autobiography and he would try then to relate all these different figures, give them motives, but on this darkening porch in Connecticut, my mother and I heading westward, he might only review their strange alliances. There were poems to be written tomorrow. Poems and articles and letters. Moreover, the Lincoln biography was still being clubbed by the press in editorials and reviews, and perhaps the day's mail had enclosed a clipping—a harsh distraction in the twilight like the painful assault by a car's headlights on the road below. 'Who's your friend on *Time*?' a nephew had asked sarcastically after a particularly negative review in that magazine.

'Why didn't you and Pop ever buy a place up there, in the country?' I ask my mother. There's been a drought this year in Iowa and the grass is brown, the leaves fall dull and unturned.

'Oh, he would say he wanted to stay in the country. Make a garden and write,' she dismisses the idea. 'But he was really a city person. Every summer, he'd begin to fidget, couldn't wait to get back to that awful dump, the Chelsea Hotel, and the city.' She leans forward, the eyes narrow and one half-closed hand seems ready to reveal a confidence. 'We nearly did buy a place one summer.'

'When was that? Where?'

'Oh, some place near Hillsdale.' She sketches a rough map of Columbia County, New York, in the Iowa air. 'I can't remember exactly now. I remember going to look at it with your father. You were along, I think. It was a small house, run-down and with a little land around it.' The green eyes dilate to accommodate the dim light of memory. 'There was a broken-down sofa on the front porch and a handpump on a well outside for water.'

'Like the house in Colebrook,' I say. My wife has gone to the kitchen to complete our dinner. 'That had a sofa on the front porch too.'

[93]

'Colebrook had no sofa,' my mother replies. 'Not on the porch.'

'I thought I remembered the two of you sitting on an old sofa on the front porch of the Colebrook place.'

Her head turns right then left; left then right as she chews up several peanuts. 'Never,' she says and the ice in her highball glass rattles. 'No, never,' she repeats as if there were still some life in the suggestion. 'There were only a couple of rockers on that porch. I bought them at an auction in Great Barrington. I remember Gladys Ficke was with me, drove me over. Anyway, he almost bought this little farmhouse but he backed away from it. No, he liked the city. Also, he never wanted to own anything after he lost everything in Chicago, after everything he had worked so hard for had been taken away from him in Chicago.' Her eyes glow and the voice flattens out as she makes these allusions to my father's divorce and the terms of the property settlement—over fifty years back.

There are only black and white portraits so I try to imagine her in color: raven hair, skin like rice paper, and the large cat's eyes. It would be impossible to turn away from her smile without a smile. I suspect Ellen Coyne was more hearty than the other girls who enrolled at the University of Chicago in 1919; her dramatic gestures and explosive laughter, supposed to suggest a maturity she did not possess, perhaps only emphasizing the shyness, the naivete the pose was meant to mask. She wanted to be an actress, to create roles and settings that were different from those she had left in Kansas City, to spin silk around the gray nub of hurt in her father's house, the shameful uselessness of being born female and therefore unable to enter West Point. So she had argued for and was sent to the University of Chicago and received orders to study either medicine or law.

'I think I played Des Moines, you know,' she says as I help her in to dinner. Arthritis has crippled her knees and hips and I wonder if another reason for her constant travel is that she is more comfortable behind the wheel of her car than pursuing a more normal pedestrian life.

'When was that?'

'It must have been 1922, after I got out of the University. I was with a stock company that toured *Cappy Ricks* and another play, I forget the name now, but we'd do the second if some other company had played *Cappy Ricks* before we arrived. Yes, Des Moines. I was the ingenue.' She steps up from the patio into the dining area of the bungalow, pauses and looks around as if she had entered another world. Her legs bend in at the knees and almost touch. 'Always the best food here than anywhere,' she says gaily.

'Quick anyhow,' my wife replies. 'Come now. Sit down, Maw, and have a good dinner.'

Was there a shadow that moved faster than the others in that Connecticut twilight, one that rattled with beads, rasped with feathered accessories as the locusts wound barbed strands around my father to bind him, rocker and porch, to that night and to the vision of a smile caught over a white shoulder, caught in the instant between a struck match and a firefly's dart? My mother says they met at some campus function to which the poet had been invited, four or five years after *Spoon River* had been published.

He probably propositioned her, as he seemed to do with every woman, almost as a matter of form or some rule in the country boy's portfolio that he still carried, would always carry with him: that the anonymity and displacement of the big city made for easy conquests, though he never tested this rule against the older axiom, that women are as interested in sex as are men; this last idea would never have occurred to him. There would be many who so trusted him, and he would mourn their belief in his sincerity, his dissemblance, in later years as the telegrams began to arrive to tell him when each had died. And who sent these wires? Who sent the telegram to tell him that Tennessee

Mitchell had died—the ghost of Sherwood Anderson? It arrived at dinner and was handed to my father as he sat among the pretty young fashion models who lived in the elegant New York boardinghouse my mother had found for them in 1944 after his near fatal illness. There among the cut flowers, the faded drapery, the silver and china pieces left from the better days of the Southern lady who ran the place, there upon this bower of beautiful young women warmed by candlelight and the heat of making their way in New York City—my father began to weep over the open telegram. 'Tennis Mitchell is dead,' he sobbed to my mother. Why did he weep? Was it his circumstances, the contrast around him, the frustration of that luscious contrast outside his grasp though within his reach, and here was this telegram to remind him cruelly of a time when he had only to stretch out his hand? Or did he weep because the woman who had just died had trusted his soul as well as enjoyed his fervor, only to be catalogued as one of those who had tried to entrap him—the word *coils* was a favorite descriptive—a woman whom he has labeled in his autobiography a victim of 'congenital nymphomania'? This is why he wept: for the cold sensuality that had enclosed the poet's heart and the smug propriety that had wronged the dead woman. I will say so.

My mother says she would have nothing to do with him in Chicago because he was a married man, though I suppose some of the family believe otherwise. She would be at the least a token for their outrage: because she married him four years after his divorce she would be suspected to be the reason for the marriage's failure; but there is evidence to suggest that the union had become bankrupt long before. Too many separations, too many family councils to force reconciliations, too many letters—especially those from his son, Hardin, as a teenager—too many reports from those who observed the marriage, to cast Ellen Coyne with any believability as 'the flapper home-breaker.' Moreover, my grandfather had hammered an iron-bound *fasces* of right and wrong into my mother's character that makes her obedient to this day to the 'correct way' of doing things, an obedience that sometimes seems ludicrous in an era that no longer counts such nuances.

And there is something else. At the age of fifty-two when he attended that function at the University of Chicago, my father entered the hall as the author of *Spoon River Anthology*. He looked fifteen years younger and was in the full rut of his fame, clothed in its glorious garments but still carrying that rude portfolio underneath. He had worked hard to become a poet and now he was working just as hard being a poet, the farm boy as Prometheus, discovering with delight the obvious but often overlooked fact in our society, that great athletes and statesmen and actors may come and go but the poet is the all-time romantic figure.

If one specific cause must be named for the breakup of his first marriage, it might be the publication of *Spoon River Anthology*. He was forty-seven when the book was published in 1915, freakishly late for a poet to come into his own—almost too late. If the lightning had not struck, if there had been no epitaphs in a country graveyard, he might have continued to practice law, to write poetry under different pseudonyms—his lack of courage to acknowledge the poetry suggests something about his character if not an unconscious evaluation of the verse—and to pay to have it published, a pathetic, seedy amorist moving through the salons of Chicago, one more bourgeois husband enduring a marriage that had become stale and boring.

'Get some of those poems by Webster Ford,' Ezra Pound wrote from Paris to the editor of *Poetry* magazine. 'He's the only poet writing in America.' But Harriet Monroe didn't know who Webster Ford was, did not know the identity of the mysterious poet whose unique poem epitaphs had begun to appear in William Marion Reedy's *St. Louis Mirror*. On the other hand, she did know Edgar Lee Masters, a prominent lawyer authoring derivative verse that she had rejected again and again and, oh—again. So he must have glistened at that reception, a shimmer from the inner glee of turning prince overnight, and though Miss Monroe's kiss had been bestowed late and perhaps under direction, it was no less sincerely given, for she read proof on the galleys of *Spoon River* when my father collapsed into a fever he attributed to pneumonia. I think he recognized the great differences the book would make in his life and one part of him tried, perversely, to abort this rebirth while another struggled to bring the dream to life.

He could not have imagined the dimensions of this dream when he came to Chicago twenty years earlier. There was nothing about it in the dog-eared volumes in his gladstone, but only the glow of that dream upon his imagination as the light of a distant city will rise in the night sky to diminish the stars. Now men like Hardy and Yeats wrote to him, and he had truly passed through the gates of that city he had only dared imagine when he arrived at the Polk Street Station.

The academic domain on the Midway to which he had been invited was only one precinct that courted his presence now, though one of the more attractive because of the florescent young women and men that were its citizenry, and it must have tickled him to be greeted by prestigious professors and deans who a few years earlier would have invited him to discuss civic issues, dry definitions of the law—never poetry. He moved with the happy nonchalance of a man who had forced recognition from the elite; moved arrogantly or even cynically as an alien who had somehow tricked the establishment into granting him full citizenship.

If I were putting this scene into a novel, I would put Ellen Coyne at this reception also. She would recognize something familiar about this man; even from across the room she might see through the raiment of his recent investiture, perhaps note the dry edge on the laugh or a near maniacal flash of eye. She had known this same mixture of smoldering anger and ecstasy in her own father, and though she had fled Tom Coyne and the loveless house he kept, Tom Coyne's daughter's blood rose to the righteousness of that anger, rejoiced with its triumphant joy. She would see the same in the poet; she would recognize him.

'He worked very hard,' my mother tells us at dinner. 'So hard.' Her face becomes more Moynihan as she grows older and her resemblance to my grandmother more apparent, especially the long jaw that suggests a sternness, an aggressiveness that is not actually a part of her character, the expression as fragile as the bone and tissue that make it. 'These people who are so free with other people's lives,' she says between bites, 'have no idea of how hard my husband worked.'

In recent years she has adopted this form when referring to my father even when she speaks to me about him, as if I were a member of an audience, unrelated and with no personal knowledge of the man. Perhaps she is right. Riding his life's circuit, her case for his defense has become a personal vindication, and to challenge any aspect of this warrant is to assault her identity; the jaw thrusts forward.

She recites some of the errors in family history she has just corrected in Petersburg on this trip, for she does know more about the Masters family than anyone born into it and still alive. But to correct the name of a minor character, to fix a proper date of birth does not affect the essential schema, for the pattern of his life remains the same as the one reviewed on that porch in Colebrook, Connecticut, the summer of 1932—whether he sat on an old sofa or a rocking chair purchased in Great Barrington.

It is true that he worked hard. Those mornings I would watch him at his desk in the Chelsea Hotel, or at the kitchen table of a rented farmhouse, my breath paired with his so I would not disturb the alchemy of the pipe smoke wound round his wizard's head: those mornings I would step carefully around the bulk of his concentration, the mass of him and his desk and chair cast like a statue moved in from a museum, and, with eyes fixed on his back, would warily reach a hand toward his right foot to snatch a paper clip off the floor. Got it! Today, I find most of the work of those mornings unreadable.

Somewhat better are the biography of Vachel Lindsay and portions of a few other books, but generally there is an abandonment of style and precision in so much of his work, even an outright sloppiness—the Lincoln biography is an example. His prodigious output in the 1930s—sometimes a novel, a collection of poems, and a biography all in one year—this production that became both legendary and wearisome to evaluate, was not so much the outpouring of a volcanic genius but the frantic rush into print of a writer in his sixties, trying to compensate for his time of neglect thirty years before. He was driven to create an *oeuvre* by a terrible urgency that pushed like an unseasonable tide into the coves of his imagination to flush out material that should have had more time to develop. He wrote poetry as if the novel had never been invented, especially the nineteenth-century English novel; long moral treatises or historical accounts in a heavy prosody that clattered on the page like lines of lead; arguments for Jeffersonian democracy, its heroes and villains, that piled up page after page on his desk like law briefs in blank verse. He had returned to writing the settled verse of his earlier days, though there was no mantel to read it by, no comfortable surroundings—not the same comfortable surroundings he was to blame for stifling his talent and which he had escaped, but escaped with the same talent.

It seemed that there would not be enough time to set down on paper all the ideas, the plots, the epics that he told himself he had had to keep buttoned up in the decorous straitjacket of law business and the first marriage, everything that had been accumulated in Chicago. Time is the ultimate adversary for every artist but my father chose to overwhelm the foe, tried to win the contest with material, so that the doing became more important than the invention. Or let me say, it was another case of trying to make up. William Rose Benét wrote him in 1933 for a poem to be included in an anthology of poems chosen by their authors as ones by which they might wish to be remembered. My father returned a long narrative entitled 'The Seven Cities of America.' 'I think as well of it as anything I have written in a long while,' he said in an accompanying note. 'It is a recent composition—last week.'

We have left the dining area and moved into the living room of this rented house. It looks like the furniture showroom of a department store, and my mother puts herself carefully into the center of a miscellaneous foam-rubber shell, like an aged goddess determined to leave the world by the same vehicle in which she arrived. She dominates the room's anonymity, gives it character if only for the brief duration of her passage through it, and I am reminded of all the strange places we have lived, the different rooms that we had taken with broken sofas, or metal lawn chairs, the small pieces of brass or hand-painted vases or the contraptions, put together out of desperation, that actually worked; all those extension cords and hot plates plugged together in Pennsylvania to make a kitchen out of a hallway.

There had been the rooms at the Chelsea, the rented farmhouses, the various apartments in all parts of New York City, the other hotel rooms; a large, eclectic suite of chambers accreted by the gimcrackery of time that were to take on my mother's shape, her aroma of sandalwood, and the sounds of her beads and bracelets, the quick click-clack of her high heels as she passed between the faded continents of old rugs, the explosive bursts of her laughter and the sharp, commanding voice she had brought from her father's house. If this domain was somewhat dilapidated it was also cozy; the daybed or old sofa might have one end fixed on bricks but it would be long enough for Pop to stretch out on for a nap, and the books and boxes of manuscripts, sometimes a metropolis for my toy cars, were always accessible and a part of the surrounding, underfoot and therefore a part of the ken, rather than suitably shelved, out of the way.

But more than any other item of furniture, it was the steamer trunks that identified those transient years. There must have been bureaus in those various rooms and apartments—I know there were—but my parents seemed to prefer using these large metal trunks that opened like great books on end, with drawers and spaces for hanging garments and compartments for odd shapes of things. My mother's trunks bore the names of the different towns she had played, while E. L. M.'s, the initials lettered in gold paint, had labels from Cunard and the German-American lines that pictured ships curling back the ocean's foam like the illustrations of Odysseus's frail craft in my father's Homer.

Wherever we moved, these trunks would be placed in the center of the bedroom, sometimes the living room, unlocked, unbuckled, and spread apart as if to establish a base camp, their musty, traveled stores left on display to support the legitimacy of the claim. Something else. Perhaps those trunks, and the transiency they suggested, also gave my parents a sense of security that, in a perverse way, was more valid for them than the usual, more permanent location of belongings; as if, upon a knock on the door, the cry of *Fire!*, everything could be tossed into those trunks: manuscripts and treasured books, clothes, cufflinks, brass incense burners, photographs, the Colt shotgun, shoes, silk kimonos, the death mask of Squire Davis Masters, the jade Buddha, bracelets, the portrait of Whitman, letters of acceptance and rejection—everything in their lives closed up, buckled, locked, and trundled out the door.

'That's not the way it was,' my mother is saying. 'It wasn't that way at all.' She shifts uncomfortably in the chair. Some scholar has published an article on the poet of *Spoon River;* it contains numerous errors. On the other hand she will not demand a correction, nor permit the use of letters and papers, nor supply information that might restrict such errors. We must piece the life together as well as we can.

Or make it up as we go along, as he did on that porch in Colebrook, Connecticut; as he was to do in his autobiography and

as he did as a young man in Chicago in 1893. When he got off
that train in the Polk Street Station, he could only find work as
a bill collector for the Edison Company, a grubby job that took
him into all parts of the city and surrounded him, as if in a hall
of mirrors, with his own reflections in the polished marble and
glass of the glittering surfaces, the lacquered doors of carriages, as
he threaded his way through their traffic to press money from
a tenement owner. There would be other contrasts. His own
dreary room in a boardinghouse, clouded with the smells of
boiled dinners, and to sit on the steps of that boardinghouse at
the end of a day, after a boiled dinner, and to peel an orange while
sitting on these steps and watching the carriages of millionaires
pass by the stoop, drawn by horses with docked tails as their
varnished wheels played roulette with the last light of day, and
there to weave a fantasy on their destinations in the first glow of
street lamps; the elegant murmur and napery of fine restaurants
and the rustling silk-on-silk passage of women moving through
those restaurants. There would be women also in the boarding-
houses, by his own account; lonely, vulnerable women who perhaps watched the same parade from the windows of their rooms,
while waiting for the young bill collector to finish his orange,
and put aside his dreams.

'[She] had caught me reading *Mademoiselle de Maupin*,' he
would write later about one such woman, 'and had sighed forth
a rebuke that one whose face was so innocent should be reading
such a book. It was that night that she stood in her nightgown
at my door knocking to come in.'

So a figure of ambition and energy emerges, a tremendous
energy that seemed to be charged by the dazzle around him; a
contradictory figure that coveted the ease and flavor of luxury
as he worked at the bedside table of his single room, working in
solitude late into the night, sometimes ignoring the soft, hesitant knock on the door. It was a 'malicious' energy, he called
it, to succeed as a poet in spite of the obstacles he felt his parents,
especially his mother, had put in his path: why had his sister

been sent to Knox College to study drawing and French when he had been allowed only a year there, before forced to read law in his father's office?

The Columbia Exposition opened in 1893, the same year he formed his first law partnership. He was no longer collecting utility bills but still writing poetry at night and already publishing some in the editorial pages of newspapers: nearly a year in the big city, a knowledgeable citizen. So the excitement of Chicago was transferred to the fairgrounds, the city's bold pretensions were exaggerated in the dimensions of this World's Fair, its naive bluster extruded into the plaster-of-paris grandeur of the imperial White City. Size was very important. The huge temples raised on the lakefront to industry, electricity, agriculture, and the arts, temporary and somehow hugely pathetic because of their great impermanence, were promoted in terms of their size or the magnitude of the collections rather than the quality of the collections: the fine-arts display catalogued thousands of paintings and pieces of sculpture from all over the world, but only the name of Mary Cassatt among a very few other artists would be familiar today.

A brochure on the Machinery Building claimed that the entire Houses of Parliament could be installed under its roof. The Manufacturers and Liberal Arts Building was even larger: press agents challenged each other with lists of the world's wonders (lists revised daily during the fair's run) that could be accommodated within this leviathan of a building: a Moby-Dick of halls, white as the plaster that formed its elaborate cornices, friezes, Ionic columns, and great entrances. It was four times larger than the Roman Colosseum. The entire Imperial Russian Army could be mobilized on its floor. On the other hand, if the Russians marched out, perhaps toward their humiliation by Japan, six baseball games could be played simultaneously—a season's schedule for the National League could be completed over a long weekend. Finally, the ultimate estimation under the steel girders of its roof and within the elaborate stage flats of its walls: the Manufacturers and Liberal Arts Building could house the United States Capitol, Madison Square Garden, Cheops's Pyramid, St. Paul's and Winchester cathedrals, and still have room for an assortment of smaller edifices. It was Chicago's answer to the Eiffel Tower, the symbol of an earlier World's Fair, though this enormous plaster model would not last a year, its gigantic vulgarity consumed by the same fire that swept the deserted fairgrounds the following summer, the Celestial City on Lake Michigan going up in smoke.

It would be tempting to put my father under this gargantuan roof during the opening-day ceremony, to have him witness the different speakers and proclamations—famous speakers of that day like Henry Watterson or Chauncey Depew or others not so famous yet, such as the young Harriet Monroe who read to the sweating, program-fanning multitude an ode she had written for the occasion. It would be nearly twenty years before she would start *Poetry* magazine, and one suspects from the nature of the verse her voice tried to carry into the farthest corners of that huge hall ('Columbia, my country, dost thou hear?/Ah! dost thou hear the song unheard of time?') that being the sister-in-law of one of the fair's architects was not an unimportant consideration in her choice as the fair's poet. On the other hand, that was the mode of the day. Perhaps my father sat too far away to be able to hear her lines, and, therefore, never mentions witnessing this historic occasion in American poetry; the young lawyer may have stood at the far edge of the multitude, strained to see and hear the ceremonies taking place, so distant that the Columbia Guards, as they escorted the different dignitaries to the speakers' platform, resembled toy soldiers. It is tempting to consider that my father may have looked upon Tom Coyne, even smiled at the comic opera getup of the guard's costume, but such speculation is the guile of popular historians and to place the two of them together in that enormous hall has no more significance than that they shared the same moment on earth with millions of others.

The fair, its size and synthentic grandeur, seemed to be a honeycomb for all my father's untutored yearnings for the aesthetic; a small-town idealization of art that confused *bathos* with *pathos*. Simultaneously, all his 'passion for Democracy and for the glory of the Republic' were focused into formal odes as monotonous and as derivative as the fair buildings that inspired them. The gigantic blandness of 'The White City' provoked his poetry. He visited the Palace of Art over and over, turning in the radiation given off by the square miles of salon art, and wrote a poem called 'Andromeda.' He stood by the reflecting pool in the Court of Honor to marvel at the statue 'The Republic' by Daniel Chester French. It was sixty-five feet tall, with fingers a yard long, cast in plaster and gilded. He wrote poems to this statue (it began to disintegrate before the fair closed, losing its nose and several fingers) because its size and symbolism excited his imagination, whereas another statue, perhaps more appropriate for a poem, was never eulogized; it stood before the Mines and Mining Building, seven feet tall and cast in pure silver —the statue of Justice.

The cafes and music halls on the fair's midway are mentioned frequently in his memoirs and particularly a restaurant called Old Vienna. 'This was one of the most glorious summers of my life,' he would write, 'if not the most glorious of all.' A practicing lawyer now, with his full name lettered on the firm's door, he would spend almost every evening dining and dancing in this ersatz fabrication, music by Strauss, accompanied by a young woman he was to lose to the more aggressive courtship of Gentleman Jim Corbett, Heavyweight Champion of the World.

The immaculate parody the White City made of everything it had been designed to extol—ideals, art, or architecture—came to an end in the late fall when its gates were closed and locked, just before a mysterious fire burned it to the ground. It was a turn of season for my father as well. He had begun a harsh and somber period in his own life; a fledgling law business barely kept him in pocket money, while he still moved through a succession of bleak boardinghouse rooms with no space for his small library and composition corner, and he dreamed of more comfortable surroundings in which his art could flourish. The majesty of the fair had promised so much, had ennobled his ambition with a dazzling varnish that proved to have been daubed over gypsum; but for that moment he could write heroic poems to heroic-sized statues and pretend to be a free citizen of this imperial city. For Tom Coyne of the Columbia Guards, there was no pretense, no intoxication with plaster glory. It was a job, a way of getting on, and any of the fair's huge wonders would be eclipsed when he moved on to South America and the ruins of the Incas and the Mayans or the authentic genius of the Panama Canal. I don't believe my father ever broke the spell cast upon him by the fair, never saw anything to surpass it in his imagination and, with the exception of *Spoon River* and a few other pieces, tried to recreate the glorious impression made upon his soul by that gypsum city, its fine purpose and gigantic forms.

My mother is preparing to leave, anxious to head back to the East, though she will have another cup of coffee as my wife clears the breakfast dishes. Because we have no spare bedroom in this small cottage, she spent the night in a nearby motel, across the street from a large veterans hospital set in spacious, well-tended grounds with a golf course and tennis courts. There are never any players on these fields, as there were at the Soldiers Home in Washington, suggesting that this most recent class of veterans from the Vietnam War do not, or cannot, or will not play golf or tennis. I wonder if she has made any association between the two places, the rare visits she made to her father in the one place and talking about her husband here last night until very late.

'Colebrook was 1932,' she declares. Last night, I had made a mistake in recollecting where we had spent different summers. 'The next year was Hillsdale and then the summer of 1934 you and I spent in Kansas City; remember all the locusts that year?

He used to catch them in jars,' she tells my wife, who receives the news calmly. 'Then in 1935 we were all at the Chelsea for the summer.'

I see her to the car and she folds herself painfully into the seat behind the wheel. She backs out of our driveway, pauses to shift gears, nods once or twice as if to answer a question, and then pulls away on the drive east. It is a road she has taken many times and I wonder if she recites her history with my father like an incantation, as we heard it last night, finding solace in familiar points in the story as she drives past familiar landmarks. In fact, I have done the same thing in these pages, revisited the same scene or gone over the same material more than once; we both trace and retrace our paths across a small field comprised of five or six summers not to find anything that may have been lost along the way but, somehow, to enlarge the perimeter of our search.

When we returned from the Yellowstone trip, my grandfather pulled the Buick into the garage behind the Roberts Street house, locked the brake, turned off the ignition, and never drove the car again. By the next summer, my mother had learned to drive and made her first drive East, my grandmother once more in the passenger seat, gloved and veiled, and I in the back. This time we left my grandfather behind, the women determined to have a rest from him, and drove to join my father in the small hamlet of Hillsdale in Columbia County, New York. He had rented a farmhouse there for the summer.

I don't remember how long it took us but I do remember many turns and detours and side journeys, and each of these separate into different itineraries, so that this one trip—one of several we were to make—becomes many trips, just as this one summer in Hillsdale, one of the few we were to share, passes through my memory as if through a prism to become many summers, sunny and carefree.

It was a hopeful time; Franklin Roosevelt had just taken office, and my father looked to the Democrat administration to restore the ideal of the Republic as interpreted by his readings of Jefferson and Mason and Madison. There was talk on the wide porch of that Hillsdale farmhouse, lazy twilight talk as the Taghkanic hills gradually soaked up the dark, of trying for a consularship; after all, Cooper and Longfellow had been so named. Hawthorne, too. The idealism and purpose of this new administration would certainly embrace such a concept.

It was also a summer of work and fun. The farmhouse was roomy and cool, with bare wooden floors carpeted by throws of sunlight, and the cozy kitchen with a kerosene stove that chug-a-lugged its fuel as my grandmother turned hotcakes or fried chicken upon it. My mother going barefoot seemed very strange to me. Then there was the one room, like a great hall, with windows that went all the way to the floor, a table and chair precisely placed in its center where my father would sit to write, immobile and distant like the jade Buddha he kept on the mantel at the Hotel Chelsea, but full-sized and pink and stern-eyed. The cool floor under my feet sends goose bumps bubbling up my legs as I watch him from the open doorway. Then he looks up: the look of an accountant who has been distracted, though there's a quizzical note in the dark eyes that grows until the whole face breaks apart in a dimpled, crooked-tooth smile that goes with the cackle and giggle. 'Howdy, Mr. It.'

He would work every morning, reading and writing or contemplating poems and articles that would make up a very productive period, and some of the best work he was to do in his later life. Vachel Lindsay had killed himself two years before and the poet's widow had asked him to do a biography. The poems that were to be published under *Invisible Landscapes* were on the desk, as were notes on his autobiography, *Across Spoon River*. There were numerous articles and incidental poems to be published in magazines and journals; every sentence, poem, or book he wrote was published and read with great interest—still.

Afterwards, he might try his hand at the flapjack griddle, standing by the kerosene range in slippers, a baggy pair of gray pants with suspenders looped over the BVD top. He'd be singing a song whose lyrics amused him all summer long, 'When I Take My Sugar to Tea.' 'Do-dee-doo-doo-doodle-dee-dee—what do you think of that song, Mr. It?' he says, flipping several cakes onto a plate and putting it before me on the white enamel surface of the kitchen table. 'There you go. Pour on the sorghum, honey . . . pour it on.'

From the kitchen window could be seen the old barn, and in between grew the good-sized garden he had planted a couple of weeks before my mother drove the Buick up the dirt lane of the white rambling farmhouse. The peas were almost ready for picking, the beans were up, and the sweet corn had burned through the brown earth. In the hot sun, after the dew had lifted, he would take hoe and rake, and work down the rows of vegetables, a misshapen straw Panama shading his face but still in slippers.

'Look at this, Mr. It.' His thumbnail has sliced open a pea pod, and nudged the young peas off their stems so they roll into his palm like smooth green stones. 'You be the poppy, and I'll be the little boy,' he says, then screws his face into a caricature of perplexity. 'Why is it, Poppy dear, that you put a seed just like this one into the ground and it grows up with more seeds?'

'Nature . . . just nature,' I remember to say.

'Nature,' he replies with great astonishment. 'Why, Poppy dear! Do nature do everything?'

'She do it all,' I reply.

Strange to me also was the sight of my grandmother moving through this New York farmhouse, almost feeling her way through its spacious rooms as if the concentration my grandfather had demanded of her in her own house had made her blind in another place, or perhaps this hesitancy was born of a shyness before my father, before his books and vast learning and occupation with words. Or her timidity might be the traditional reaction of a mother-in-law in the house of her daughter's husband, a man she hardly knew and only a couple of years younger than herself; at any rate, she came to enjoy the side trips we made that summer, the visits to auction barns, and made herself even more at home by putting up preserves and jellies. She and I shared a bedroom and it was a comfort to me, and to her as well I think, when I crawled into her bed at night and lay against her soft warmth.

The Buick, this veteran of Custer's Last Stand, now turned down roads to Chatham and the Shaker settlement, Martin Van Buren's grave, the old Livingston manor, and similar sites that seemed to refresh my father's imagination like the pools of spring water in which he would insist everyone, except my grandmother, take daily dips. Also, with my mother at the wheel, her silver bracelets sounding every change of gear, we'd make jaunts after naps in the heat of the day to those friends who lived nearby, Jack Powys or Edna Millay or summer residents who invited the famed poet and his family for a supper, a picnic by a pond clogged with water lilies.

This summer also came to be known as the-summer-my-mother-won-a-blue-ribbon-at-the-Columbia-County-Fair, for her giant cosmos, or the-summer-my-father-shot-the-groundhog; as if all the mornings and afternoons and evenings of those few weeks had been taken up with preparing the soil, sorting out the seeds, tending the young plants, and arranging the blooms; or perhaps days had been required to break open the shotgun, slowly insert the shell, close it; days lengthening into weeks to raise the heavy weapon to take aim and then the report finally sounding throughout the last month as the groundhog tumbles over and over, out of date and timeless. Or the-summer-we-looked-for-a-place-to-buy, though my memory is apparently faulty on this episode; yet it is another multiple that can be made of the one integral.

Every daily routine assumes its own season as time fragments, so that an entire summer can be made of the walk down to the Hillsdale station to meet the late afternoon train. Into the haze and buzz of that August afternoon, my father and I would follow the dirt road before the house to where it joined the cement state highway, turn right toward the village center, around the Union soldier standing watch in the small park, and down the hill to the railroad station. It would be about two miles and so the hike would be broken by a visit to the small tavern behind the Civil War monument, since another ingredient of that summer's lightheartedness had been the repeal of Prohibition. 'Sterle,' my father would address the owner, 'give us a beer.' A glass jigger of beer was set before me.

But it was the arrival of the steam engine that was our obsession, not the mail car it pulled with letters and books, nor the passengers that might step down from its oven-hot coaches—but the coal-fired, steam-driven locomotive. The suspense on the platform squeezed us into fidgets as every click-clack of the station agent's telegraph key wound up the tension like the sound of a gear about to strip. We paced the length of the platform. We tested the baggage cart. Frequent trips were made to the water fountain in the waiting room that smelled of old wax and printed forms and unclaimed luggage and resembled the varnished lapstraked hull of a longboat upside down.

Judiciously my father would pull a large gold watch from its small pocket at the top of his pants, flip open its lid and observe its face, then mine, and then compare both with the large clock that tick-tocked on the wall of the station agent's cubicle, next to the large calendar for the New York Central. 'By God, where is that engine?' he sighs. 'Where is that engine, Mr. It?'

'I dunno,' I say.

'Say,' he disturbs the agent. 'Is that engine going to get in here today? We've come down to see that engine. Where's it got to?' The railroad man goes along with the play; yes, it's due any time now.

Back on the platform. The name board on the end of the building: HILLSDALE. Another metal imprint: RAILWAY EXPRESS AGENCY. The phone rings in the station agent's office. H-I-L-L-S-D-A-L-E. 'Chicken Supper and Social—North Hillsdale, Adults, One Dollar—Children, Fifty Cents.' New Schedule, Harlem Valley Division, New York Central Railroad Company. Hillsdale, arrv . . . . . . 4:48.

And there it would be. It had appeared at a bend in the track, silently, like a great shy beast that had suddenly popped out from the tall woods by the cut; a black, one-eyed monster poised on the rails and ready to scramble the hard-cooked hour of the afternoon with its white plumed shriek of a whistle. It was as if it had been there on the track all along, there at the curve, waiting with a good-mannered patience for the two of us to see it, to recognize it before it let go with a blast of sound, a clang of bell that charged the air and ruffled the announcements tacked to the bulletin board.

The wide boards beneath our feet began to shift and vibrate as if the engine's signal had unlocked some frightful energy stored in the earth, a power that had only been waiting for this disturbance to trigger its eruption. Another blast, more raucous and ear-splitting than the last, and the engine had grown even larger, unbelievably larger—it could get no larger. But it did. It got larger and larger and its sound more and more and more until I cannot even hear its sound nor hear my father as he holds the straw Panama onto his head, but I know he shouts, 'Oh, Poppy dear, it's here, it's here!'

Then it shot past, like a hot tenement building rushing by, even with the ubiquitous face in the window high above and looking down, waving back to us through the blackened sweat of coal dust, the heat of the locomotive flushes over and by us to load our eyes with grit, its gears and pistons almost jumbled, almost throwing themselves into a mangle of machinery with every turn of the gliding wheels.

There would be some passengers to disembark, mail and freight to unload, perhaps milk cans to put aboard, and then the train would pull away, almost silently; the rectangular doorway of its last car, braced open for ventilation, would grow smaller and close up tight just before the whistle saluted the Craryville crossing a few miles down the track. It would be silent once more on the platform, save for the cricket notes of the telegraph key, and we would be alone once again. We turn back.

When we turned back for Kansas City in August the corn in the garden outside the kitchen window was not yet ready to pick. I have no memory of that leave-taking—say, peering out the oval rear window of the Buick to see my father standing by the garden and waving good-bye to us. Whatever words or gestures that accompanied that departure remain behind a narrowing aperture and it would be as unlikely to recall them as it would have been unnatural for that train down the track to stop and back up. He would have picked the corn alone, perhaps shared it with friends—though they had their own gardens—and continued to work every morning at his desk in the center of the bare room. He would walk to Sterle's tap for an afternoon beer, go to the station, check the post office, and get Hartigan to drive him around. And in the evening, he would sit on the porch and smoke and watch the fireflies among the field lilies as the last caps of daylight on the Berkshires melted and disappeared.

6

The ambulance attendants had left my grandmother on the living room sofa like a hastily wrapped package from Woolf Brothers, a white bandage around her head and a sling of muslin folded and pinned around her left shoulder, encased in plaster. There had been no one home when they arrived and there were other accidents to answer that day, other victims to be delivered around Kansas City. She had been downtown on a daily pilgrimage of stores and tea shop and movie matinee, and had been knocked down by a truck as she crossed a street.

Her eyes, where pain and shame vied for the singular expression, looked up at me from beneath a visor of gauze, and she managed a scrap of laugh as if to say, *Hello there. Here we are. Here we are.* The pupils seemed to enlarge, to encompass in their brown velvet depths a recognition of my presence, my standing there in my high school ROTC uniform and what that meant in terms of time, of the afternoon hour, for the morning had gone like a cup of tea at Emery-Byrd-Thayer; it was all very confusing but one thing became clear to her. If I were home from school, then it was time to get supper on because Tom Coyne would come striding through the door at any moment.

'Here,' she does say, 'here,' putting out her right hand for me to take, to help her up from the couch, and she rises unsteadily and off balance because of the left arm being wrapped tight and fixed against her bosom, and the two of us head for the kitchen like a tableau in some coffee-and-cake social where parents and children are pressed into unsuitable roles: *The Retreat from Gettysburg* with Mrs. Thos. Coyne as the wounded soldier supported by her grandson, thirteen-year-old Hilary in his olive drabs and Sam Browne belt, playing the old comrade.

'I'm all right,' she says, her right hand gripping my shoulder. Then she repeats the phrase, a lyrical lilt in her mellow voice, says it a third time as if there is a charm in the words that will benefit her, assuage her injuries more than the treatment they had received at the hospital emergency room. 'I'm all right.'

We pass the heavy mahogany sideboard in the dining room, the large table of the same suite, as she leans on me and laughs with some apology for her lameness. She is a big woman, tall and large-boned, and for the first time I feel the weight of her on my shoulder and resent the weight, and I'm impatient with the halting step. Indeed, there had been tableaux played out here in these rooms, make-believe but happier scenes.

Woman's

DEMOCRATIC

Meeting

Saturday, March 22nd

2 o'clock p.m.

Residence

Mrs. Thos. Coyne

3228 Roberts Street

Everybody Welcome   Especially the Ladies

My grandmother had found in the loam of Tom Pendergast's political machine a nourishment not supplied by the spare landscape my grandfather had transposed from the Montana of his army days. Her statuesque beauty, her soft, easygoing nature and graceful expression were great assets to the party and to its leaders, who were quick to use such natural gifts for their own ends. Her prominence in Church affairs, as president of the women's auxiliary of the Knights of Columbus, together with the associations she held as Capt. John Moynihan's daughter, presented the organization with a fabric of allegiances and goodwill already woven and ready to wear.

To be both Irish and a Democrat those early days in Kansas City was to be doubly punished, and to be a woman as well was to take that punishment into exile, but she must have sensed something was about to happen that would reverse this situation, some demographic shift that would alter the registration books and the voting slips, though she would never think of it in those terms but something more immediate, more personal, like a remembrance of her girlhood in the Bottoms, one of Capt. John Moynihan's three talented daughters, in the same neighborhood where the Pendergast brothers ran an honest saloon. She would make that connection, out of nostalgia, out of pride, out of self-preservation.

And it was a chance that paid off, beginning on the hot morning of April 10, 1930. According to the *Kansas City Journal-Post*, it was the hottest April 10th in forty-two years, 88° at one P.M., so that on that morning the council chamber in the old city hall was a blur of fans and programs, the air heated up even more by the klieg lights set up for motion-picture cameras, as a new mayor and city council were to be inaugurated, establishing another record: the first Democratic administration, mayor and city council, to be elected in Kansas City in living memory. Shoulder to shoulder the jammed crowd of loyal workers patiently followed the outgoing Republican mayor as he conducted the final business with the lame duck council; the programs and fans of the patient crowd worked the air, redolent with sweat and the fragrance of the floral tributes, hundreds of dollars' worth of flowers banked on a temporary platform built at the end of the hall. The fans and programs worked as if the temperature of the day might conspire with the temper of the recent political debate to raise a heat that would melt the Democratic victory. Then,

With my grandparents, Mollie and Tom Coyne, on the steps of the house on Roberts Street in Kansas City.

Left: Here I am a chubby eleven-year-old-year posed with Mother.

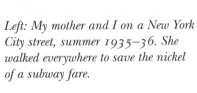

Above: With my grandfather ("Gee-Gee") at the site of Fort Custer, Montana, where he soldiered in the cavalry around 1880. This picture was taken on the same day as the one with me and the Indian [on the cover].

Left: My mother and I on a New York City street, summer 1935–36. She walked everywhere to save the nickel of a subway fare.

Ellen Coyne, taken in her senior year at the University of Chicago in 1922 when she was 22–23.

Left: With my grandmother, Mollie Moynihan Coyne, in the backyard of Roberts Street. In the background is some of the pampas grass my grandfather brought back from South America. Its leaves were like razor wires.

Right: With my father on one of my summer visits to New York. I am about six.

At age five, with my father and grandmother at the farmhouse he rented in Hillsdale, New York.

the mayor-elect entered, Bryce B. Smith, and the crowd stood and gave a great cheer.

The youngest Democrat in the council chamber was Hillary [*sic*] Thomas Masters, 2-year-old son of Edgar Lee Masters, noted poet and author of New York. The child lives with his maternal grandmother, Mrs. T. F. Coyne, 3228 Roberts Street, an active Democratic worker. She had a seat just outside the railing of the room and little Hillary, dressed in a bright yellow suit, sat on the railing above the heads of most of the crowd and applauded vigorously every time his grandmother gave him the cue. He was the only child at the inaugural.

The only child at the inaugural, and dressed in a yellow suit, held high above the crowd, told when to applaud: a scene stealer, and meant to steal that scene, and to be sure the theft was recorded, put in the paper, there was the mention of the father's identity. The Moynihan calculation here at work: the facility for dramatic presentation, for playing all the points at once. I can see the pair of us: the little boy sitting on his grandmother's shoulder as she bends forward in her seat and leans on the wooden railing that separates the audience from the council table, see her touch the boy on the leg, urge him to applaud at the right moments in Mayor Smith's inaugural address, her eyes fixed forward and aglow as she waits for the recognition she has set a trap for. She was handsome, capable, accomplished, full of grace, and she wanted to be recognized.

I support her now in this kitchen in 1941, this dark, high-ceilinged kitchen, as she directs me with her one good arm to the tall-doored cabinets where I lift down a bag of cornmeal, her dark eyes on a slant to my regard and dulled by pain, standing like the last of a species stunned with the perception of its own extinction. In fact, she is still in a daze, but manages to direct me to bowls, to a beater, and to eggs, milk, and baking powder, and gives me the step-by-step instructions for corn bread. What else would there be for supper? Chicken, probably. There always seemed to be chicken in the miraculous Montgomery Ward refrigerator, and she lifts a heavy iron skillet to the top of the stove with her one good arm and hand. There had been dessert, she tells me, a small cake she had bought at Wolferman's, but it had been knocked from her grasp and had fallen under the truck's wheels. But there were peach preserves downstairs in the basement, she had put them up last summer, and I was sent to fetch a jar. *He* would be home soon and the table still had to be set. She places the silverware at the three appointed places, and I help, less anxious now to see her about a familiar routine. She will be all right, I assure myself; she's getting the table ready for supper. She'll be all right. We do not speak, I do not remember that we speak, but then her voice has never sounded anything much more than calls to meals, and she would be shy about my day's activities at school, as if I had passed into a realm beyond her ken when I entered high school, like entering the priesthood or some such withdrawal from the world, with an aura of the supernatural about it. Indeed, to pass into the upper grades and adolescence was to abandon her in other ways, for now there was no one for her to cuddle, to spoil and spend her abundant affection on, a spendthrift love. What time is it?

'Come,' she says, trying to turn our dilemma into a skit. 'We'll make the potatoes. You can peel them and I'll mash them. It will be like the army,' she adds with a dry laugh, though it is not funny to me. I take my ROTC training and its uniform, a half size too large and like thick scratchy cardboard, very seriously.

In 1941, my grandfather, at the age of eighty, would be jaunting home down Roberts Street with that same light gait as if he had just left his mount at Benton Boulevard, swung down off his horse at the head of the block to approach the rest and refreshment of the camp that was due a trooper after his tour of duty. Though of what that tour of duty might consist can only be conjectured: long trolley rides, a sunny bivouac on the courthouse steps, or an inspection tour of his different properties around town, especially those he had sold—to see how they had been 'run down' by the new owners.

There was nothing else for him to do in 1941, but he maintained the same schedule that had regulated his days when he worked at the municipal water department: to rise early, to read the morning paper and perhaps peruse a volume of the encyclopedia, and then to take the breakfast my grandmother would lay out for him just as the sky grew light. Then gone for the day, he would return exactly at five. My grandmother had got him the job.

He had not needed the minor clerk's salary (it could not have been much; the Official State Manual for 1935 lists the salary for the Director of the Kansas City Water Department to be $6000), but it was a post for him in an uneventful stretch, all the old deeds and glories far beyond the horizon and only subjects for bedtime stories now, his manual of spirit yet unsatisfied; but here was a routine to pacify it, though armed only with pen points and dedicated to the regular transcription of water usages from ledger to ledger in a neat, graceful hand. Moreover, from my grandmother's point of view, it was a way of getting him out of the house and away from the fire in the backyard that he had begun to feed with the artifacts of a life that had become ungenuine.

'Can't you do something for Tom?' she must have asked of Jim Alyward or young Jim Pendergast or perhaps even Joe Shannon, leaning toward the round, pink ear set in the smooth silvery expanse of the politician's face, her broad-brimmed hat of orchid straw rounding a frame for her own oval face so that she and the politician resembled a pair of those saints in pictures who were always whispering to each other about something. Or the soft conspiracy of her request might be plotted at a funeral; that would be more likely the case, and she would be in a black, broad-brimmed hat, and gloved. She would have become one of the shadows that moved on the wide dark porch of a funeral

home or a private home, or in a somber rear hallway near the
kitchen where the hushed talk would be of Roosevelt and registration figures, while the rosary droned in the front parlor.
Can't you do something for Tom?

'Is that him? Is that him?' she asks anxiously as I peel the potatoes. A shoe had scraped against the cement steps of the porch.
We listen. The Montgomery Ward refrigerator hums. The gas in
the oven sighs. Yes, the front door has opened, closed, but the
footsteps go upstairs. We fall back to our chores. To go upstairs
meant that a ritual would be observed that would give us
another twenty minutes: the hairs of the moustache were to be
trimmed, the high-topped shoes shined or some new remedy,
some cure for the terminal condition of life would be readied
for application. One evening, several years before, we were also
in the kitchen, awaiting his arrival. My mother was with us this
time, scraping carrots, even eating some of them raw as she went
along—another one of those astonishing customs she had brought
back to us from New York City. On her previous visit, she had
left the small brass incense burners in the living room. Her appearance always astonished me, and she dressed as if to accentu-
ate her exotic coloring, the raven hair and white, white skin and
green eyes. Even now, as she peeled the carrots, she wore an array
of bracelets and necklaces that clattered with every move of the
paring knife. 'He's home,' my grandmother had said and looked
at the roast. My mother chomped a carrot stick in two.

My grandfather was upstairs and preparing the evening's ablutions, but there was to be something different about them this
particular night. He explained at the table, for my mother's
benefit, for she had arrived only that afternoon at Union Station,
that his feet had become infected with certain microbes, a condition popularly known as 'athlete's foot,' and that he had tried
everything. He had even talked to the head pharmacist at the
Katz Drug Store downtown and nothing the man had recommended, no balm, lotion, or ointment had been effective, no

elixir had eliminated the persistent itch and nibble at his toes, the toothing by the little monsters that consumed the pads of his feet.

'Is it from the running they get it?' my grandmother had asked as she passed the rolls.

'Get what?' Gee Gee had stopped short, a fork of roast pork halfway to his mouth.

'The foot,' my grandmother replied. 'The athletes,' she expanded her explanation and sat down. She pulled her napkin across her lap with eyes downcast, an expression that was more regal than demure. 'Is it all the running the athletes do that gives them this foot disease?' she had said and sipped some water.

He chewed as he observed her, as if reconnoitering an innocent-seeming landscape for covert hostility. A whiteness had risen to the surface of the skin around his nose and over his cheekbones, like spots of lye, and his eyes probed her placid manner. 'It's these microbes.' He turned to my mother. 'Have you read the book by this fellow de Kruif?'

'Lee says he did all the medical research for *Arrowsmith*, the novel by Sinclair Lewis,' my mother replied. Even then she talked in anecdotes, didactically.

'*Microbe Hunters*,' my grandfather had continued, a pause in his manner as if my mother had answered him in Arabic. 'It's all in that book. But I have a cure for them. I've got something that will do the job now.'

Not from running, but from time running out did his feet itch as the blood slowed, and his arteries and their tributaries began to dry up and harden, extremities pricked and needled by age. He was being consumed, but not by bugs or a disease advertised in the Sunday papers, and he knew it, knew it as surely as he had seen the same carrion feast placed upon the Western plains or in the jungles of South America, sometimes prepared with violence and by his own hand sometimes; now it was coming to him but slowly, bit by bit and without the honor of the apocalypse that was due him. So he would meet this sneaky, cowardly adversary, flush him out, force him to put up a fight, sting him and corner him and harass him until he was forced to put up or shut up. He had found the formula.

From the bathroom, I heard my mother and grandmother speaking together in the bedroom across the hall. My mother would be unpacking, and their conversation would be light and casual, about clothes or about old acquaintances and family gossip—a sisterly talk of women at ease. My grandmother would laugh and grow almost loquacious when my mother visited, initially, for she would have someone to talk to, another woman who understood her life with Tom Coyne and, at the same time, a daughter of whom she was very proud, though in an ignorant and unknowing way so that this adulation contained for its object as much nourishment as a glass of water.

But after a few days, my mother would become bored with the talk of family and politics; the kind practiced in Kansas City she felt to be rather vulgar and coarse. Nor did my grandmother, after the initial enthusiastic exchange, respond to my mother's main conversation; the newest books she had read, the names of the authors she had met meant nothing to my grandmother, nor did the poetry of Philip Freneau—the elite poet of the Revolution and the subject of my mother's graduate dissertation at Columbia University. So my mother spent her time home, after the first couple of days, with people she knew at the University of Kansas City, luncheons that featured creamed tuna and peas in pastry shells, or she might look up some of the members of the American Association of University Women since the local chapter had shown an interest in her reading some of her husband's work, the long narrative poems dedicated to Oliver Hazard Perry or Daniel Webster given the full benefit of her theatrical experience. But she grew bored with these diversions; their attractions were relative, no comparison to the life she lived in New York City or the work she was trying to complete for her master's degree.

But this was her first evening home and they would be together in the bedroom, a room never used except during her visits—I still shared a room with my grandmother—the older woman sitting on the bed as my mother passed from closet to bed and back to hang up her clothes from the suitcase. And I am in the bathroom with my grandfather who prepares his solution.

A small seat had been placed athwart the white tub's sides; my grandfather had had it especially made so that he could bathe his feet without removing his underwear. The hot water spigot had been turned on full and the oversized boiler in the basement pumped a stream of water into the tub that curdled on the edge of steam. Gee Gee sat on a chair, his pants removed but the rest of him fully clothed, the legs of the long underwear pulled up just below the knees, one shoe and sock removed and the other sock being carefully peeled off. I looked at his pink and white feet, small and delicate for the feet of a warrior, but there were no signs of the ravages he had described at the supper table, no tracks or marks made by the infestation of bugs that I had expected to see scurry between his toes when the socks were removed.

'Now, take that small sack there,' he directed me. 'Let me have the bottle in it.' I handed him a small dark bottle. L-Y-S-O-L.

'What's Lysol, Gee Gee?' I asked.

'It will do the trick,' he replied and pulled out the stopper. He poured the brown liquid into the vat of water, and we began to cough from the fumes vaporized by the steam. It was as though a poison gas had attacked our throats and clawed at the confinement of our lungs. The swirling water in the tub had become an evil color, like the final essence in a rendering vat, and it bubbled and popped, and brought tears to our eyes. 'By God, it will do the job,' he said as he poured the last of the chemical, replaced the stopper, and returned the empty bottle to me.

He seemed to brace his shoulders and pause for a second, but there was no turning back. He sat on the suspended seat and swung his legs up and over the side of the tub and down. He plunged them both into the seething brew. His hands gripped the sides of the tub, and the knuckles turned white. His face had become mottled, a range of cyanic blues. The eyes had hardened and shrunk, and the cheekbones flashed the messages censored by the clenched teeth. 'There, by God,' he finally growled through stiff lips. '*There!*' He pressed his feet against the bottom of the tub, held them there with supreme effort as if some force were trying to push them out from underneath.

'Ah-ha,' he panted, his face in a sudden sweat. He smiled with a curious distance but just as quickly, the expression became fierce, warlike. 'Get them!' he shouted. 'Get those sons-uv-bitches. Get them!' he yelled and pressed his feet more firmly against the tub, even half rose from the seat to push down, to hurry the attack. 'Kill those sons-uv-bitches. Kill 'em!' he commanded.

My mother and grandmother had rushed through the door but stood behind me helplessly, either put off by the fumes or the furious figure that swayed and strained in the clouds of bitter steam. I have never seen my grandfather look so angry, so fearful. Years later I will see the same expression on a cavalryman, a sergeant at that, painted by Frederic Remington: the eyes blind with fury, the moustachios serpentine, and the face gaunt with a charging blood lust.

'Get them, get them!' he shouts. 'Get those bastards! By God, get them!' How long we stood there, mesmerized by this torturous battle between him and his mortality is difficult to say— the scene is suspended in a seamless continuity in my memory, reinforced with details of subsequent baths he gave his feet, for he repeated the treatment night after night for a week until his toes became the size and purplish hue of the knockwurst my grandmother would spear from boiling water for my lunch. Large raw patches opened the soles of his feet, the flesh like new veal, and my grandmother and mother would help him walk to his bed, a temporary retreat before a new attack could be mounted the next day. The microbes were putting up a stiff resistance, and it was their counterattack that caused the pain and ravaged the flesh, but he would take them. 'By God, I'll have them yet,' he promised as he smeared balm on the cooked meat and bandaged up the wounds.

Finally, it was left to an old doctor down the street, a trusted croquet partner, to advise him that he had fought the enemy to a standstill, no one could have performed better or served more brilliantly, and a truce was in order. When he recovered, when he could once more lace the stiff, high-topped shoes, his walk had even more of a swing to it, more of a privateer's challenge as he came down Roberts Street and up our steps at the end of the day, to scoop up the evening paper and open the front door—all in one smooth dip—and up the stairs to the bathroom to clean up for supper.

'Listen,' my grandmother says now. 'Listen.' The chicken snaps in the skillet. The potatoes bubble. But there has been no sound from upstairs; the house seems to yearn for a footstep. 'Yes, all right. All right,' she says, busy once more about the stove and, tucking a strand of gray hair beneath the gauze bandage, she peers through the cracked oven door at the rising corn bread within. I cut the lemon for the iced tea; she supervises and urges me to be careful with the knife. Her guardianship of me is a never-ending source of anxiety. 'Let's do the potatoes. I'll hold the pot and you do the masher.'

Our days in Kansas City had become mixed, a grayish combination of flat business, salted occasionally by my mother's visits or, in my case, the two summers I spent at a camp in the East and a third with Aunt Kit in California, but the day-to-day concoction that composed my grandparents' life had become zestless. In 1941, Roosevelt had been elected for a third term, and Senator Truman was about to be chosen for a second one, but the Democrats in Kansas City were once more in disarray. Tom Pendergast was serving time in Leavenworth Penitentiary for income tax evasion.

Our house on Roberts Street had become dark and silent. No longer was it the informal headquarters for the Fourteenth

Ward, no more did the large LaSalles and Pierce Arrows idle
smugly at our curb as their passengers conferred with my grandmother on the porch or, if my grandfather were not home, in the
living room. The newspaper in 1930 had described her as 'an
active Democratic worker,' but four years later, Mrs. Thos.
Coyne had risen from that anonymous file to be elected to the
State Committee, representing the Fourth Congressional Dis-
trict, and when Judge Truman had been nominated for the U.S.
Senate, the first time, she had risen to make a seconding speech.
I can hear her fruity, sensuous voice pouring over that smoky
convention like the rich cream she would make me use on my
oatmeal.

Nor in 1941 did we attend any funerals as we used to do; those
wonderful wakes that seemed to occur every week as if they came
with the fish on Friday, where each bier of a fallen worker for the
Democratic cause seemed more magnificent than the last, as if
the glorious solemnity of each occasion was meant to illuminate
the majesty and ascendancy of the Democratic Party even as
each death reduced its ranks. In this period I spent a good bit of
one night a week on my knees reciting the rosary in private
homes, funeral parlors, and a rare apartment.

'Who's the little one on his knees?'

'Ah, that's Mollie Coyne's grandson, you know. His father's
the writer.'

'The who?'

'The writer.'

'Ah, the writer. Isn't he an angel, though.'

Some of the Moynihan calculation at work again, for no one
kept me from the keen around the dead man, and I'm sure my
grandmother had nudged me forward, I can feel her gentle push
in the shoulder, before she joined the caucus in the back room
or, in good weather, on the dark front porch where cigarettes
and cigars glowed, a visual pulse for the cicadas sounding in the
dark tree tops. My grandfather rarely attended these wakes,
even though it might be said he owed his job to them, but one

time he saw me on my knees at one and I can remember some of the discussion as we went home on the Independence Avenue streetcar.

'But he doesn't even know the words, for Christ's sake,' he said to my grandmother.

'Ah well, it does no harm,' she replied smoothly.

'No harm!' The eyes grew lighter. 'The boy's not a Catholic and you have him on his knees going through the holy motions?' He turned and looked her full in the face.

'Well, now, every little bit helps. His nibs,' she referred to the deceased, 'was not the best of sinners and needed all the prayers he could get.' She turned away from him, looked at her own reflection in the trolley's darkened window.

'By God.' Gee Gee laughed dryly after a moment's pause. 'You beat them all. I've never seen anyone like you.' And he laughed again, a short cough of a laugh as if he had been kicked in the chest. 'You beat them all.' He slapped his thigh.

Death smelled of gardenias and roses and a thick peachy fragrance that seemed to bubble up and drip from the urns and large inverted lamps with colored bulbs cleverly hidden inside them to illuminate vestibules hung with velvet and to bathe family member and friend with a false glow of health, an embalmed sunshine. The men my grandmother conferred with on these occasions all looked as if they had spent too much time under these lamps, had acquired a peculiar color from them, an unnatural roseate that suggested a casual familiarity with, a handling of sources of power that burned in places ordinary people did not go. Their smiles, deep-dimpled and assured, were given like surplus jewels handed out to the bereaved, and the expression also distracted this audience from moves made by their manicured hands that with a mere rotation of the palms could rearrange lives, raise or lower the lights of a family's destiny.

Even the dead sunk in their floral tributes were bathed in this peculiar color, though tinged with a dusty yellow as if they had become vainly pollenated by the blossoms banked around them; moreover, more than one lay in his coffin with a smile as if he had known something and had got away with it. We children who attended these funerals would study the dead. Our families were all involved with the Pendergast machine, and we would meet regularly at the wakes, coming from different parts of town by streetcar, taxi, plain auto, or liveried limousine to contribute our innocent, imperfect prayers for those who had passed on. These were riotous times; the Democratic Party had split apart and some of the deceased had made unnatural if not untimely exits from the world—the reports were in the papers all the time—so the group of us would study a corpse for wax-plugged bullet holes or for a pipe welt painted over. Our attention was ascribed to respect, a tender display of childish sorrow.

The bunch of us could have written a survey of funeral homes in Kansas City: which had the best yard for outdoor games, which had the spookiest interior for indoor charades; and we became connoisseurs of lighting, of music systems, of flower arrangements—even priests were evaluated, particularly in terms of the time they took; *brief with the breviary* was a high compliment, rarely bestowed.

Private homes were also rated, for many wakes were held in the deceased's residence, and the food and drink were carefully noted by us. There were big spreads of ham and sliced turkey, different kinds of pickles and preserves, tureens of chili con carne, and bowls of spareribs—some of these feasts we'd talk about for weeks—and there would be the more modest offerings of meat pies and potato chips, or a large pot of coleslaw. There was never any fish. But it was the cakes that really made the difference between a first-class funeral and your usual neighborhood layout. In the latter case, they would be thin, layered, and sloped on one side as if in the rush from the neighbor's next door the wind had misshaped them. The icing was brittle and cracked like paraffin when touched and sometimes the interior tasted like one of the new ready-mixes. But it was the other cakes, in the better homes, that raised us from our knees, that drew us from our sentinel at the bier, for it was cakes we were after. There were creations of lemon and orange, mocha, coconut, and chocolate; cakes that rose so high that they resembled the ornate, unstable carriages that would pop up from the pages of a book on Cinderella; cakes that clung to the fingers like paste and had to be licked off and sucked clean and sent the eyes rolling deep into the head; cakes so encrusted with thick sugared icing that they burned the throat all the way down.

For drink there would be tea and lemonade; there would be bottles and flasks also and a keg on the back porch. The lemonade too would be unusually sweet, almost a syrup; it was given up quickly when one of our group, more imaginative if not as addicted to sweets as the rest of us, started the rumor that it was the same sort of stuff that had been pumped into the corpse in the living room.

We searched storage rooms and learned all about caskets: how they were put together, fitted, and sealed, and how to tell real copper from embossed tin over gumwood. We discovered a sure way of telling the quality item, and that was by the coffin's lining: was it of real silk and good padding, or was it only some cheap rayon made to look soft and cozy under the lights? There was only one way to tell for sure: touch it. Someone would have to touch it. Right beside the pillow, under the right ear—for some reason they always seemed to be laid out from left to right —go ahead, touch it. I touched it last time. We'd gather around, close together, our little faces puffed with sweet sorrow, to form a screen for a hand pale and impervious to the dye of the colored lights, as it descended into the shimmering interior of the casket, one finger sprung out like the antenna of a spacecraft about to land on the moon. Then it would pause, hover. Get on with it. Touch it. Touch it! A quick probe and a quicker return as if the resiliency of the quilted surface had bounced it back. It's the real stuff.

We ranged far and wide over Kansas City but never met in our own neighborhoods, would not recognize each other in our own neighborhoods, and certainly would not have the intimate, intense discussions that eliminated class differences, the compelling questions that we tried to resolve as equals: was the rosary held in the stiff fingers a family heirloom or one bought quickly for the occasion? Why was a particular casket completely closed up? And what really happened to the lining? Did it go with everything underground? Or was it slipped out—especially if it were expensive, the real stuff—by some Houdini trick of the undertaker's, somehow pulled out just before the casket was sealed, and used again? We envisioned the poor devil sent to rattle about eternity in a bare coffin like the last piece of candy in a box.

There has been a crick-crack of the front stairs. My grandmother and I hasten our preparations in the kitchen as my grandfather descends to the living room. Just enough time to make gravy; yes, just enough time, and my grandmother alternately pours flour and then stirs it in the chicken drippings, her one good hand taking turns with flour bag and cooking spoon. I've run the corn bread to the table, the mashed potatoes, iced tea, and then comes the chicken, crisp and hot on its platter. With a final toss of black pepper, she declares the gravy done, and I pour it into an ironstone boat; she refers to it as her Askew Avenue dish. It is the only piece left from a set she once used in a house Gee Gee owned on Askew Avenue, one of the many camps he had made in his trek around Kansas City.

He does pause at the dining room, his eyes do take the two of us in, as we stand by the sideboard like the last members of a lost platoon; I in my oversized uniform, the boy recruit, and my grandmother displaying the hasty bandages and splints of the battle-line aid station. A yellowish-purple bruise has begun to spread beneath her left eye. But it is only a hesitation, enough to let us know that he knows, but not so much as to spoil us by too much recognition. He still wears the brown fedora, pulled low and straight across his brow, wears it as he takes his seat at the end, makes the chair square and right to the table; then he removes the hat, furls the brim, and sets it neatly beneath chair. We pass plates around and begin to eat.

Our meals were always quiet and what talk there was, was based on my school work, my day's events, or what letters I may have had from the East, from my mother and father, each letter from a different address these days. Sometimes Gee Gee would recite a vignette from his tour of Walnut Street or of how someone had died or had met with similar justice, usually personalities from my grandmother's era of political eminence; personages as faded, as bland as the newsprint on which their obituaries appeared so that one wondered why they had been important, so colorful, in the first place.

My grandmother said nothing, never acknowledged or answered his bait and returned the lofty demeanor of a queen who might agree to hear a peasant's complaint. At the most, and only if my mother were present, she might slip a soft, fine aside, a remark that only the two women seemed to hear, to understand.

'What's that? What's that?' my grandfather would demand, his eyes become sharp points.

'I said the rose is known for its bloom,' my grandmother would answer majestically, 'and not for its thorn.' Gee Gee would stare, the hard gems of the eyes trying to cut through the confection of her delivery into the core of meaning.

So this evening we tend our supper in silence, my grandmother awkwardly lifting the food to her swollen lips with her left hand, and my grandfather stealing a look now and then at her bandaged head, her shoulder and arm fixed in plaster. He was trying to find the words. He poured gravy into a white volcano of mashed potatoes and tried to find something to say. He was looking for a gesture to accommodate the situation, to sympathize while not weakening his own position. He doused the entire plate before him with salt; he always used large amounts of salt. He sipped the iced tea.

'Well, sergeant,' he spoke to me, 'how was your day?'

'I'm not a sergeant, I'm only a private,' I reply.

'Ah, but you will be. I've written Congressman Bell about nominating you to the Point.' I say nothing and eat my chicken but I have no intention of going to West Point. 'Well,' he continues, 'there's a story in the evening papers about an accident downtown. Some woman was hit by a trailer truck on Twelfth Street.'

The report of my grandmother's accident might have made the evening paper, but our copy of the journal still lay rolled up on a chair in the living room; more likely he had heard about the accident during his daily tour. My grandmother's eyes had become heavy and she lifted her one good arm to fix a strand of hair back beneath the bandage: a soiled frame around a damaged portrait.

'She was crossing and this truck turned in on her and she never saw it coming,' he has continued as he looks over the dish of fried chicken, fork poised to spear a piece. 'Never saw it. More likely,' and his voice falters into a whistle, a thin whinny like a horse in the distance—a sound that meant he had been touched by humor or pathos, and he does laugh abruptly; and continues: 'More likely she had been drinking beer.'

Again he had been trying to sympathize, to recognize her injuries and pain and still make light of the situation, to treat it humorously, as one comrade might joke to another, but he had stumbled, put his foot into a deep hole. My grandmother had jerked, her chair creaked, and she sighed as if his remark had chased out the last breath of air, one she had been saving for an emergency. Her eyes had quickly sought mine, a fearful question in them. Had I told? Had I given her secret away? No, I had never said anything about the stops we made on the way home from the grocery store, usually at the Linwood Tavern, where with a wink and a quarter for me (which was the bribe?), she would have a glass or two of beer. Nor had I revealed the place in the basement, behind the jars of preserves, where she sometimes kept an extra quart of Pilsner, kept it as cool as and certainly more secretly than the Montgomery Ward refrigerator. Somehow, Gee Gee had found these things out himself, had known about her tippling all along; perhaps she had even suspected he knew, but now it was out; he had put it into words, and before me. Once again he had disgraced her.

'What is it? What's the matter?' Gee Gee cries with astonishment. My grandmother has risen like a character in an O'Casey play, dignity strengthened by the suffering in her face—a suffering given full range in pantomime by the Moynihan dramatic gift—and then slowly walks from the table, each step easier than the last as the bruised joints and muscles are exercised. 'What did I say?' Gee Gee asks me.

'Ah, by God.' He returns to his plate, angry now, his eyes sapphirine. 'By God, it's too much,' he says, as she mounts the stairs—the tread a little too fateful even to my sense—and he consumes a large glob of potato and gravy. Her response to his joke, intended by him to be a signal that he was sorry and that all was forgiven, had once more put him back in the stables behind the grand mansion of manners kept by the Moynihan family. Her response had snagged the resentment buried deep within his gut and had pulled out all the old grievances, steaming and covered with bile.

It was a long line, a familiar list but, nonetheless, I was treated to it all again for the rest of supper. How he had rescued the Moynihan family from bankruptcy, from ignominious servitude. How he had had to give up his job as chief engineer for the construction of the Quito-Guayaquil railroad and return to Kansas City when Capt. John had fallen ill. How he had set up the whole family on a section of land in the Ozarks, stocked it with the best breeds money could buy, only to have old Moynihan run it into the ground. How he had sent my mother to the University of Chicago. How he had provided homes for all of them, wherever they wanted. How Aunt Kit's husband, the Swede, had gypped him out of fifteen hundred dollars on that grain elevator deal in Kansas—he still had the notes the sonuvabitch signed to prove it. How he had wanted to stay on the Panama, to take the jobs Goethals and Wood had offered him, good jobs in a fine climate and with authority and respect, but how she—Mollie Moynihan—had to live in Kansas City, had to become the big shebang, and sniff around the pot for a chop. 'Ah, by God, Hilary, it's enough to kill a man. If it weren't for me, they'd all be still wiping their tails on tree bark. Ah, who can eat like this,' he concludes and pushes his plate away, the surface polished clean beneath a stack of bones.

Homework was my excuse for retreat, an excuse he would not question. In fact, there may have been algebra lessons to do in the corner I had set up in the bedroom my mother used when she visited.

In fact, from this night on I slept in that room, no more shared a room with my grandmother because I somehow knew she now had withdrawn completely, even from me; that she wanted no more to do with any of us, either of the men in her house. Gee Gee and I cooked and cleaned, pretending the chores to be temporary while she recovered, pretending we were camping out in the Black Hills, but her injuries were more serious than we knew, her wounds never healed, and she sought explanations, perhaps relief, in the wallpaper's obscure calligraphy beside her bed. She turned her face to the wall like one of James's misunderstood heroines, her doom setting up around her on Roberts Street with the certainty of cement.

*   *   *

'Grandma is dead.' Gee Gee and I sit in a large sun parlor at the end of his hospital ward in the Soldiers Home. It is cold and wet outside, as only Washington can be cold and wet in the fall, and it is 1951. I had come without notice so I found him on his bed, napping fully clothed and with the dark blue robe of issue pulled around him, prepared, it would seem, for any caller, for anything. With no show of surprise he had unfolded and fitted the steel-wire glasses to his face and guided me between rows of white enameled iron beds to this large alcove at the end of the wing, a good-sized room with high windows where a few heavy chairs and a sofa had been set down casually. One old veteran watches a range of gray tones on a small television set in the corner. There's a strong scent of pine disinfectant.

He asked me about college; we had talked about the war in Korea, about the crooks in Truman's administration; and then he leaned forward to say with a whippet laugh that his pension checks hadn't arrived yet and if I had come to see him for some money, had made the four-hundred-mile trip from Providence to put the touch on him, then I had come too soon.

'Grandma is dead.' His head nods quickly, almost a reflex action as if a nerve had been jabbed, but it was also a gesture that accommodated, officially recorded the information.

'Do you watch much of this business?' he says, a thumb toward the television set. 'They have some pretty good shows now and then.'

'Gee Gee, my mother wants you to ask them if she can be buried in Arlington, in a plot next to yours.'

'Ah, so that's it.' He laughs silently, head back. 'Out of the question,' he says softly. 'There's no more room in Arlington. They won't permit spouses to be buried there anymore.'

'Well—' I take a breath and raise the next proposal my mother rehearsed on the drive to Washington. 'What about in the same grave, both of you together?' I had almost added on top of each other, but a flash of wisdom silenced me.

'Ha!' He seems to explode like a stick figure, all of his thin parts—arms and legs, neck and head—flying apart and then snapping back together on elastic strings. 'By God, she beats everything,' he says with honest admiration. 'That schoolmarm of yours beats 'em all. If she had just left well enough alone—I had it all taken care of, Hilary. She's made a mess of it, your mother has made a mess of it.'

'Well, she's here,' I say, impatient to end the interview.

'Who's here?' he replies, almost frightened. There's a checked gathering of energies, as if he were about to spring to the window, as if he had expected to see my grandmother below, laid out in the rain.

'My mother brought her to Washington this morning. She's arranged for a mass tomorrow at St. Matthew's—you're invited, of course—and we'll find a place to bury her here.'

'But why here?' he cries. The eyes burned deep in the hollows of his skull and the large nose became warlike, the shape of a tomahawk. 'Why here?' It is in three years that I am to stand in Arlington, listening to the bugle blow taps over him. My grandmother is buried across the river, somewhere in Washington in a large, promiscuous cemetery whose location I cannot recall.

'She has family here.' I try to repeat the reasoning my mother had fashioned, but it comes undone before I can use the words. True, there were cousins living in Washington, but Nona, the eldest of the Moynihan sisters, had had little contact with the family before she died some years before and there was no room near her cemetery plot either. My mother had already inquired. So why had she brought my grandmother here, arranged for a funeral mass at the prestigious St. Matthew's and sent out obituary notices to all the papers? Why not just bury her in Philadelphia where she had been living with my mother and where she had died? Why not Kansas City?

'The schoolmarm couldn't leave well enough alone,' my grandfather says, his voice tinged more by regret than anger. His attention passes to the flipflopping image on the television screen; an airplane overhead has distorted the picture.

When, on the evening of the accident, my grandmother took to her bed and pulled the covers over her head, she also pulled awry the smooth counterpane of fiction my mother had made up, so the odd ends of our life that had been tucked underneath were suddenly exposed. The singular dormitory my grandmother maintained for me in Kansas City allowed my mother to complete her graduate work in New York and to begin her career as a teacher without the encumbrance of a child to care for.

Her determination to commence work on a master's degree at

Columbia University had been a sore point between my parents, a contention that formed my earliest memory of domestic quarrels and poked at my father's peculiar sense of inferiority: that decision, so many years back, to take him from Knox College after only a year. It still rankled and embarrassed him on occasion. Moreover, he had no liking for the contemporary literature and was suspicious of the academy that taught it (Frost's campus courtships and his subsequent promotion by English departments especially stung him), so that with all of his vaunted perception of human aspirations, motives, and desires, my father refused to acknowledge my mother's need for distinction. Perhaps it was too close to recognize or perhaps he interpreted her studies as a challenge, an attempt to compete intellectually with him.

On the other hand, this phantom that haunted my mother was easier to see in Kansas City, in my grandparents' house, as the rooms of that house and the facades of that old cow town caught her attitudes, reflected her scorn for that provincial domain. She became a silhouette to me, a mirror of expectations I would have before each of her visits, so that I never knew how to look at her or where to look for the image I had had of her. Could I even trust her appearances?

When she unpacked in the bedroom there would be flat packages underneath the slippery, scented contents of her suitcase, packages that crinkled fancifully and turned out to be brand new skill books for spelling, grammar, and vocabulary; new techniques to teach and test these disciplines she had just learned from Thorndike at Columbia and brought home for me to practice, to fill in the blanks at the dining room table when I would rather pack gelatine capsules with the quinine Gee Gee took for his malaria. I earned movie money this way. Was I so backward as to require these remedial labors that took me away from ball games on the corner, that made me unavailable and therefore fatally different from the playmates who had come by on their bikes to pick me up? Or was the school system in Kansas

City so poor that these extra efforts were necessary to make up for the deficiencies suffered in the winter term? As she corrected the tests, her red pencil seemed to grade me and Kansas City and the system.

'Why don't you take him out of here, then?' my grandfather spoke to her scorn one evening at supper. All of our important arguments took place at the dinner table. Their eyes had met, different in color, but with the same fierce light. My mother snapped off a piece of celery in her teeth and chewed it.

'Oh, please,' my grandmother soothed them. 'Let's all have a pleasant meal.'

My parents had moved apart. My mother had left the Chelsea, unable to concentrate on her studies there and, I guess, unwilling to put up with my father's hostile opposition to them. So when I made the summer trip East in 1937, my mother brought me to a tiny apartment and not to the old hotel that had become my second home and whose corridors, elevators, and marble staircase had entertained me in my memory on the Greyhound bus from Kansas City. I roller-skated and played stick ball with the kids on this New York City block while in the small back apartment upstairs my mother typed and typed and moved in and around piles of books and leaves of manuscripts and folders, whispering phrases, trying one on the typewriter to see how it looked and then discarding it to try another. It was camping out again but even more delightful because of the covert nature of our operation, set up only a few blocks from the Chelsea and unknown to my father; if luck were with us we could play a happy joke on him before I would have to return to Kansas City. But it was more than luck, for she worked very hard.

There was something else. In 1937, my father published three of the more important books of his late career: the biography of Whitman, the novel *Tide of Time,* and *The New World,* which was to be the last of the long narrative poems. The urge to be a part of this good year, not to compete with any of its achievements but rather to contribute to its successful aura, raced my mother up the flights of steps to the cluttered apartment where she talked to herself, tested and scored herself; turned up the pace and lengthened her stride, already difficult to match as she walked to the main Public Library or sometimes all the way to Morningside Heights.

It came out right, or seemed to have worked. The day she received her degree with honors, we took the Seventh Avenue subway from Columbia down to 23rd Street and I was once more in the familiar, musty lobby of the Chelsea Hotel. But my father was not there and the desk clerk was even hesitant about giving up the keys to his apartment.

My father's rooms were still and hot, the windows were closed and the air hung with the odors of ink and tobacco and paper and clothing—smells that sometimes came to me in the middle of the night in Kansas City. But even stronger was the aroma of absence. He had been gone for some time; all the while my mother had typed and studied, all the nights we had joked about living secretly a few blocks away doing all these things while he sat in his rooms at the Chelsea reading and smoking his pipe; it turned out he hadn't been there at all. He had gone; and gone, apparently, in the company of another woman.

'My God, kid, you've done it.' That's what she had hoped to hear after she had passed through the revolving door into the lobby. There, she had planned to say, the bright, challenging look of her father's eye forcing the poet to smile, to dimple his primness—see, I told you I'd do it and I have. Here's the paper, the degree, and with second honors too. 'My God, kid, you've done it,' he was supposed to say and cackle like some old country character who's been outfoxed and then we would all go downstairs and outside and around the corner to Pappa's Restaurant for a big meal.

But this scene had never been written into the script and she had only just discovered that, a frustrating discovery made more painful by the knowledge that it would never be played. This was the hurt that rolled her onto the old double bed by the locked-up wardrobe trunks, to sob the rest of the afternoon in that airless hotel suite, and not the disclosure of my father's affairs; for she regarded his sexual casualties, so to speak, on the level of itches to be scratched—an attitude that reflected his own, though at seventy years of age his interpretation may have been more acute and less philosophical than hers. I spent the afternoon looking through the books of his library, books that would open with a sudden familiarity, like rounding a corner to come upon an old neighborhood.

'I had it all worked out,' my grandfather is saying. We have gone to the small canteen in the basement of his hospital building and sit at a square table beneath an old-fashioned ceiling fan. There's a small bar and short-order grill and a television set perched in one corner of the room, that is going and goes unnoticed. 'If your mother had just left things be, let them stay the way I had fixed it up.'

In his bathrobe, pants, slippers, and with the fedora set straight, he resembles someone who has been routed out of bed by a fire and has grabbed whatever belongings were close at hand. What he had worked out was to put my grandmother into a place run by Catholic charities in Kansas City and then retire, himself, into the Soldiers Home in Washington, D.C. My grandmother had willingly signed her own commitment papers, perhaps happily signed to certify her separation and freedom from this bad bargain, this poor match. But my mother had made a quick flight to Kansas City—this was in 1946—and brought Mollie Coyne to live with us in Philadelphia, to share the small faculty apartment on the campus of the junior college where my mother taught.

This all happened five years after my grandmother's accident and probably happened because of that accident downtown, all the routines of our lives flattened and made unrecognizable like the cake from Wolferman's that had rolled from her grasp. Through the fall and winter months, Gee Gee and I had cooked and cleaned while my grandmother lay in bed upstairs, kept the outpost alive until the relief might come, but by spring some old instinct had urged him to move to another site where conditions might be better; so they went to the large house on Troost Avenue, a last refuge.

'Come and get your kid, is what he wrote me,' my mother will say when we discuss this time of our lives. Her tone is accusatory and meant to make me an ally in the old contest. 'Come and get your kid,' she repeats, mimicking his harsh rhythm. But, in truth, when my grandfather sold the house on Roberts Street and moved to the large, rambling place on Troost, I was fourteen years of age, he was eighty-two, and my grandmother, disabled and destroyed, only ten years younger. Perhaps it was time for me to be got.

When Gee Gee had sold the Roberts Street house he had sold all of its contents with it: furniture, drapes, dishes, silverware, the dining room sideboard and table, the desks and bookcases— everything but the beds, which were moved. What he did not sell, he burned. It was an obsession to burn out the rot, to cauterize the wound his life had become. He would stand day after day like a sentry by the fire in the backyard, in shirtsleeves and vest and the grayish-brown fedora, the rake poised to stir the embers and turn the last of family pictures, journals, worthless bonds, or an irreplaceable diploma from the University of Chicago into ash.

It was to retrieve that diploma, to look for it, that my mother made the side trip to Roberts Street on our way to Union Station and our last departure from Kansas City. But he had beat her to it—that would be his way of looking at it. She had mocked him, challenged him, so he had put a torch to the certificate of this recognition she foolishly craved, the same need for recognition that had brought her back to Kansas City on brief visits, to seek it in places and from people she held in contempt.

'Well, your father's gone,' Gee Gee says, lifting and resetting the fedora in the exact same ageless angle across his brow. 'And now Mollie.' His eyes become watery and he looks around the hospital canteen; we are almost alone, for it is midmorning. 'Even the Goddamn Swede is dead!' He refers to Aunt Kit's husband, and the anger clears his eyes. 'And here I am, still going on. Do you know I'm the last Indian Wars veteran alive here? The other day, that old gink O'Rourke kicked the bucket. He and I were the last two.'

'Did you know him?' I ask. There's a game quiz on the television. 'I mean, then—did you know him out there?'

'Naw, he was with Miles against the Apache. Did I ever tell you the time we all slept in our saddles because we was supposed to move in the morning down to Mexico, after Geronimo?'

'Yes, you did. Word came that he had been captured or something like that, so you didn't go?'

' 'Course he hadn't been captured at all,' he muses. 'Not then, anyways.' He sounds sorry, sighs and takes another deep breath and his back straightens. He stands up. 'Tell your mother I can't do anything for her. She should have left well enough alone.'

My appearance must have shocked my grandmother as much as the changes in her horrified me, for it had been four years since I had last seen her in Kansas City, moving through the rooms and hallways of the large house on Troost Avenue as if in a trance. It was 1946 and I had come home on leave from the navy to find her living with my parents in the faculty apartment. Perhaps 'confused' would be a more appropriate description of the poor old lady's reaction, because the last time she had seen me I had worn the olive drab uniform of my high school ROTC and here I reappeared four years later, wearing the blue uniform of the U.S. Navy.

She had become wasted; the luxuriance of her body that had warmed and soothed me as I lay against her with the early morning spasms of a nightmare had become abstracted, all sharp angles and hollows. The shock of the accident had reactivated a thyroid goiter and her flesh seemed to dissolve in its poisons. My grandfather was quick to remind us that he had begged her to let Gorgas remove the goiter when they were on the Panama, but her vanity forbade anything that might scar the full, smooth throat.

Her teeth were gone also, replaced by awkward dentures fixed behind her lips like small saucers to stretch the jaundiced skin over cheekbones; she resembled a mask from some old ritual. But the eyes held the same craft of a prima donna ready to steal a scene, and they moved imperially in their deep sockets—though there was little content behind them; it was all technique. No thought accompanied the grand study.

'How is he? Did you see him?' she would inquire if she knew I had recently visited Gee Gee at the Soldiers Home. 'Did you see him?' Her fingers, turned into boled twigs by arthritis, pinch my arm, and she looks close into my face, looks for the squint of a falsehood as I gradually pull away from her. Her expression becomes almost jocular, a good-natured butt of a jest, and I am transported back to those days when I would sit in my yellow suit and watch her rise to address a committee or a convention, her round, sensuous face dimpled by the pleasantry, the witty turn of phrase that lay just beneath that expression, that was about to be spoken, but first came—like the artist, the pro she was—the throw-away glimmer of amusement to prepare the audience for the joke to come. 'Ah, you didn't see him,' she said, her smile a grotesquerie of false teeth and bone and sallow skin. 'He's *not* still alive?'

7

'W here are you from, Masters?' Prints of English fox hunters hung on the paneled walls of the student union where our football team had been invited to share cocoa and cookies with their team. We had lost the game 42–3.

'I'm from Missouri.' In fact, still wanted in Kansas City, I almost added; still waited for and wanted by a guy with a long knife standing at the intersection of Benton Boulevard and Independence Avenue. The austere manner of my gray-flanneled host urged me to shake his cocoa cup with such gory admissions.

'Oh, re-ah-lly.' Most of the people I had just met in New Hampshire neatly parceled their words, but not this fellow nor any of his peers at the other schools our football schedule included. They all spoke as if the consonants had got caught crosswise in the back of their throats and had to be turned straight before passing the lips. That's if they spoke at all. Usually, they only smiled, as if relishing a secret joke, perhaps our recent sacrifice on their gridiron. Someone seemed to have taught them it was better to give less information and fewer opinions in ordinary conversation, certainly less than what I had been accustomed to hear in the free flow of Roberts Street, and to speak openly and without constraint would be to betray a code of good conduct. 'That's where the buffalo roam, isn't it?'

They knew nothing about geography either. All those times I had traveled between Kansas City and the East by car, by train and bus, even by air once on a DC-3, had taught me the different dimensions the same distance between two places could have. It was as though a shuttle had woven the two points together, as I moved back and forth between them, put them into one fabric, but this pattern all came apart after my grandmother's accident and my grandfather's determination to burn the fort down rather than surrender it. So I had made one more trip East, this one in 1942 and with no return ticket.

Or maybe those preppies offered me an insight that I was too unsophisticated to perceive: that there are certain things that can never be spoken of directly, or described as they happen, but if one is lucky, the attempt can be made later to talk about them, even write about them. The emphasis is on the preposition: to talk or write around, on the outside of a subject but never inside. So, here's the problem with this transition. The signal fires and phone lines and letters that I had assumed to be a permanent field, like the prairie that turned endlessly outside my train windows, were a network that had come unraveled without my knowing it. Now, it must be pieced together from the outside and long after the incidents took place.

Somehow, my mother had been able to locate a small, dilapidated school on the shore of Lake Winnipesaukee, an academy established by a local benefactor to give free secondary education to the children of the village while it also accepted a small number of boarders. It was not a very good school, its curriculum and instruction on a par with the teams it fielded in outmoded, cracked uniforms, but it was cheap and it accepted me quickly. It was good enough, my mother would say.

In a letter, H. L. Mencken called her a 'stupid woman,' though it seems that Mencken had no genuine understanding of the character of an independent woman. Nor did he seem to have sympathy, certainly in my mother's instance, for a woman who would not give in to the circumstances, acquiesce to the limitations and realities imposed by the man's world she was supposed to accommodate. All this is to come later, but for now,

Mencken's comment exemplified my father's attitude, his frustration and anger, as my mother persisted in her career as a teacher, the frustration toothed by astonishment when it seemed she could take care of herself.

She had offered him a divorce but he had refused. Perhaps he did not wish to lose contact with me completely, but more likely the horror that had been the divorce from his first wife still caused him anguish. The cost in time, in distraction, and finally in emotional and financial exhaustion vetoed any idea of a second divorce, particularly now that his resources were so diminished. Moreover, he and my mother continued to get together for a drink or dinner to discuss plans that might affect me or ideas for books and articles, or just for him to air a writer's complaints. Harold Ickes had offered him a post as secretary to the governor of the Virgin Islands, clearly an honor the Roosevelt administration meant to give him to afford his last years a comfortable place to live and work. It was the post that had been hoped for on the porch in Hillsdale. Should he take it? he asked my mother. Yes. Would she come with him and bring Hilary? No. Her own professional credits were beginning to accumulate and she had more than one future to worry about. He rejected the offer.

Moreover, in spite of their conflicts, she provided a continuity for him, a channel into the landlocked memory of his boyhood in Illinois, and this may have been his strongest reason to maintain the marriage, at least formally. They could talk about old Hannah Armstrong, about schoolmates from Petersburg she had met, or members of his family, their history. She knew his family as no other person knew its secrets, joys, and tragedies and this frame of reference was important to him. So as I was the thin wire through which my grandparents and my father and mother were able to talk to each other, like a country party line, like the illustration in *Projects for Boys and Girls*—a book Pop had given me and so archaic that the boys who tugged the wired tin cans tightly to their ears wore caps and high-buttoned shoes and knickers with drooping socks—my mother, in the same way, was a transmission into the past from which he drew for inspiration and if the calling up of that inspiration had now become so weak, the power turned down, that it could only be plotted on the red checkered tablecloths of Cavanaugh's Restaurant, the impulse of its messages was still important. 'We write about what we have loved and lost,' someone has said, and perhaps, I might add, what we have lost before we can give it love—and so, if one can no longer write, one talks.

He had been arrogant and lofty and short-tempered with his contemporaries and they had finally left him alone, all save for Dreiser, who would visit him when in town. His work had lost focus, become sodden, but in this year of 1942 he was to publish *The Sangamon*, a pleasant book and a worthy contribution to the River Series put out by Farrar and Rinehart; and it was to be his last important publication. Moreover, the Eastern Establishment—the junior members of which I was encountering on the playing fields of Exeter and St. Paul's—had begun to work the revenge demanded for the embarrassment *Spoon River Anthology* had always caused them in their orderly declension of American Literature, and the term 'one-book author' began to be used as anthologies appeared without him on the pejorative grounds that his work had only 'historical importance.' Where are you from, Masters?

So he would get on the phone at the Chelsea and call my mother, put the telephone on top of the half-opened steamer trunk in the bedroom of the hotel suite and shout into it, not out of anger, though the roundness of the face echoed by the round glasses would be pink and the flesh tight, but because he never liked to use the telephone, felt awkward with it as he did with the automobile, and talked into it as if it were still a box hanging on some farm kitchen wall that was to be used only for emergencies and powered by the tone of voice.

'Hello. Hello. Ellen. Ellen, I want you to get over here straight away!' he'd shout, the twang in his voice like the snap of dry willow.

He was alone now; yet not alone, enduring the worst sort of solitude; visited by a retinue whose level of ordinary dullness made exile from his peers even more painful. Like pests invading an empty house, they consumed his days with worthless distractions and jabber that only amused or benefited or complimented themselves with a sense of importance; they were *seeing* the 'author of *Spoon River*,' a counterfeit currency that could be successfully passed at the next meeting of the Poetry Society of America or exchanged for some attention they might not otherwise receive at a dinner.

'They're always coming here,' he tells my mother one time, 'talking about the wonderful lunch they just left at the Lafayette or some such place. Goddammit,' the glasses glint, 'I have to eat too! Why don't they take me to lunch?'

He made notes about them in his journal and gave them the name *anonkorai*, the term made more appropriate by the services some of the women performed—the same old services Xenophon attributed to his camp followers—for they would arrive to spend a part of some nights or some afternoons in the rooms that overlooked the ailanthus trees and the howling fence-stuck cats below. They came to his rooms with no lust nor love; but at the age of seventy-four, he must have opened the door with a wonder and gratitude that overlooked their motives.

It is an old story, this bedding down of a celebrity. Ironically these poor women revealed more of themselves than they may have intended, for like Chekhov's Anna Sergeyevna, their bourgeois pretensions fell away with their clothes, so that they told him of their other affairs, how their husbands were impotent, or flunkies, or fools—or all three—and they confessed to their abortions, their bouts with gonorrhea, their experiments with lesbianism, a litany of afflictions put upon women who break the rules, and however venal or superficial they were in public they showed him their secret wounds, thinking he looked with a poet's compassionate eye when actually their confessions were recorded by an attorney's cool mind. He made notes, copious and detailed notes like briefs to be used in some countersuit. Some of their confessions would even be transcribed into pornographic heroic couplets, sonnets dedicated to fellatio or buggery, run off at the desk by the bay window the morning after; 'typed without revision in 1 min. 42 seconds' noted at the bottom of the page, as if the same impulse that had driven him earlier to produce an opus had become trivialized by this pathetic frenzy.

July 10, 1942

Dear Mr. Ittie; the war, the hot weather, a thousand things have me stymied. I want you to have the Sangamon but just now I haven't any here, and have to send to Farrar and Rinehardt's [sic] to get them. A woman in Petersburg sent me a check to fill in to buy one; and I had to do that, then I have to wrap it up and autograph it and get it off. Something like this every day, till I get tired of it.

I am truly sorry that your grandma is so ill. Give her my best. Don't forget that I love de. I am proud of your studies. I am glad you picked 'Weekend by the Sea.' It is one of the best of my recent things. Write when you can and I'll try to answer. I have no secretary and have to do everything for myself.

Your loving Pa,
E. L. M.

I received this letter as my grandfather moved from Roberts Street to Troost Avenue and as my mother prepared my final move to the East, and as all the familiar lines of my life were erased, I began to share the aggravation my father and grandfather felt for my mother's obstinate behavior, my new manhood made ally to their scorn. Why couldn't she leave well enough alone? Why didn't she leave me in Kansas City to live on Troost Avenue and finish high school? Why didn't she give up this playing the 'schoolmarm,' to use Gee Gee's term, and go back to live at the Chelsea? Why didn't she let things go back the way they were? Angry questions for me at night. She now shared a tiny apartment with the owner of a bookstore on East End Avenue near Gracie Mansion. Two rooms set behind the bookstore, not enough room for me to sleep over when I came to New York on school vacations, so a bed would be 'borrowed' at a neighbor's place. I slept on couches in strange apartments. On the other hand, it was a bookstore and I read from morning to night: bestsellers and detective novels and romances.

Even the way she walked me around Manhattan spurred my exasperation, the pace she kept, the distances we covered, but it never occurred to me why we walked, at least one way, to a friend's apartment in the Village for dinner, or to a store downtown to buy me a new suit for school or to a meeting at the Bentley School on the West Side where she taught English. Subway and bus fare was still only a nickel—but she was saving dimes. Block after block, my sullen anger burrowed within me while I tried to keep up with the long strides of her handsome legs; East and West, uptown and down, while she hummed show tunes interrupted by crisp bulletins on the state of the marriage, the problems my father's new friends caused him, the family betrayals and alliances; all this as we cut across parks, jogged between stalled cars, and dodged into shortcuts through the subterranean passageways of department stores. When I would lag behind, unwilling to keep up and weary of her grievances, a braceleted arm would wave me forward, a command gesture exactly as Gee Gee would have used, but with the cry, 'C'mon, Snookums, c'mon,' and I would race far ahead to escape the appellation. She would catch up.

'Did you tell them about these times?' I ask her. 'About walking around New York and living at the bookstore and making out the way you did?' Lionel Trilling has invited her to record her recollections for the oral history archives at Columbia University and she's visiting us, in Columbia County, after one of the interviews. My question has challenged the order of events, her command of them, and her thoughts have stopped short to clear the obstruction.

'Oh, they don't want to hear about that sort of thing,' she replies, wrinkling her nose. Her hand tosses the idea into the shadows outside our house.

Beginning in the summer of 1938, after my parents moved apart, my mother had a summer job as a counselor in a girls' camp in the Pocono Mountains, and part of her compensation was free tuition for me at a companion camp for boys. So I was able to visit my father at the Chelsea within the brief parentheses formed by the different arrivals and departures that composed each summer's journey. The old hotel was the only familiar landmark left in the territory behind me but even the Chelsea was different, off center, as if it had shifted slightly on its coordinates each time one looked away. That late summer of 1942, there were men in uniform who moved through the lobby with an easy gallantry that challenged, shamed, my adolescence. I had come to visit my father before going to New Hampshire, to my new school. The cozy restaurant next door had been transformed into a club for merchant marine officers, and its doors were closed to civilians—certainly fourteen-year-old civilians. On the other side, a record store had set up its bins of heavy shellac records in the space once occupied by the drugstore.

Something more had changed. I was silent and faced the front in the elevator as it lifted me to my father's floor. A peculiar glance had passed between the desk clerks when I announced myself. There was soft talk, a suggestive laugh, as I turned away. Moreover, there were new tenants whom I did not know, but who knew my father, and one or two women who, I guessed, knew him very well. I shared the elevator with one on more than one occasion, silently rising to our different floors together, while a thought was pulled up into my consciousness, a thought so breathed upon by her closeness as she stood behind me as to ignite a mutual, unspoken understanding: if I were not on the elevator, she would be the one to get off on the second floor.

The halls were dark and closed in against my intrusion, though when his door opened the light from the large bay window momentarily dazzled me so that I was an easy prey to his embrace, and suffered the scrape of his grizzled cheek as he kissed me. I was no longer patient with such affection, too old to be called 'Mr. Ittie'—though he insisted on using the name—and I had outgrown all the Poppy-dear games, had been to all the museums, zoos, and aquariums. 'The Washington Post March' no longer interested me as did the Benny Goodman record I had bought at the store downstairs on my way up to his rooms.

'Turn that damn thing off,' he'd growl. 'What kind of racket is that?'

'That's swing, Pop,' I'd say, lifting the heavy playing arm of the old wind-up Victrola off the record.

'Swing? That's utter nonsense. Utter nonsense that's what that is. Doobie-doobie-dum-dum,' he mocked the beat of 'Sing, Sing, Sing.' 'Straight out of the jungle,' he said sternly.

He didn't like my music nor did he know what to do with me when I visited him. We read a good deal. He seemed to read more than write these days and it would be rare for me to wake on the sofa in the front room to the scratch of pen on paper. There was a silence between us, not without contentment, nor unusual—as I now know it not to be strange for a father and son to share silences at this time of their lives. When he did speak he told me stories about his boyhood in Petersburg, about fishing in the Sangamon, playing pranks on pompous villagers; all stories I had heard many times, stories he had already put into prose or poetry. Abruptly, the volume of Goethe would be lowered, the brier pipe relit—almost all in one motion—and he'd start to talk.

'One day my father took me down to the courthouse there in Petersburg.' *Draw—draw*—puff-puff; head gone up in smoke. 'Just as we were on the steps, this old man comes out. He looked like a bum, a crazy bum. And he comes up to my pa and starts to talk to him and my pa talks to him and then this old bum staggers off, like he was on the likker, and my pa says to me, "You know who that was, Lee?" and I say no and then he says, "That's Mentor Graham." So what do you think of that, Mr. It?'

I made some noise of astonishment that seemed appropriate, though I did not know who Mentor Graham was, and we returned to our different books. Or, as if to signal the end of some determined interval, he would throw aside his book and say, 'Oh, fiddle-dee-dee. Let's get out of this place, Mr. It.'

He'd clamp on the soiled Panama hat—it would be summer—and we would take the elevator to the lobby where he would introduce me gratuitously to every member of the staff we met along the way: maids, bellhops, desk clerks, and porters. 'This is my boy, Hilary,' he'd say and I would be forced to look into faces which had deadpanned my presence minutes before. Sometimes we'd walk down to Madison Park, or go across 23rd Street to the Y for a swim, or stop into a bar where he would order one beer, a soda for me, and pass a few words to the bartender about Babe Ruth or Joe Louis or Jack Dempsey—a swaggering exchange for my benefit and professionally served by the bartender.

His steps were slowly measured and we halted frequently at window displays or to review minor landmarks in the area, their examination also affording a brief rest. I was as irked by his slow pace as I was exasperated by my mother's quick-march tempo—no one walked to suit my pace anymore—and it seemed that the great bulk of his belly had become a terrible burden, for it jutted far out under his vest, setting and braking his course, all at once.

He continued to swim at the YMCA across the street, enjoying the exercise and probably the illusion of fitness given by the water's buoyancy as he pushed the large roundness of his head, more bald without glasses, across the surface of the chlorinated water, a pink, blinking ball propelled by the steady, serious breaststroke like an ancient water sport that celebrated some heroic myth. His body offended and shocked me so I never swam with him but fooled around the pool's edge or poked around the locker room or hallway; the poor man would swim but a few laps before my antics would harry him from the water and he would rise up and get dressed. This had been the purpose of my behavior: for him to get dressed; his bloated nakedness embarrassed me and I did not wish anyone else to see him. All the strength and suppleness I had remembered displayed in powerful arms and thighs seemed to have drained into and soured in the swollen mass of his abdomen, and though the chest and shoulders were still broad they had lost a third dimension, a depth.

'I had so many things to think about then,' my mother says. There are fireflies tonight, perhaps the descendents, several hundred generations down, of those we used to watch forty years ago in Hillsdale, just twelve miles north of here. 'There was your grandmother to take care of, and you in school, and your father falling apart and your grandfather acting crazy. Then there was my own work. My own work!' She leans forward, a hand spread against her bosom as if to keep it from tumbling out.

I need no persuasion, though she has the chronology wrong, has compressed events. She did not bring my grandmother East until 1946. My father suffered his physical collapse in December of 1943. By 1944 I was in college, and in the navy by 1946. But the pressure she must have been under, the balancing act she had begun to put together, apparently puts a net beneath these separate events and catches them up in her memory.

It seems clear now that she was working out our separate destinies in 1942, preparing for each future with the same sort of frantic dexterity she was to employ in the preparation of four-course meals on pyramided hot plates. The school in New Hampshire was not the best—if there had been more time maybe a better one could have been found—but it was all right and it was also a place where I could live—sleep and eat—for nine months of the year. It was good enough. Meantime, she could tend to my father and his demands, his arguments and desperations, keeping an eye on his deteriorating situation while trying, at long distance, to say in touch with my grandfather's suicidal impulses in Kansas City; he was now threatening to sell all of his property, including that on Troost Avenue, if my grandmother did not get out of bed and start running the rooming house properly. Then there was, as she says, her own work.

The intricacies of this balancing act in New York were difficult to see from New Hampshire, and in any event I was too busy trying to change the way I talked and dressed, so that now when I was asked, 'Where are you from, Masters?' I would casually answer New York City. Where in New York City?

'My mother lives on the East Side,' I'd say. 'Near Beekman Place,' I would add. Ah yes, the patrician snouts would rise in recognition, a herd scenting one of its own. 'But my father lives at the Hotel Chelsea.' Two domiciles, parents living apart; surely this was a way of life familiar to many of my new associates, and I could weld, in fantasy, a bond with them, though it would be cruelly tested on the hard edge of reality when I visited New York City during holidays.

The resources my father had laid aside from the old lucrative law practice in order to write had long been depleted by the terms of the divorce settlement and the years since he had left Chicago for New York. Royalties had fallen off; nor had they far to fall, being those of a poet. Contracts for prose books were not forthcoming; his kind of fiction was no longer read and his name could not guarantee sales nor any longer excuse the slightness of such prose efforts as his life of Mark Twain, published in 1938. He had written several universities and colleges, inquiring if some position could be made for him on their campus, such as the now familiar post of 'writer in residence.' The few who bothered to answer him complained of hard times, tight budgets.

The word was out that he had become bitter and sour and difficult to deal with, and he had the reputation of trying to bite anyone who offered to help. So he lived on dwindling savings, selling a poem to a magazine or newspaper, sometimes a prose piece, the sum total this side of penury. There were still friends in editorial positions who helped out, but occasionally even some of these surprised him with rejections.

'One day on a train going from Baltimore to New York,' William Saroyan wrote me a few years ago, 'H. L. Mencken told me the old gent used to take bad poems to the *American Mercury* and would become enraged because Mencken wouldn't publish them. I said, you should have bought them anyhow, and maybe even published them, maybe with some improvements by him, or by yourself.'

My father's bitterness was the anger of a lover betrayed, for he felt he had made some contribution to American literature, given some definition to the American character, but he discovered the legislature of poets had voted him out, the *Kosmos* that Walt Whitman proposed had expelled him; there was no room for him on the mountain.

When my mother used his old charge account at John Wanamaker's to buy me some shirts and underwear, his anger was Jovian. After all, she was the one with the job, the schoolmarm. He could not support these expenditures. If she was going to be so damn independent, she could damn well pay the bills, too.

The gas ring set up next to the small sink in the rooms behind the bookstore could boil water for tea and coffee, cook a light breakfast, but it could not cook the meals required by an adolescent, so my mother became very good at locating cheap restaurants in which to feed me those times I came down to New York from New Hampshire. German, Chinese, Czech—the ethnic character of the restaurants was not so important as the amount of food served for a dollar. Her annual salary at the Bentley School was only a thousand of those dollars, which should have explained the walking tours and the other ignoble frugalities, for in addition to my school costs and her own expenses, she was also putting a small amount aside for the emergency she feared might billow at either end of her horizon. There was an Italian restaurant on West 32nd Street near Eighth Avenue where one could get a five-course meal: minestrone, spaghetti or ravioli, baked chicken, salad, and biscuit tortoni—all for fifty cents.

So when I came down from New Hampshire that first year for the Christmas holidays it was to arrive into this penurious existence. I would leave school warmed by the illusion that I was a member of that large pack of boys who poured from the New England woods in seasonal migration: sleek athletes and scholars, tweedy and carefully spoken on their certain journeys to a comfortable apartment overlooking the East River or to a snug house in Connecticut, cozily chimnied and snowbound, or to the old home place in Westchester County after a long drive through the poplars. I would look out the bus windows and imagine an arrival put together from other arrivals, a fiction of snips collected from the best of all my travels. Then I would step off the Greyhound bus into the freezing slush of 34th Street and be walked crosstown to the Lexington Avenue subway for the trip to 86th Street and then another walk over to East End Avenue and the bookstore, my shoes wet through, with the suitcase clipping my legs as I endeavored to bury my chagrin and keep up with my mother's galoshed gait.

She had set up a life for us that was not meant to be permanent but which would be fun for the time we had together, using all her theatrical skills, the logistical savvy from the old stock companies that could set up a show in one night and then move it fifty miles for the next performance; ingenious in her salvage of materials, and probably inspired by Mollie Coyne's imagination which could turn an ordinary cup of tea into an elegant occasion, and with her exotic good looks and eagerness for good times, her open-hearted laughter and ready spirit—Ellen Coyne must have been an astonishing if not frightening creature for any man to encounter in those days, especially my father, but I could not see that then.

I wandered through the gypsy camp she had set up for me like every stuffy young man in legend and life, insisting the baubles were not real and lifting the scrim to discover the unpainted wall behind. There was no adventure in the different restaurants—their cheapness embarrassed me—nor in the odd side streets where most of them were located. We passed through barricades of garbage cans and around trucks that were either abandoned or that surely were about to receive stolen goods, as I slumped inside my overcoat, pulled up the collar as she led me down the stairs into one of these places (another thing: the restaurants always seemed to be in the basement of a building—the basement!), for I was terrified that one of the chaps from New Hampshire might see me, might just be passing by on the leather lounge seat of a Sky-Vue cab, probably on his way to the Waldorf-Astoria for dinner, and see me going into this dump for a fifty-cent meal, beverage not included.

'You'll be spending Christmas Eve and the next day with your father,' she said to me. I turned to the shelf of new novels in the lending library section of the bookstore; I can't remember their titles, only the bosoms on their covers. I barely heard the itinerary she had planned for my vacation because my mind was already at the Chelsea, the good old Chelsea: run down, different yet familiar to me because I had a historical place there, a legitimacy, quite different from the cramped studio behind the bookstore. Moreover, my father might take me to Lüchow's for dinner, and the sparkle and aromas of the grand restaurant rose in my imagination like a glazed meringue. 'I've arranged with a woman up the street,' my mother said, 'for you to sleep on her couch. It's a pull-out and comfortable. Did you bring your bathrobe?'

We have been talking of these times since dinner, old names in a familiar narrative, but now the darkness here in Columbia County seems to remove us from the past as we are apart from but yet a part of the occasional traffic on the county road below. Then my mother's voice cuts through the night's fabric. 'They would have let him die, those people.' Her voice is flat, matter-of-fact. 'Let him die.'

When I arrived at the Chelsea on Christmas Eve of 1942, I had a fair idea of who 'those people' were: some family, some of the new courtiers and courtesans. It had been a long, awkward trip down from the Upper East Side and over to West 23rd Street, but the lobby of the hotel was warm and there were strands of small lights draped over the mirrors and mantel. A small tree was fixed in one corner, strung with blue lights, and the whole right wall thudded with the rhythm of the celebrations next door at the Merchant Marine Club. I had never been in the hotel in winter, never seen it turned out for a holiday, and the absent summer airs left a graceless vacancy; the bare wires of electric bulbs denoted more than the season, like plastic flowers pinned to a threadbare coat.

'I'll wait here,' my mother said, and sat down on the round settee before the fireplace. 'Call me from upstairs.'

There was no one at the desk, but I was expected anyhow, so I turned to the left and the elevator and stepped into the cab with an operator who was new to me, part of the winter staff perhaps —Sydney was gone—and gave myself up to the wobbly, clunk-clunk ascent, every inch of altitude releasing my spirit from the pressure of my mother's bitterness and hurt, rising away from her voice and the catalogue of wrongs it always seemed to carry. At the second floor I turned to the left and down the corridor. I carried a small nightbag with pajamas, toothbrush, a change of underwear and socks, and a one-pound tin of Prince Albert smoking tobacco. It had come already boxed and wrapped in paper patterned with green holly leaves but with no trade name visible, so my mother had demanded the drugstore clerk carefully unwrap one end of the package to verify that it really *was* Prince Albert tobacco and not some other brand my father would not smoke.

A turn to the right down a very short hallway, an entryway,

with the familiar door directly ahead. There was no sound, no response after I knocked, but the walls are soundproof. The door opened before I could knock again, but only partly, as if my father were on guard to contain what was inside rather than keep me out; but the noise of the party had already escaped through the aperture. He looked freshly shaved, his complexion was flushed, and the hazel eyes snapped behind the glasses; the tie was neatly knotted within the crisp white collar of the shirt. He was dressed, I remember thinking, as if he were going out, but he wasn't going out.

There had been a mistake, he told me, still holding the door almost closed, speaking forcefully but not sternly; not sternly but only at a level above the broken laughter and talk behind him, music and the kiss of glassware and ice. I was meant to visit him tomorrow, on Christmas Day, he said. Come back tomorrow. She's waiting downstairs? Good. Come back tomorrow.

The elevator operator said nothing, showed no surprise when he opened the doors, as if he had known all along that I had made a mistake about the floor, about the night, but who was he to say anything about it? So down we passed to the lobby, and out I stepped with a curious elation as if I had passed some test only to be confronted with another.

'There's been no mistake,' my mother said evenly. She snapped her purse shut and stood up. 'Go right back up there and tell him you're to stay here tonight.'

The elevator operator sprang to his post when he saw me return; this was a scene that had been played before; even now, a couple of desk clerks had appeared and leaned on the register to observe our rehearsal. The chains and steel joints of the machinery clashed and the Brown Knight rose again, but without armor, for at fourteen, wrapping paper would no longer suffice.

This time members of the party came to look over my father's shoulder as he stood in the doorway, their expression bemused, quizzical, as if they had come upon a street accident but finding it not serious, not really interesting, turn and go about their business with a satisfied nod. My father's look was hard and crimsoned. He called me by name, something he only did in anger or gravity. No. No. No. Not tonight. I could not stay there tonight. Go back to the lobby. Come back tomorrow. Once again the elevator operator opened the doors with the disciplined drift of a patient retainer, but I knew he was thinking. I could tell he was thinking as I stared at the back of his head. He even cleared his throat.

'There had been some mix-up,' my mother says uncertainly, as she sorts through her memory. The leaves of the old maples that tower above us are burnished by the moonlight. 'But it wasn't anything like the way you remember it. You didn't make all those trips up and down in the elevator. Now I remember. Your father called me from upstairs.' Her voice has gained confidence, a Sybilline authority set down on a canvas lawn chair in Columbia County. 'He called me from upstairs—I remember going to the house phone in the lobby, all those awful hotel clerks listening—but he had forgot the date.'

So we disagree on the number of times I used the elevator, but I do not care to sully the fine air with argument; like her own father, she will never surrender a point, so she settles back into the lawn chair—her version unquestioned.

'Wait there a minute,' my father said, as I appeared at his door for the second or the third or perhaps the fourth time. The door closed, shutting me off from the party, and I leaned against the coarse vanilla surface of the hotel hallway. No doubt he had gone to use the telephone in the bedroom, perhaps closing the door of the bedroom so that his guests would not hear, perhaps one or two permitted to stand beside him, a clucking chorus, as he bent over the top of the steamer trunk and yelled into the mouthpiece. 'Your mother wants you to come downstairs,' he told me at the door. 'Then come back tomorrow.'

I walked down to the lobby this last time (it would be unseemly to ring for the elevator once more, to disturb the operator once more on Christmas Eve), each step on the worn marble treads bringing me down to where my mother waited, her face blanked by the abrupt change of plan, her pose stiff beside the round settee, awkward and out of season with the casual drape of the lobby's decorations; each step down closer to street level to join her in a brisk walk toward a Chinese restaurant near 28th Street; each step taking me deeper into a revelation I hoped to lose before I reached the lobby. Whatever the cost in loyalty, in self-respect and pride, I had wanted to join the party.

About Hilary

If through our separation, fate enforced,
Against which I have struggled to no avail,
Misfortune should be yours, from good divorced,
Tangled in circumstances to make you fail,
And stay your steps along the upward path
Of years ahead, the path which even at best
Is difficult—even now the aftermath
Of my regret is always in my breast.

Your spirit beautiful, serene and good.
Your gifts already budding make the call
Upon my strength to guide you, as I should,
And be your father, close to you in all.
Since I have never been this, nor can be,
But must somehow make numb my aching love,
The measure of regret and agony
Has grown a grief that cannot grieve enough.

My mother's feet were always swollen as she prepared for bed, as she sat on the day couch in the corner of the small apartment at the rear of the bookstore; it would be two in the morning and she would have worked the check counter at a hotel banquet, and she would be up at six to grade papers, review her class work. Her share of the tips that night had been fifteen dollars and change. The urgency to meet her needs and my welfare by taking part-time jobs as a hat-check girl offended my newly won snobbery.

The features of her face were still firm but the eyes had become underscored by fatigue, and there was now a hesitancy in her laugh that censored the response. Making plans and then making alternate plans and then making more plans as she slipped off her shoes and lay back on the narrow bed. She had little time and small energy for a social life of her own, but lived through her students or from behind the counters where she checked coats for a society affair, and she would describe these occasions later with the rush of a girl's impressions as if she had been a member of the debutante's court: what celebrities had attended and how natural they had behaved to her; the magnificent gowns, the music.

She was in her early forties and very attractive, so there would be an occasional dinner out, an evening at the theater; away from the papers to be graded and the making of plans but never far away, it seemed, for I remember one such night (sometimes the bookstore owner would be away and I could use her bed), listening to her bid an early good-night—perhaps that's why I was there, to assure an early good-night—hearing her humored, graceful excuses become more forceful, a kiss bestowed to stay the man's ardor, hearing all this take place in the vestibule outside the bookstore as I sat on the floor in the darkness surrounded by the passionate romances of the lending library.

But these few hours out of the clocked drudgery of her life were like found money, some fun that would freshen her parched spirit though she would be too tired to drink a glass of water; only able to lift her feet upon the daybed but too tired to soak them in a basin of hot water with Epsom salts as someone, perhaps one of the other women who worked the hotel function, had recommended, or was it one of her father's recipes? She couldn't remember, though she thought of him taking care of his feet and thought of her mother also lying down in Kansas City and also worn out, and then there was Lee, across town, his vanity curried by those who ignored his degeneration, and so she drifted into a wakeful napping that waited upon the early alarm. She would review the plans she had for each of us as a resident in a ramshackle hotel might review the different escape routes before closing his eyes; finally closing her mind around the one plan, already in motion, already working—Hilary in school in New Hampshire—it seemed to be working. Everything was going to plan. Everything had been planned, and she could sleep.

New Hampshire had become my South America, a remote place where I could create my own identity, a fictional persona that functioned for nine months of the year at least, and a place where I was granted first-class citizenship in the same way my grandfather had been assumed to have full citizenship by the natives of Mexico or South America who knew no better. But now, I was an émigré, an alien from the Midwest, restricted in my movements whenever I came to New York, and confined to dull passages of time until I could return North and to freedom, and this peculiar statelessness incensed me, the same rage that had convulsed the thick vein on Gee Gee's forehead and fed his furious stare with the reflection of flames, though he had earned his anger with the contract that had committed him to a neighborhood of paved streets and pedestrian rules. Even now he would be making his own plans to break this contract that he had sought, to make one more dash into a territory that would grant him citizenship; even now planning his last stand as my grandmother lay in her bed of abandonment, a dreadful freedom of her own making; even now as my mother was making her plans.

None of this was clear to me then, though all the elements were lightly clothed; my vision was too far-fixed by the New Hampshire mountains to focus on anything so close, my senses too caught in the aroma of my new-mown freedom, my own plans.

And my mother interfered with these plans. Right or wrong, it had been my impression that she was someone to take trips with, someone who would visit us in Kansas City, if only to test my language skills, sometimes to stand on the front steps of Roberts Street and halloo me home from the corner lot when I was accustomed to leave the game in my own time. Now her supervision had become full time and the normal parental concerns seemed to me meddling interferences. Christmas of 1943 approached; the chill in the New England air turned up the cold dread within me as the school term neared the holiday recess. I had nowhere to go but New York. I envisioned a holiday spent on the elevator of the Hotel Chelsea, but the prospect must have been even more anxious for her: what to do with a fifteen-year-old boy in New York City for two weeks, with no money, no place for him to sleep, no community for him to join?

But our holiday had already been organized. As I packed, inserting only the good reports and papers into folds of clothing, a classmate entered my room with a letter from his parents. They wrote that my father had been found starving in his hotel room and was near death. It had been in all the New York papers and on the radio.

'I didn't want to bother you,' my mother now says on this summer night. 'You were having exams and anyway it had been greatly exaggerated by the newspapers. Also, what could you do about it?' Ice rattles in her glass.

Joseph Nicolosi, a sculptor, an old friend, had called for my father at the Chelsea—they were to have dinner together—and found him feverish, barely able to breathe or move. Nicolosi made two phone calls: the first for an ambulance and the second, at my father's request, to my mother. A woman who claimed to be my father's secretary strenuously objected to both calls. She lived in the hotel.

'She keep saying to me,' Joseph told my mother, 'about the disgrace of taking him to Bellevue, how the newspapers will print it up.' New York's Bellevue is associated with the insane and the indigent, but it was also the most important emergency hospital facility in the city during wartime. 'I say to her—"What kinda disgrace you want—like when he's dead? You want them to write his obituary, maybe?" So then I call you, Ellen. He tell me, he whisper in my ear to call you.'

In any event, it was a cliché guaranteed to find space in any newspaper—poet found starving in dingy hotel room—and the 'malnutrition' that patterned the pneumonia was amplified. Moreover, in this day before the National Endowment and university positions, poets were supposed to die hungry. Those who did not were suspect. The formula, its credibility, were further enforced when a bed had been set up for him in a hospital hallway—not even in the charity ward—though the copy desk editor neglected to remind readers of the wartime shortages of beds, or that this was an emergency.

Something else. Ellen Coyne, the child of immigrants, and Joseph Nicolosi, himself an immigrant, neither had any false pride; they knew only an obligation to save a man's life in the most expeditious way available, regardless of how it might 'look' to others. Incidentally, two bottles of prescribed medicine were found in his coat pocket, unopened and untaken. Curiously, this lack of decorum seems to be what H. L. Mencken referred to as my mother's 'stupid' behavior, as if it would have been more proper to let the old poet die within the comfortable outlines of the cliché.

'He's all right,' my mother said as I stepped off the Greyhound bus. 'He's very sick, but he's all right. We've just moved him to a good hospital and he has a room of his own and a good doctor.' The Authors League Fund had volunteered generous funds and the Carnegie Fund, through Daniel Henderson, had also helped with the cost. Other donations came in the mail, some anonymously but others signed. A check for fifty dollars arrived from Edna St. Vincent Millay, herself suffering hardships then, but my father directed the check go uncashed.

Unaccountably, he also seemed to be directing his own recovery, the realignment of his life, from the hospital bed: who would be admitted to visit him, what members of the *anonkorai* were to be excluded. He lay propped up against the crisp linen, all the cocky, ironic crackle restored though his stern, matter-of-fact demeanor grew in the firm ground my mother once again provided him, her onstage presence. He was like a sailor who had endured a perilous voyage, buffeted by storms, waylaid in strange ports, and torn by temptations to lose ships and companions and then miraculously finding his way home again—swept up miraculously, just when all seemed lost, on the clean white sheets of this hospital bed to bask in the warmth of a family reunion. But only to wonder for a little bit.

'By God, Mr. It, there you are,' he said when I came through the door.

'Hi, Pop.' I kissed his pink cheek, freshly shaved by a solicitous nurse. 'Merry Christmas.'

'By God.' His handclasp was slight but resolute. 'How old are you now, It?' He studied me, an intimate, welcoming gaze.

'Almost sixteen, Pop,' I answered.

'Think of that. Sixteen. Almost a man—maybe you are a man.' He cackled, the eyes flashed. 'Think of that, kid.' He turned to my mother who sat in the corner. She had opened her briefcase and prepared to take down the letters he would dictate. 'Our Mr. It has come of age.'

In the same letter in which Mencken spoke so disapprovingly of my mother, he mentions also that he donated one hundred dollars toward the payment of my father's overdue account at the Chelsea. He gave the check to one of 'those people.' Mencken had a genuine affection and regard for my father and there's no reason to doubt his word, but the hotel bill had not been paid. No monies were subscribed by family or friends, though one check from a nephew was found. It was for eleven dollars and made out, curiously, to the woman who claimed to be my father's secretary. My mother paid the hotel bill and, over a period of many years, returned to the Authors League Fund the entire sum it had supplied for my father's hospital expenses.

8

My father served a time of convalescence in a Bronx nursing home whose distance from Manhattan was the subject of petulant petitions passed among the *anonkorai*, as if my mother had committed some outrage, swiped a national treasure and stashed it in a foreign country—certainly beyond the taxi range limited by wartime gasoline rationing. The members of this entourage rarely used public transportation.

But it was a comfortable place, and it had been approved by his doctors. Moreover, it charged a rate my mother could afford, for the bills were hers alone and sometimes the cost of medicines equaled her week's income.

Like every husband since Ulysses who has strayed, my father quickly reclaimed the shore of domesticity and, as if to prove his virtue as well as gratuitously salute my mother's banner, turned scorn upon the companions of his wayward journey. He was the first to ridicule them and invented nicknames for them.

'Well, I had visitors today,' he'd say to my mother with a dryness of tone that gave a poor estimate of the visit.

It was January and it would be dark when she arrived at the nursing home to unwind her scarf and kick off galoshes, pull gloves and coat off as he watched her, his expectant eyes like those of an impatient lover though the cackle hatched deep in his throat suggested another sport. Usually, she sat by his bed to grade compositions while he ate the evening meal from a tray.

'The Three Roses,' he would say, no longer able to hold back his rooster laugh so that it flapped around the room, around my mother's head as she nodded to recognize the joke, nodded to accept the tribute it offered. 'By God, all three of them showed up here.' He paused to replay the scene in his mind. 'Hired a limousine together.'

These were three women who, like others, thought they were intimate with him because they had shared an intimacy with him, and they had made the mistake of visiting him earlier at the hospital, also together. Each had carried a single rose, and they arrived like a trio of creaky dryads flushed out of the woods and into the open, finding courage in their number, only to have their sentiment appear foolish in the banal light of the hospital. 'The Three Roses,' he would repeat, enjoying the joke with each spoon of syrup from a dish of peaches, because the title was also an allusion to a cheap brand of blended whiskey.

From this small camp in what some considered to be a wilderness, my mother began to put our community back together. Circumstances dictated every move she made: this was not one of the plans she had made as she stretched out on her narrow bed, but rather she met each factor as it developed. As she corrected the grammar and punctuation in her students' papers, she also corrected the errors of our lives, gave them a new construction; patiently and firmly going over them again and again in her mind and on paper until she had them—not right, for she would be the first to say there was no right way, no one way—but had them aligned within the possibility of circumstances and her resources. This can wear down a mind, can be more exhausting than the physical effort such a prospectus proposes, for there is no end to the list, the list becomes the main work, subject to constant revision, symbiotic with frustration though releasing a curious, anxious energy, a self-perpetuating energy that can drive a person beyond her normal physical capacity as it had driven my grandmother before she stepped off that curb, probably going over a list in her mind as she stepped off the curb in front of that truck; a complicated order of the day for which the small cake and quarter pound of gunpowder tea in her reticule represented merit awards.

My mother was forty-five that spring of 1944, though she seemed older when she met me at the bus station. She had aged between my Christmas holiday and when I returned for the last time with a diploma from New Hampshire. 'Well, how did it go?' she asked, acknowledging my graduation.

'Fine,' I replied. This time we walked across 34th Street to Madison Avenue and took a bus uptown. 'They rang every church bell in town just as we were getting our diplomas.'

'That's nice.' She nodded. We stepped on the bus and she paid both fares.

'It wasn't for us,' I said as we sat down. 'It was for D-Day. The invasion of Normandy.'

'Listen, I think you'll like where we're staying.' She had been looking out the big window and now faced me. The large green eyes lay deep in hollows of fatigue, though there was a flicker within them, a secret-keeping joy. Then she told me of the rooms she had taken in an elegant boardinghouse maintained by a genteel Southern lady. The other roomers were all young women— just the sort of environment to perk up my father—and, she continued, in a couple of weeks she would be returning to the girls' camp in Pennsylvania as its director, my father with her— there would be a counselor's job for me at the boys' camp—then, here's the big news, in the fall we were all moving to North Carolina where she would teach English in a new country day school in Charlotte—she had just signed the contract—and there was a very good college nearby for me.

'I'd rather go to Chapel Hill,' I said.

'You're too young for Chapel Hill,' she replied. 'You're going to Davidson. I've already enrolled you. It's known as the Princeton of the South. Woodrow Wilson went there for a year. Here's where we get off.'

Much of her exhilaration came from the knowledge that she was winning the contest thrown at her by some of the *anonkorai,* some members of my father's family, who 'surrendered' him to her with gestures as falsely grand as they were sour. 'Well, if she thinks she can do better, let her try,' and no other contribution toward his recovery was made though the challenge they presented to her was more than enough; indeed, it was overgenerous, for none of them understood how alien blood can rise to a challenge; how competition is the game of immigrants.

The change in him was nearly miraculous, as if energy and animation had been fed into him by transfusion, perhaps my mother's youth and spirit going through the tube; and though his walk was hesitant, would always be a slowly measured shuffle from now on, his face had filled out rosily, the eyes sparkled, and it seemed as if my mother's raucous laugh, harsh in some ears, had pumped him up, pushed out the slack and wrinkled parts of his personality. He had even begun to write again, only short sketches and prose vignettes, but the old black Parker fountain pen was gripped firmly in the right hand in the mornings.

'Well, here we are, Mr. It,' he greeted me from a chair by a large window that opened above a handsome rear garden. The room was large and sunny; a bathroom adjoined and connected with a smaller bedroom that would be mine. There were books and papers, the same brass knickknacks, the green jade Buddha, the photograph of Whitman—two steamer trunks half open in a corner, it seemed as if they had been living there for a long time. 'We're fixed up pretty well here,' he said as I leaned over to kiss him. 'How old are you now, It?'

'I'm sixteen, Pop.'

'By God, I hope this war is over before you have to go. It's an awful business. They're fighting like hell in Normandy.'

'They rang all the church bells in town for the invasion when we graduated.'

'Ah,' he said, gripping the chair and hoisting himself up.

'There's the dinner gong. We do things very stylish around here.
But the grub is good stuff.' He took my arm and we went slowly
downstairs.

All the dark splendor of the old townhouse had been polished
and buffed by this Southern aristocrat who had brought her own
family heirlooms to the place: the family silver and plate, the
cut crystal vases for fresh flowers, the family carpets on the main
floor, the family black cook in the kitchen. Our hostess had married a Russian painter, rumored to have been a fourth-string
Romanov. There were photographs of him on a long table in
the front hallway that showed the falcon profile of this fierce
prince who had dived and disappeared into the soft divan of an
American heiress, leaving behind some melancholy seascapes on
the wall above.

The grub set down on the table in the dining room, a gracious
room that opened onto the garden through French doors, was
plentiful and nicely done, but there were more attractions here
than the food. Every evening, a dozen young women took their
places around that table and around my father. Some were
fashion models, others worked on magazines or in advertising
or as executive secretaries, but all would take their places, loose-
limbed and relaxed yet still tuned to the city's challenge as they
slipped the linen cloths from the silver napkin rings at their
plates, talking and laughing and giving off an aura that the
candles in the old candelabra seemed about to ignite: a volatile
mixture of success and independence and the curious sexual heat
that accompanied that war.

My father was dinner companion to them all. He was tutor
and grandfather, lover and story teller, celebrity and historian
and poet, and they listened to him like obedient children with
dilated eyes and parted lips, perhaps not quite believing everything he said but never having heard stories like his before either.
Personalities they had only read about, studied in school, were
referred to casually or with a knowing chuckle that suggested

[174]

something not to be found in a college text. There were anecdotes, some lines of verse, perhaps even a song crooned between courses. He had been making notes on some of his old law cases; perhaps he would tell them about defending the *Chicago Tribune* in a slander suit brought by Annie Oakley. Who was Annie Oakley? Well, Annie Oakley had been married to Buffalo Bill and was a crack shot herself and—the narrative would run on into the sherbet.

Their audience provided him with a nutrition as important as that contained in the food on his plate and he grew full from it. His cheeks stood out rounder and were burnished, and if his step still faltered his eyes moved nimbly; more than once, his gaze crossed mine as we both glanced up the banistered stairway to look upon a pair of slim legs on the landing. He put on the paradoxical personality that had always charmed women: the Puck within the schoolmaster, the hick with the encyclopedic knowledge, the poet in spite of himself. My mother would sit at the table beside him, at the same time giving the impression she also sat a little behind him, ready to raise a corroborative nod for his narrative, supply a straight line, a footnote. 'Yes, that's right,' she'd assure the others. 'That's the way it happened.'

In the same way she would succeed him into a room or a restaurant, even pushing me ahead so that she could bring up the rear in some kind of self-imposed purdah that suggested a humility that did not exist. Sometimes a small royalty check had arrived in the day's mail, not large enough to affect practical expenses but sufficient for a 'blow-out' at Bleek's or Lüchow's or some similar establishment where an entrance could be made: the poet and his family coming to dine, a presentation that delighted them both, I think, since he had been proclaimed nearly dead from starvation, forlorn and abandoned, and yet only a few months later, here was the poet of *Spoon River*—if not yet an obituary, already an historical oddity in some minds—leading his small family to a special table at the front or near the orchestra;

slow of step to be sure, but perhaps stately under the circumstances and, by the way, providing an interval in which unbelievers could come to terms with the miracle.

'We've come for some of that roast beef of yours,' he would command the maître d'.

'Certainly, Mr. Masters. It is excellent tonight. A cocktail first, perhaps?'

'What about it, Ellen?' my father would inquire almost sternly.

'Oh, I don't know,' my mother would reply, looking over the menu, the prices.

'Why the hell not,' he'd urge. 'Let's blow the whole kit. I'll have one of those Manhattan cocktails. How about you, Mr. It? What's your poison?'

'A ginger ale, a Coke—it doesn't matter,' I'd reply. My mother would have a whiskey sour.

'Well, here we are.' He would tuck the napkin in under his chin and break open a roll. 'The Holy Trinity,' or maybe he meant 'Holy Family'; I never knew whether he thought of himself as Joseph or the Holy Spirit, but he would look no more mortal than on these occasions. The white counterpane of the large restaurant napkin served up the round happiness of his countenance, for he relished these few hours of once more being in charge. He spread sweet butter on a piece of roll and laid out advice to my mother. She had received a letter from my grandfather that day; my grandmother's depression seemed to be worse.

'It's a hellish thing, this getting old,' he said between bites. 'He's a fine man with a strong spirit. But he can only do so much. He's doing the best he can, I'm sure.' His attempt to soothe her seemed to have the opposite effect, for she had begun a subtle realignment of her place setting, the water glass moved here, the butter plate there. 'We owe them a good deal for taking care of Hilary.'

'Oh, yes, yes.' There was no agreement in her voice, only a

weary recognition. 'But he's destroying everything around him. Selling his property like that for a price, any price. Asking her to manage a rooming house. A rooming house. My mother running a rooming house?' She leaned across the table, a hand at her throat to emphasize the protest.

'Well, what's to be done. What's to be done? Eh, Mr. It, what's to be done?' I would have no answer. Roberts Street already seemed another life away to me, nor did I cry in my sleep anymore for my grandmother.

Halfway through the meal (my father and I had ordered the roast beef), my mother would lean over her plate of fillet of sole and say, in a low voice, something like, 'Lee, here is someone coming over to talk to you,' or 'Here is so-and-so,' supplying the name. 'Now be pleasant.'

His face would harden, and a disagreeable sound would slip from his lips as he chewed, juices and sigh both escaping to be blotted by the napkin; the full-lipped, jocular mouth was transformed into a thin, hard line, even the dimples became brittle. Health had also returned the old arrogance, the impatience with fools, a broad and densely populated category, and though part of the fun of these 'blow-outs' was to be seen in public, it was meant to be a public that kept its distance from the table. The interview would go something like this:

'Mr. Masters, I just wanted to stop and say how wonderful it is to see you in such good health.'

'Yes,' my father would drawl. 'Better and better every day.' He would continue to cut through the roast beef.

'I'm a great admirer, one of many. Only yesterday I was re-reading some of those poems in *Poems of People*.'

'Oh, yes? Which ones were they? Pass me that Worcestershire sauce there, Hilary.'

'This is your son?'

'That's he.'

'And this is Mrs. . . .'—for some reason there was always a

hesitation here, as if my mother might have a different name—
'. . . Masters.'

'That's the boss,' my father would say laconically. My mother
would guffaw and bat her eyes, try with an appealing look to
soften the exchange.

'It's very nice to see you,' she would say in one of her better
stage-drawing-room inflections.

'Are you spending the summer in the city?' the person would
continue. It was always difficult to leave gracefully.

'Ask her.' My father would point his fork across the table.
'She's running things.'

My mother would laugh again, a balcony laugh that would
carry to the farthest tables, then grow serious, very professional.
'We'll be in the Pocono Mountains of Pennsylvania,' she would
say flatly. 'I've been named the director of a girls' camp there
and we'll all be there for the summer.'

'Wonderful, getting away from the city's heat.'

'Yes, yes,' my father would say dryly as he bent over his plate.

'Well, stay in good health. Again, it's . . . good-bye.'

'Yes, yes.' Then when the person was out of hearing, 'Ha-Ha-
Ha.'

'You could have been a little more agreeable,' she admonished
him.

'Oh, what's the bother.' His head twisted with impatience, a
turn of dismissal. Then, as if overcome with the sweetness of the
occasion, of being alive and having roast beef and being with
us and of the interruption even—for the hard shell of his annoy-
ance enclosed a grain of vanity—a chorus of some old song would
flow from his lips, time beat on the table with a spoon.

> *Ole Zip Coon is a very learned scholar,*
> *Ole Zip Coon is a very learned scholar,*
> *Ole Zip Coon is a very learned scho-lar,*
> *And he plays on de banjo . . .*
> > *Cooney in de holler.*

Better than any piece of apple strudel would be the ceremony raised by the dinner check. The total was judiciously reviewed, as the fingers of the right hand went to a vest pocket to slip out a small square of folded currency. The bills were carefully unfolded and then, just as carefully, as if some sudden draught in the restaurant might blow them away, each would be placed directly upon the face of the check—one, two, three—counted out one after one with a frown of uncertainty that all three would be needed though he would know they would be. It was a honeyed moment, but not without its bitter aftertaste. Sometimes my mother would have to pay the taxi fare home.

Here again was the old rub that made for the raw places between them, that had wrinkled up his disapproval of her graduate work, of her teaching; though at the same time he recognized the diminished figures of his royalty statements. If we were to live together as a family, someone would have to pay the rent, and he knew this, but to identify a dilemma and to live with it are two different matters. So he could speak admiringly of my grandfather's wild ride through his real estate in Kansas City, though he knew the charge was a disaster. Tom Coyne was still astride his destiny.

'By God, I don't see how anyone can afford to live in this country anymore,' he'd say in the taxi. I would have to sit on one of the jump seats and my mother perched on the edge of the far side, in the corner, for my father lay athwart the rear seat like a diner at a Roman banquet, a position he had half fallen, half lurched into when he climbed into the vehicle outside the restaurant. Neither of us had been strong enough to right him. He spoke to us like a tilted oracle. 'Only the Jews are making money out of this war and they are into everything, own everything. Restaurants. Publishing. They own it all. They run everything. How did that happen?'

He spoke with one ear close to the rumble of the automobile's transmission. He may have been listening to the ironical turn of his life as well; a murmur of incidents that began when he got off that train in Chicago with the purpose of being a poet, to make any deal in order to be a poet, comfortably, and driven to the role by something that can only be speculated upon now. There are hints in his autobiography: the dismay caused by his mother's hard verdict on that Illinois summer day long ago: sister Madeline would pursue college and an artistic career while Lee would return home and read law in his father's office.

Many years cover the sharp stone of memory, but the vibrations set off in that taxi prodded old bruises to sour the digestion and spoil the festive occasion and to inflame the same anger that had fueled his lust for recognition as a poet. It is true, as my mother will say, he worked very hard; but I wonder if the role became more important to him than the art. His success in that role was never recognized enough to heal that early wound, certainly never recognized enough by those who, in his estimation, had done the wounding, and no amount of tribute paid him in restaurants as he cut up a piece of roast beef could make up for those accounts receivable, now uncollectible.

'Good night, Pop. Thanks for dinner.' I kissed the bald spot above his brow. It was like a baby's head. He read in a chair by the window of the large rear room as my mother folded and packed clothes. Trunks and suitcases were ranked into a miniature skyline in the center of the room. We were to leave for the camps in Pennsylvania the next day.

'Good night, Mr. It.' He replaced the pipe stem in his mouth and drew on it. 'We had a good feed tonight. And tomorrow we'll have another one. On to Penn-syl-van-aye-ay. Eh, kid?'

' "On to Pennsylvania," ' my mother hummed as she put together the last of our belongings.

*   *   *

'She beats everything,' my grandfather says to me two years later. There's a whisker of respect in his voice as there might be for an adversary he had finally conceded to be his equal. My mother had not meant to challenge him, but she would not let Mollie Coyne remain in the charity home where Gee Gee had consigned her before he retired to the Soldiers Home in Washington. I hardly recognized my grandmother: the goiter and the effects of her accident had ravaged her; she was deaf and nearly blind, and she covered her ruined beauty with the latticework of arthritic fingers. She would live with my parents in a small faculty apartment.

'She wanted for nothing,' my grandfather continues. We walk across the grounds of the Soldiers Home. It has been five years since I have seen him, too, but he has not changed; the same wiry energy, same bluff and swagger and identical fierce light in the eyes. 'I left the sisters that run that place a good amount of money to take care of her,' he tells me. 'It was a clean place too. Clean with wholesome food.' He must be about eighty-five years of age now, but keeps the same quick-march pace that I had to skip beside coming down Roberts Street. I am able to keep up with him now, but he still has a small lead on me as we tour the grounds.

'They give musical concerts here.' He gestures toward an ornate bandstand. 'And over there, Lincoln lived for a while when he thought Washington would fall to the Confederates.' He swings around, one fist grinding into the other palm. 'There you have it. There you have it. That schoolmarm couldn't leave well enough alone. She had to meddle.' Then the whitish-blue eyes blink, as if he has only just noticed my navy uniform. 'So, you had to go and become a gob. A gob.' He laughs soundlessly.

*　　*　　*

My mission—apparently it went with the uniform—had been to report my grandmother's whereabouts, not so much because he should know her location on the map—the junior college near Philadelphia where my mother now taught—but because my mother wished to present Gee Gee with an Irish *aidos:* a public exposure of something that should shame him, though it caused her even more hardship and worry to do it—which made the maneuver Irish. It never bothered him.

On the other hand, bringing my grandmother East was the

last piece to the collection my mother had commenced that winter of 1944. As she gathered up the school papers and books she had reviewed by my father's bedside, as she had prepared to leave him for the night and take the subway back to Manhattan, she had also begun to gather us together; to put us into a community that she was to fashion seemingly overnight, one made of scraps, extension cords, and sheer pluck.

When she packed our belongings for the trip to the Pocono Mountains in 1944, she also put my father and me together in a way that was new to us, a day-to-day relationship that was strange to us; our syllabus of conversations only covered short courses, not an extended curriculum. Moreover, I resented his weight upon my arm, his slow step and hesitancy before a curb or taxi door. His body would begin to vibrate, as if all the machinery that operated the leg were running at full throttle but had not engaged, so that the leg did not lift and the foot remained fixed to the ground.

'Ellen, I can't do this,' he said sternly. We had just managed him out of the taxi at Pennsylvania Station. Camp was over and we were going to North Carolina. 'I can't do it.'

'Of course you can,' she said and turned to pay the driver, check the luggage. We were traveling light; furniture and a couple of steamer trunks had been put into storage.

'I tell you I can't do it.' Anger wound the Midwestern accent tight, a fiddle string about to break, and his voice twanged. He did not wish to leave New York. To leave the city in summer was normal, if not for the Pocono Mountains then Columbia County, but to leave in the fall and for North Carolina and, maybe, for good—that was something else again.

'Here. You there,' she commanded a porter. The man, stopped short by the authority in her voice, looked astonished that anyone would still address him that way, but wheeled his cart around. 'We're on that Southern Seaboard for Charlotte. This trunk goes into freight. These bags go with us on the coach.

We'll meet you at the train. Here. I'll give you the rest when we get on board.' She handed him a quarter.

My father's feet had become unstuck from the pavement and we began a slow passage into the station and through the long arcade of the building's main entrance. He had shrugged off my mother's supportive hand to wield his cane with a splendid flourish that was crazily out of rhythm to his snail-like shuffle. My shoulder and arm began to cramp under his heavy grasp.

'I don't like the looks of that fellow,' my mother said. 'I'll just go and make sure that trunk gets checked through all right.' She leaves us, high heels sounding on the marble floor, each step threatening to craze the stone, to put distance between us with the comic exaggeration of a cartoon, though she walked at a normal rate.

My father stops as she disappears into the press of travelers, pauses to take a breath as if to refresh himself in her absence, and then with a visible summoning of energy, goes on. 'Now what?' he mutters. 'What's she up to now? Eh, what's she up to now?' I look at the floor so as not to see the crowds of people rushing around and by us.

He knew what she was about, but he resented her efforts to salvage him, physically or artistically, resented the way she had pragmatically sliced through his fictions. After nearly fifteen years of residency, he had checked out of the Chelsea Hotel for good. He no longer had rooms that were his own, a pad where he might sing or croak, as he willed, and even though the last years proved his vulnerability to the climate and the appetites of that place, the illusion that he was yet in charge could be sustained there. Now he had been taken in charge, and those short intervals of independence bought by the occasional royalty check could not relieve the chagrin that burned him: to be cared for and paid for by a woman and, especially, by a woman whom he had tried to discourage in a profession that now supported them both.

[183]

'I have to sit down, Hilary.' We had reached the end of the majestic colonnade and had come to the top of the grand marble staircase that overlooked the formal canyon of the waiting room. Stanford White and his colleagues had reproduced the Baths of Caracalla with a perverse purity, for there was not a single bench, ledge, or slab, nothing to support the human figure in the whole expanse. And there were many human figures, all in military uniforms, stretched out on the floor or sitting hunched over on duffel bags and luggage. 'I must sit down,' my father repeated, and his knees began to buckle.

'Wait. Wait. We have to wait,' I pleaded. 'Where the train gates are, the concourse. There are seats there.'

He sighed and cursed and we boarded the escalator installed over the marble cascade that swept down onto the main level. This brief ride offered a little rest, but he was unprepared for the abrupt end of the trip, or the muscles of his legs did not respond quickly enough to the mind's orders, for when the moving belt met the unmoving floor, the momentum propelled him onto the polished marble in a stiff-legged, runaway hop and slide that tested all my strength to control, to keep his great bulk upright while slowing him down. A picture flashed through my mind of those strong men in Robert Ripley's 'Believe It Or Not' who grappled with steam locomotives and pushed them backward. Ever so slowly, his balance returned, and then he stopped.

'Whew!' He pulled his shoulders back and reset his hat. Then, seeing the terror still fixed in my expression, he grinned, a yellowed, gap-toothed leer of a jack-o'-lantern. 'By God, Mr. It, you're a strong boy. All that sorghum and flapjacks, I bet.' Then looking over his shoulder at the escalator, he giggled. 'Dear, oh dear, oh dear. Let's have another go at it, want to?' When he saw me smile, his mood changed to one of impatience again, worry and a slow anger. 'Now where has she got to?' he asked. His cane tapped out the inquiry against the marble floor. 'Where in hell is she? How in hell is she ever going to find us in all this?' Armies surrounded us, at ease.

[184]

'Let's go in where the train gates are. She'll look for us there,' I urged him. We began to move slowly, his feet sliding with that peculiar loose-slippered slip-slop, around piles of duffel bags, through camps of sprawled military. We looked like two non-combatants who had stumbled into a war zone. 'There are seats in the other room,' I promised.

There were seats in the concourse, but they were all occupied, every branch of the armed services represented by men who lay like casualties upon them. Even if a place were vacated, we could not move quickly enough; someone would take the space before we could make two steps.

'It's like hell in here,' my father said with a matter-of-fact tone. 'This is the way hell looks.' There was an eerie quality about the great hall, like one of Piranesi's bizarre engravings. Girders and arches of intricate ironwork supported the glass canopy through which a flat light sifted, like light coming through water, shadow-less and without heat, to illuminate the hundreds of figures making their departures. There was a continuous rush, an androgy-nous sound layered with unintelligible announcements from the public address system and punctured by sharp echoes of things being dropped on the stone pavement.

'There's a seat. I'll grab it. You follow me.'

'Here. Don't leave me,' he called, but I had already run to the location, a distance of about twenty yards, to cut out a sailor and a woman with a small child. I sat down on the bench.

'C'mon!' I waved to my father. 'You can do it. Keep coming. C'mon.' He had straightened his shoulders and taken a deep breath. The exercise seemed to thrust his stomach out even more, to make him even more top-heavy, but, trembling the whole time, he began to move one foot, then the other, his eyes fixed on me as if wired. His slow progress across the distance did seem like a tightrope act, the suspense increasing as he neared the bench. He had begun to shake more violently but I dared not go to him, dared not leave the seat.

'You can do it,' I cried when he was within ten feet. He had put out his left hand, the heavy green jade ring on the little finger like a beacon, and I reached for it, leaning forward on the bench. The distance between our hands slowly became less and, finally, our fingers touched, and his hand worked its way up mine until he was able to seize it completely with a bone-cracking grip as his knees began to bend and the whole mass of him began to sink toward the floor like a dirigible slowly coming to rest. 'Not yet. Not yet,' I said desperately. If he went all the way down, I'd never be able to get him back on his feet. With one great effort, he took a long step, as if stepping across an abyss; it threw him off balance, but I managed to pivot his body and slip out from beneath him just in time.

'Ouch. Goddamn,' he exclaimed as he fell against the hard back of the wooden seat. The impact knocked his hat askew, but that was all. He replaced the fedora to the proper angle with a businesslike expression. 'Well, here we are. Now where has she got to?' He held his hands out, palms down, as if to study their steadiness, the shovel-shaped evenness of the well-manicured fingernails. His eyes had become wintry behind the panes of his glasses. 'I suppose she'll have us wait here all day for her.'

I stood to one side and looked over the vast court. A baby's wail rose like cigarette smoke, absorbed by the neutral space. 'By God, you're a strong boy, Mr. It. I guess that comes from playing that football.' I turned away. None of the others on the bench seemed to have heard him. 'Say—' He fished in a vest pocket. 'Maybe that newsstand over there sells apples. Here's a dime. Go buy yourself an apple. Here's another dime—get me a couple of White Owls.'

He knew newsstands no longer sold fruit, but it was a ruse to give me some freedom, to release me from duty, for he sensed my impatience if not my embarrassment. I bought his cigars, and then browsed through the picture magazines before choosing between a model airplane magazine that I really wanted and a paperback collection of Bret Harte stories that I thought I should buy. I never read the stories.

When I returned, he seemed more content, puffing on his pipe and chatting with a soldier who sat beside him. A civilian slept like a large, sodden embryo on the other side. 'This corporal here is from Missouri,' he introduced me. 'I told him you were raised there.' We eyed each other and nodded. 'Well, it looks like she's gone and left us,' he said flatly and relit his pipe. Then he added, throwing the match away, 'I may have to use the toilet soon.' We would never make such a trip before train time.

Then, my mother appeared, or made an entrance on the enormous Grand Concourse. She was down at the far end, but her vivid coloring, the dark-dark hair and white skin and the scarlet of her heavily lipsticked mouth seemed to challenge the ambivalence of that atmosphere. I cannot remember what she wore but it was summery and light, and the long strands of green turquoise beads my father had given her years before swung from around her neck with the cadence of her walk, a confident, cocky cadence. Just as I had turned away to look for the men's lavatory, should we need to use it, I saw her step into a shaft of light that slanted down from the vaulted roof and splash into a doorway.

With no hesitation, she walked directly toward us, as if she had known before she stepped into that huge gallery where to find us among the thousands of transients, where in those communities of travelers we had found a place. Her bearing carried success, and no small success such as the safe disposition of the heavier baggage, but larger triumphs were paraded: the better teaching position in North Carolina, being able to move the three of us there, to make the arrangements and pay the bills. There was a freedom in her stride, a sense of moving out of the dark, near tragic times and into the brighter prospect that she had put together, and though none of those she passed knew these details, they followed her with their eyes—not just because she was an attractive woman, but because there was something special about her that raised their curiosity to a higher level.

'Well, here we are,' she commenced, still talking like the

camp director of that summer, an official gaiety. 'No, thank you. Keep your seat,' she told the soldier who had risen slowly. 'Our train will be called soon. Here are the checks for the trunks.' She handed them to me. 'They'll be checked straight through to Charlotte. My, isn't it crowded?' she said looking around, as if she had only now noticed the wartime conditions.

My father had remained silent, had made no gesture or acknowledgment of her but looked straight ahead, his cane fixed between his legs and perpendicular to the floor. He puffed and puffed, and the irises of his eyes seemed to grow until there was no white space around them. A tremor went through him. 'I nearly fell down twice,' he said, removing the pipe. 'If it hadn't been for Hilary, I would have fallen down.'

'Well, he's very strong.' My mother smiled and put an arm around my waist.

'But I nearly fell down,' my father repeated like a patient attorney leading a dull witness.

'But you didn't fall down,' my mother replied.

'But I nearly did,' he repeated.

'Well, you didn't,' she said.

'But I almost did.'

'But . . .'

'What I'm saying,' he continued, his eyes still straight ahead, 'is that I cannot make this trip. Nor will I make this trip. I cannot leave New York nor will I leave New York.'

'Nonsense.' My mother waved away his words with a handkerchief, blew her nose and deposited the linen in her purse. She turned her back to check the time on the great clock suspended above us.

'Listen to me, Ellen.' He raised his cane and cracked it once, twice upon the stone floor. 'I am not going to leave here. You can go, but I am not leaving here to . . .'

'Not leave here?' she shouted. I jumped. Everyone around us jumped and stared. 'Not leave here?' She whirled around, her face like a mask in a Noh play, the full lips pulled back over the large teeth, the eyes rounded with fury. Even the fingernails of her hands seemed to have grown as she reached out and seized him by the shoulders and shook him.

'What do you mean you won't leave here? What do you mean? Where can you stay? With what? With whom?' I was afraid she would bite her tongue in two as she rocked him back and forth against the bench. 'What are you talking about?' The drunk got up quickly, shook himself, and disappeared; the soldier from Missouri drew back from the conflict.

'Here now,' my father responded, trying to hold his hat on. 'Look out there.'

'You foolish man,' my mother continued to wool him about. 'You silly, foolish man! What do you mean, you won't go?'

'Now, just a minute,' my father said in a small, reasonable voice.

'Stand up,' my mother commanded. The soldier almost obeyed. 'Stand up. I want to get to the train early to make sure we get seats.' My father had stood up quickly.

'Well, which way? Which way?' he demanded with an angry impatience, as if he had been waiting for directions all along.

'This way,' she replied and struck off without looking back.

He had gestured for my arm and we followed her, his step remarkably quick and flexible; his movement spurred by an eagerness to quit the site of the fuss. Her public outburst had been guaranteed to stimulate this response, sting that part of his nature that always hoped to avoid a public scene whatever the cost. She was from a different background where there was no such false decorum, no holding back.

We negotiated the stairs down to the track level with a surprising ease, and at the bottom my father even looked around as if for more challenges. My mother was already talking to a conductor, her feet squarely planted before the trainman, a man obviously working beyond his retirement because of the war emergency, who finally threw up his hands and walked away from her.

'There's another one,' she muttered darkly. 'Here, get on.'

'Can we get on?' my father asked, trying to resume a normality between them. 'Is this where we get on?'

'Get on, get on. Here's our redcap. Here we are! Put those on right here.' She pointed to the open vestibule of the coach. 'Right there. Fine. Thank you. Here. This is for you.' He took the tip without looking at it and hurried away.

What the conductor had been trying to explain to her was that the train had been almost completely taken over by the military, and every seat had already been occupied by soldiers with all their gear. Even the aisles were filled.

'Look here—' My mother halted another conductor who had been making his way over the men and baggage slumped in the aisle. 'You must find us some seats.' He shrugged and began to move around us. 'I have a sick man here,' her voice began to rise. 'My husband is just out of the hospital. You'll have to find a seat for him.' It looked like she was about to grab him by the shoulders and shake him also until a couple of soldiers jumped up and offered their places. 'Oh my,' her eyes softened, her whole posture melted, a helpless woman, 'isn't that nice of you? Thank you, so much. Here, Lee, these nice young men have given us their seats.'

I rode in the vestibule, standing or sitting on our luggage the whole way to North Carolina, and that was all right, for I was able to smoke the cigarettes I had hidden under my shirt and I could listen to the stories of the soldiers who shared the space with me.

*　　　*　　　*

'Those Japs made a mistake chasing MacArthur out of the Philippines,' my grandfather says. 'It was like a second home for him. His father set up an empire there for himself.' He had brought two glasses of beer to the table. We sat in the small canteen located in the basement of one of the hospital buildings. 'No, that only made him mad, so he just wore 'em down—just like his father did with the Sioux, like Crook did the Apache. Truman had no need to drop that bomb.'

He tilts the glass to funnel the beer in almost one long draught into his mouth in the same way he used to down a concoction of Bromo-Seltzer every night in Kansas City. 'But there's one thing to be said. All the shooting is over now that you're in the service. I'm glad for that. But why the navy?' He laughs and wipes the small moustache he keeps above his lips. The eyes have cooled, his mind has slid back to the subject of my visit.

'Those Goddamned Moynihans. I wish to God I never laid eyes on them. I spent a fortune on them. Took care of that old man, gave him a place to live. I lost a fortune on them. You don't know what it was like with your grandmother out there. The house had become filthy. She was filthy. Stayed in bed the whole time. Eggs and oatmeal and hamburger were our meals.' He laughs, such fare still unbelievable. 'Never washed herself. Never looked after the place. I had to do everything. Do it all. Blue balls of fire, I'm eighty-seven, maybe ninety years of age— I don't know how old. I can't do it anymore.' His brow hoods the fierce eyes. 'Well, your mother can have her. Where in hell can they all live? Your father is not well, I guess. How can she take care of them both and still meet her classes?'

'The college provides a small apartment,' I tell him. 'She can manage. I'm only home a little bit now, and use a couch in the apartment above.'

'By Jesus Christ.' There's wonder, a curious admiration in his half-laugh. 'She just rolls over everything like a steam roller.' I finish the beer in my glass as he stands abruptly. 'Tell her I can't help her. I've done all I can. There comes a time when you have to cut your way out, if you have the equipment. I did my best in Kansas City and that wasn't good enough. She can do it now.'

*   *   *

What appeared to my grandfather, to all of us sometimes, to be an all-out assault, an interference with our lives, was really the manifestation of my mother's frantic efforts to keep those lives going on a day-to-day basis. She had begun that juggling act that was to go on for the next several years, the last years, and it was rehearsed in the small hotel room she had rented after we arrived in Charlotte.

'We have everything we need here,' my father would dictate as he sat by the room's window that overlooked an old church yard. *'There's good food in the hotel restaurant downstairs. I spend the day reading or working. Ellen is busy with her English classes and can bring me any book I want from the library. Hilary is attending a college nearby. The beds are fine and we have good sleeps.'*

He sent out the same message to relatives and acquaintances, or even to strangers who had written him on his receipt of an award from the American Academy of Poets.

'All right, now, who else?' my mother would say as she typed an address on an envelope.

'Oh, that's all for tonight,' he'd answer, drawing deep on the pipe. It had gone out and he would sort through the papers and books on the table next to him for matches.

'What about . . . ?' and she would suggest another correspondent.

'Oh, let's do him tomorrow.' He picked up a book from the table. 'You have your own papers to do.'

'Let's do him now. Get him out of the way,' she said firmly and rolled a fresh piece of hotel stationery into the portable machine.

'Well, all right. Give him the same one,' he replied, no longer interested. He looked over at me. 'Where are you staying tonight, It?' I sat on one of the twin beds that were crammed into the room along with two steamer trunks, a bureau, a table, and two chairs seemingly wedged into the space as a concession.

'I'm just down the hall,' I replied. When I came home for a

weekend, my mother would arrange with the hotel to set up a cot in a large sample room where traveling salesmen, on weekdays, would lay out their wares on large sheets of plywood placed upon sawhorses. By contrast, my room would be vast and empty.

'Now you have to sign these.' She had handed him several letters.

'By God, you really go to it, don't you?'' He laughed with admiration.

'Someone has to,' she replied with a mock severity and then a playful expression came over her as she lifted up the letters when he had finished. 'Say, let me tell you what happened today.' He responded to her eagerness by putting aside his book and shifting in his chair to prepare for the story.

'Now then, you remember what the director said to me about my classes and how certain people . . . well,' and then a bark of a narrative would be launched on which she took all the roles; deep-voiced, 'Mrs. Masters, you don't mean to say,' or suddenly chandelled to a wee register to imitate another. 'That's the way she talks,' my mother would assure him, 'she even holds her hands up like this, like a chipmunk—and then, and then, oh wait until you hear this'—a slight pause to go to another part of the story—'while all this was going on here—down in the office,' several skits put in motion, all running simultaneously, the whole tale observing the classical pattern she taught in class, climax followed by a resolution, supplementary clauses everywhere turning on irony, lubricated by wit, every scene given its time on the stage by the bathroom door. 'No, wait. Wait,' she commands as my father's laughter deepens, his paunch quakes. 'Wait, not yet—you haven't heard the best yet—here we are, standing there. My dear, you couldn't believe my astonishment,' and her face breaks into a geode of surprise, and she pauses, leans against the doorway, then delivers the final line that brings down the house. 'Now isn't that something. Isn't that dreadful?' She kicks off her shoes and joins our laughter.

Every day there would be some scrap of academic politics, a piece of student folly, some incident that had caught on the fiber of her imagination and which she would reproduce with a gush: 'Wait'll you hear!' She would take her position by the proscenium of the open steamer trunk in the same way, a couple of years later, she'd stand in the middle of the cluttered but cozy living room of the small faculty apartment at the junior college near Philadelphia. 'Now listen to this!' she'd strike the overture and my father would lay aside his book, relight his pipe. His eyes would already glow.

By then, my grandmother would also be in the audience, but a darkness had slid over her eyes and into her ears and mind, so that she was only able to follow the dazzling shadows of my mother's gestures, responding instinctively at the right moment, perhaps the old habits of a committeewoman prompting her to react to the rhythm of the monologue rather than its substance. 'Oh, Fay-fay,' she would exclaim, using the family diminutive. 'Oh dear,' she'd half laugh and look around the room for the ghosts of loyal workers to follow her lead, imitate her response.

She herself resembled a ghost: a tall, thin negative of her former rosy contours, and there was no soft place about her but only the bony angles of her wasted body and arthritic hands. Her skeleton threatened to poke through the envelope of her skin and, in fact, she had stuffed wads of toilet tissue or scraps of material into her stockings at the knee to cushion her bones when she knelt on the floor to inspect the run-off tray beneath the old-fashioned ice chest my mother had installed in the hallway.

The imperious woman who owned and presided over this junior college, a place for rich and weary girls, made no provision for a kitchen in this faculty apartment, though my mother was invited to take her meals in the student dining room. The invitation was also extended to my father and grandmother, but it was impossible for them to accept, so my mother plugged together a series of hot plates in the hallway to develop a unique if not surreptitious cuisine. She had also located a small, top-loading, old-fashioned icebox made of wood.

'It will make a nice planter,' she firmly answered the suspicions of the faculty couple who lived on the first floor below. The box had just been carried through their foyer and up our stairs. She never bothered to explain or even acknowledge the ice deliveries.

'By God, she's at that thing every five minutes,' my father would report when my mother returned from school. He sat in a metal lawn chair placed beside the window and his old writing table, retrieved from storage. 'I can see her from here. She moves like smoke—I wish to God I could move around the way she does —and when I look up, there she comes again. Down on her knees. Out comes the pan. There's not more than a spoonful of water in it when she brings it into the bathroom.'

'She's only supposed to check it once a day,' my mother said. 'It gives her something to do.'

'She do it,' my father laughed.

It had been my mother, remember, who had forced my grandmother to exchange the old icebox in Kansas City for the electric refrigerator from Montgomery Ward and perhaps the anxiousness that brought her so often to the task of emptying that drain pan in the hallway was pricked by a memory of that old time: perhaps she had lingered too long at some meeting, had indulged herself, only to return home to find Tom Coyne mopping up the kitchen floor, his eyes as icy as the water on the linoleum. Perhaps now, as she came to this icebox, whispering like a druid on the way to a hollow oak, perhaps now as she knelt on her padded knees to find the tray almost empty she could tell herself that she had beaten him home again and again, and yet again.

For even from the Soldiers Home, he could harry her by his absence, a physical absence at last accompanying the spirit's exile that had gone before, so she constructed a husk of apprehension

[195]

in order to press a form, something, from the nothingness of their lives.

In a different way, my father's serene presence in his metal chair rocked and bobbed in my mother's consciousness as he smoked and read every day, all day, by the window, passing into a reverie of words as my grandfather had withdrawn into a Valhalla of memories. Sometimes, I would see him read one of his own poems or pieces of prose over and over, as if to discover how they had been written. There were no more arguments. He had surrendered to the circumstances of his age and condition, though sometimes a wry light would come into his eyes as if he might be plotting some escape out the window, might throw himself out the window as he had thrown a pair of Oriental rugs out the window of that Chicago mansion thirty years before, to smuggle them downtown for quick cash and temporarily evade the harsh financial strictures of that divorce settlement.

Whatever his expressions or the thoughts behind them, his being alive to have such expressions and thoughts reminded my mother of her responsibility for him. She worked to provide him good food, good company, and, when needed, good medical care; worked with an attention to detail as if she might be called upon to offer proof, be asked to open up the books on his miraculous recovery by a surprise audit.

It was no coincidence, I believe, that most visits from friends or relatives, interviews with journalists or scholars, were scheduled in the summer months, after the three of them had moved for the school's recess into a stone mansion put at their disposal by the college president. During the school year, its thirty rooms were turned into a dormitory, but during summer vacation its sunny porches, sunken living rooms and library, and the prospects of the extensive grounds from French windows provided a refreshing change from the small apartment my parents and grandmother shared in the winter. My grandmother roamed from room to room on the third floor, day and night.

'We have everything we need here,' my father would say to the journalist-scholar. They would be sitting on the outside terrace that resembled the second-act set of an old melodrama, the place where lovers always took their misunderstandings.

'I dare say,' the person would reply. 'Tell me. Does this—I mean does this, this house . . .?' He would wave his hand to encompass the grounds, the stonework, and mullioned window casements.

'It all comes with her job,' my father would say casually. A groundskeeper, one of the school's maintenance men, turned a small mowing tractor at the far end of the broad lawn.

'It must be quite a job,' the interviewer would say. His eyes had lifted above, to measure the rise of the mansion's floors and linger on the tile roof. Something had caught his gaze in one of the top windows, a flicker of a face, something, then was gone. 'She teaches . . .'

'She's a marvelous woman,' my father dictates. They both look at her. She is on the other end of the terrace, cutting roses. 'I would have died like a dog if it hadn't been for her. She's from Missouri, you know, and has that determination. Her father was a soldier on the frontier; also a builder of railroads in South America.'

'Yes, how interesting. Can we talk about your early influences? Whitman, of course, and then . . .'

'There were many. Chicago was a boiling pot.' My father's voice is flat, matter-of-fact, but he continues to observe my mother as she clips another rose. She looks rested, relaxed, and wears silver bracelets and a seersucker dress. 'It was also a place of leeches.'

'Leeches?' The scholar leans forward.

'Yes. They would get their suction on you. Some of them never let go. Take Sandburg, for example. He follows me everywhere I go. He followed me down to North Carolina, you know.'

'Really?'

'Now, Lee'—my mother has joined them—'you don't really mean that.' She laughs a little and looks at the reporter, though her expression does not entirely discredit the idea.

'Why, he's followed me everywhere since I left Chicago. When we went down to North Carolina, didn't I tell you he'd show up? Didn't I?'

'I guess you did.' She laughs again.

'Sometimes, I look out there of a morning and half expect him to pop up here, too.' The group turns as one to regard the immense slope of lawn, the formal garden and hedgerows, perhaps to see a head of thick white hair suddenly appear.

'Here's Virginia.' My mother would break the spell. She had hired this woman several days a week to keep the house and cook some meals, or for such occasions as this interview when she would appear in one of the open French doors with a tea cart.

'What do you have there?' my father would inquire pleasantly.

'We got blueberry muffins today, Mistuh Mastuhs,' Virginia would reply. She was aware of the role, seemed to enjoy playing it. 'I remembered you liked them last time.'

'Ah!' My father's head would accept her thoughtfulness with a nod. 'Virginia's a great help to us here,' he'd say authoritatively. 'Almost one of the family.'

'That's right,' Virginia would say. 'Anything else, Miz Mastuhs?'

'No, thank you, Virginia. Do have one of these muffins,' the visitor would be told. 'Or perhaps some of this cake. Milk or lemon?' The interviewer would be loaded up, have to juggle cup, plate, and notebook—finally putting aside the latter, along with any possibility of writing anything down other than what my mother wished him to write, and perhaps this was her ultimate provision: to give my father a sunny, tranquil place from which he could send out the word, 'We have everything we need here.'

There is time, then, to make one last picture. It is a group picture, one of the few we were to make together; it does not include my grandfather, but the particles of his presence will linger in the air as if he had only just stepped out of the room, beyond the frame.

It would be winter. My mother has borrowed a car to meet my train at North Philadelphia, and she manages to drive and talk, to shift gears and change topics with a fluid power, a narrative that can never be overtaken, that never needs to refuel.

'Well, how is he?' she asks about my grandfather. I have just visited him at the Soldiers Home. 'He'd never think of sending a note. The great hero. Napoleon at Elba, I suppose. You'll notice a change in your father. His walking has become poorer and his alimentary functions—well, I don't know how much longer I'll be able to take care of him at home. My schedule this term is very heavy, now that I'm chairman of the department. I know your grandfather gives you money. I hope you are saving it. We'll need all we can save. Oscar Williams is going to use more poems in his next anthology, also there's a new German translation being done and we heard today about an opera based on some of the poems—that's in Italy. I don't know what to do with your grandmother, you'll see for yourself. Well, what can I do? These people all just collapsed in the middle of the floor on me. She eats very little. Says her new teeth hurt her. I guess they do. You wouldn't believe the correspondence I had to do this week. The requests for your father's work have risen quite a bit. We ask a fixed amount for the poems in anthologies, but I charge very little for textbooks. It's important that he's read in schools. I don't suppose the great hero said anything about the furniture he left behind on Roberts Street, did he? That highboy secretary. There was that walnut desk and cabinet—you remember that, those cartoon books you used to look at were in the bottom of it—you see, none of it belonged to him, but so what? That didn't matter to him. Then your grandmother. You wouldn't believe the scene I was met with. My mother eating out of a wooden bowl with a wooden spoon! She probably raised money for this place when she was president of the Daughters of Isabella. That's where he had put her—like a castoff. What was I to do? They all

just fell in on me. Oh, yes—you have a bed in the apartment upstairs. We have a holiday now and Dr. Mitchell is away, so you
have it to yourself. Now one thing more: don't talk to the people
downstairs, if they are around. You wouldn't believe what happened. I came home the other day to find him upstairs, sketching
your father. Not a word to me about it, no permission, nothing.
Very bold. Now, here we are. Remember, go right upstairs.
Don't even say hello if they're around.'

Her manner softens once we gain the realm of our second floor
and she assumes a passive, almost seconding role. There is also
something of the camp counselor, a cheery authority that em-
braces and directs her charges all at once. She turns to the dinner's preparation as I pass through the bony turnstile of my
grandmother's embrace. Unaccountably, she was aware of my
arrival and had been waiting at the top of the steps.

'There you are, Mr. It.' My father waves to me from the metal
chair in the bedroom. 'Just in time. This Goddamn pipe can't
be smoked. It's all plugged up.' I kiss him. There are bits of
toilet paper stuck to his cheeks where he had nicked the flesh
while shaving. 'What do they say on that newspaper of yours
about Truman? I'm afraid this Dewey is going to get him. Then
there'll be hell to pay.' We pass small talk as I scoop out the tar
that has clogged up the brier. The heady tobacco aroma is laced
with an astringent smell that rises from his clothes. 'Thank you.'
He puts the pipe stem in his lips and makes several toots.
'That's the stuff. Say, there's something else you can fix. That
phonograph over there. It's stopped working.'

He packs the cleaned pipe bowl with fresh tobacco and lights
up as I bend over the simple equipment. It is a plain turntable
and amplifier. There is a scrape of cutlery, a kiss of metal pans
in the hallway; then, the pleasing stutter of escaping steam as
the pressure cookers begin to hiss on their roost of hot plates.
The windows fog up and the small apartment is cozied with
moist fragrances.

'Tell your father about your advancement on the newspaper,' my mother shouts from the hallway. My mother was never comfortable with silence and the silence in the bedroom, as he smoked and I reconnected the phonograph, was to be discouraged. He is mildly interested in the fact that the Washington newspaper that employs me as a copy boy has permitted me to do the weather and a few obituaries.

'Fixed?' he asks. 'What was it?'

'Just a loose connection. Want to play something?'

'There's some Sibelius there. Let's hear some of that.' These are heavy, shellac records that turn at 78 rpm as the needle transmits a grandiose passage, threatening to burst the fragile plastic of the radio. The lower register of the arrangement is homogenized thunder. 'Say, Ellen,' he calls. She comes into the room, a potholder in one hand. 'Any of that applejack left?'

'Good idea,' she says and turns back. We hear her in the living room. 'Maw,' she shouts. 'Come into the bedroom. We're going to have a drink before dinner.'

'A drink?' my grandmother says with feigned astonishment. 'Oh, Fay-fay. Do you think we . . .'

'C'mon,' my mother urges. There's the clink of glassware, bottles. Their steps approach. 'No, don't stop. It's all right.'

'It might spill over,' my grandmother protests.

'It's all right. Keep moving.'

My father chuckles. He's been able to see through to the hall from where he sits. 'She's at that ice tray morning, noon, and night,' he says to me, then shouts, 'Hello there, Mollie,' as my grandmother pauses at the door of the room. He greets her as if they had just met after an absence of years, though they spend every day together in this three-room apartment. 'Come in. Come in,' he says in a tone that strives to be gracious while still reaching through her deafness.

Shyly, she sits in a straight-back chair that complements her rail of a body. Her legs wind around each other and one hand lifts to cover her face though it cannot hide the ceaseless movement of her jaw as her gums work against themselves. There is sherry for her. She watches as my mother pours some in a glass, a keen eye peering through the screen of fingers to appraise the level. 'Oh my,' she expresses alarm as my mother nudges her. 'That's too much, isn't it?' she asks almost hopefully but, after a small but perfected display of distaste, downs the wine like medicine—something to be swallowed and done with. She makes a slight burp as she fits the glass to the precise edge of the table, a ladylike suggestion of duty performed. 'Hilary's not in the navy anymore?' she asks, suddenly discerning my civilian clothes.

'No,' my mother shouts. She hands my father a glass of whiskey. 'He's working on a newspaper. In Washington.'

'Washington,' my grandmother repeats. Her jaws work—then stop working—then start working. 'Washington? Do you—have you—is he . . .''

'I just saw Gee Gee,' I yell across the room. 'He's in the hospital.'

'Hospital?' she says, alarmed.

'He's all right,' my mother assures her. 'It's just the way they live there. He takes care of himself, don't worry.' Abruptly, my grandmother covers her face again and falls silent.

'This is good stuff.' My father smacks his lips over the glass. 'But not like what we would get in Hillsdale.'

'That *was* good,' my mother agrees. She lounges against the edge of the large bed my father uses. There's a dish towel over one arm and a drink in the other hand. 'In fact, it was supposed to have saved my life that time the rattlesnake bit me. You remember that, Hilary?'

Yes, I remember. We had gone berry picking one afternoon. I was standing next to her when she moved deeper into the brush. There had been the sound of dried peas when the snake struck. 'Of course, that was the worst thing to do,' I say. 'Drink any kind of alcohol.'

'I don't know,' she replies with a speculative rise. 'Then your father put some tobacco on it.'

'Yes, I cut the fang marks and made a poultice of Prince Albert. We got back to the house and took out the homemade applejack. Why, hell, we cured the bite in no time. No problem at all.'

'No problem?' My mother guffaws. 'My leg turned coal black, that was all.'

'Wonder what happened to that snake?' he says, a light in his eyes.

'It died.' She laughs in bursts. 'It died from the bite.'

'We had some good times. There was Felix and Hartigan and the old Doc who sewed up your knee that time. Do you remember those times, Hilary? I did good work up there.' He reached for one of the several books piled on the table beside him. It was the table that used to be centered in the bay window of the Chelsea rooms, where I would see him work in the morning.

'Read something,' my mother says. She motions for me to lift the record player's arm, as he starts to turn the pages of a book entitled *More People,* then comes back to the first page. He looks pleased and happy, and begins to read in that quick, falling drone of a voice in which he always read his work, as if to give an inflection or dramatic emphasis would be to take an unfair advantage of the listener.

> This is the spot where Black Hawk, fully dressed
> In the uniform that Andrew Jackson gave,
> Was buried upright, this is that West
> Which cured at last his wrong, his heart's unrest,
> The wound of loneliness in his hawk-like breast.
> This spot is Black Hawk's grave.
>
> His body became a fellow to the rain,
> And prairie winds . . .

It is a long poem and one of the best of his late years, its theme the waste and betrayal of the American spirit, the soil and soul of America. He reads rapidly, pausing only to take a deep breath at each stanza's end, no rest on the rhyme or caesura. My mother listens with half-closed eyes, pleasure in all the lines of her face, like a student mesmerized by his mind's play and never cool to his accomplishments. That afternoon my grandfather had also spoken of the Indians, different from the Saux and Fox my father wrote about in this poem, but with the same fate. I had heard him out, listening to the usual litany of sorrow and praise he delivered over one civilization he had helped put down in order to be accepted by another, patiently listened to Gee Gee, as I heard my father address the settlers' grab of the rich soil of the Illinois prairie, patiently listened to my grandfather until that point of departure came round, that poor moment between us when he would slip a stiff pension check from its envelope and sign it over to me. There were debts to be paid.

'Hello, up there.' It is a man's voice from the bottom of the stairs. My mother's face twists to one side.

'Now, who can that be?' she mutters, though her sour expression betrays her knowledge. 'Just a minute,' she cries in a gay voice and leaves the room.

'We seem to have blown a fuse,' the man's voice says from below.

'Oh my,' my mother replies, struck with wonder. 'What can be the matter? It must be the smothered cabbage,' she tells him graciously. 'But it's done, anyway. You can put another fuse in and I'll turn them off. I'm sure they're done. Thank you.' The door below is closed without a word.

My father has paused, looked sternly over the top of his glasses toward the source of the interruption (he must have glared the same way, twenty years before, when the rustlings of late arrivals disturbed his readings), but then he takes up the poem again, continues through the exchange with the man downstairs and while my mother completes the meal's preparations. He reads to

me and he reads to himself, but mostly to himself. My grandmother, one hand over her face, continues to chew her gums.

'. . . as they starved Chief Black Hawk, so they killed
The land they took. They did not fertilize as they tilled;
They scooped the strip mines leaving deep ravines,
Where once the banners of corn unfurled,
While cities shot up to the sky, the world
Became their province, conquered by machines.

The Land was lost to Black Hawk, then to us
Through years calamitous—
The White man now needs corn.'

He reads the last lines rapidly, almost garbles them, as if he
were aware of the end of the poem and wished to get it over with
or as if he had suddenly become bored with the recitation, with
listening to his own words. He snaps the book shut and tosses it
onto the table, but there is a curious, shy bravado in the gesture,
as if he has made his statement and that is all there is to it. He
pulls on the cold pipe a few times, then puts a match to it to raise
a screen of smoke around himself.

'Yes. Yes,' my mother says from the doorway. Her face has
taken on that half-closed, intense expression. 'Those were terrible days. I remember all those farms when we drove across the
country to Hillsdale that summer—all going into dust. The
drought was terrible. The dust bowl.'

'We still need corn,' my father replies, taking the pipe from
his mouth and scratching the skin of his scalp. He inspects his
fingernail. 'Still need it.' He puffs.

'Well, we have some supper ready,' my mother says. 'Come into
the living room.' She touches my grandmother under an elbow,
and my grandmother rises immediately, as if she had been waiting for this signal. The two women leave the room.

I help my father rise from his chair. 'That's called an inverse

construction, isn't it?' I say. 'That line about the "years calamitous"?'

He is half risen from the chair, knees bent. My question seems
to have stuck him in that position. 'Oh, is that it?' he says, a dan-
gerous dryness in his voice. 'Is that what it's called?'

'Yes. It's when the adjective or modifier follows the object.'
We walk through the bathroom that joins the bedroom to the
rest of the apartment. 'They used it a lot in . . .'

'In that line, the force of the poem's meaning is in the word
calamitous, which is why it is singled out and given that importance. A mistake was made, some time ago, that took the
Latin *calamus* to mean corn being turned into straw, made use-
less stuff by drought or mildew . . . those were some of my con-
siderations with the usage you question.'

There is a small step down into the living room, and I support
his entire weight as he edges one foot over the sill, the knee of the
other leg slowly bending, the torso sinking to a lower level. My
mother has set places at the large cherry table, also a familiar
landmark within those rooms at the Chelsea and now returned
from storage. A candle burns in one of the two heavy brass Russian candlesticks. There's a mixture of plate and glassware and
dishes of beef brisket with horseradish sauce, potatoes, green
beans, and smothered cabbage. There are sweet potatoes also.
'They don't go with the rest of the meal,' she says, 'but your
grandmother can eat them without her teeth. There's gingerbread and applesauce for dessert.'

My grandmother is already at the table, trying not to appear
too eager, disguising her anticipation with the remnants of good
manners as she unfolds and pulls the napkin across her lap; a
parody of the old full-fleshed smile pries apart her sunken
mouth. The depth of her brown eyes pulls at my every move.
My father has sat at one end and hooks his cane over the edge of
the table. He tucks the napkin under his chin. 'Well, how are
you, Mollie?' he shouts.

'Yes. Fine, thank you,' she replies in a mellow voice. She is uncomfortable, uneasy that he has addressed her directly. She clears her throat, importantly, as if she might stand to offer an amendment but then passes a hand beneath the collar of her dress to look for an undergarment strap to adjust.

'Now, you're going to have to move that cane. I've told you about that before,' my mother says as she arrives with a basket of hot rolls.

'You're the boss,' he says, putting the stick between his knees.

'By God, this is a feast. We eat pretty well here, Mr. It. Your ma does wonders in that kitchen she's rigged up.'

'If I don't burn the house down.' She laughs and takes her place. 'We have beer. Anyone want a beer?'

'A bee-ah,' my father drawls in a way I remember from times past. He has used a lot of sauce on his beef; it's one of his favorite meals. There's little talk until dessert and coffee. My grandmother leans toward my mother and whispers something behind knotted fingers.

'Yes. Yes . . .' My mother nods. Then, to me. 'She wants to know if you've seen Gee Gee.'

'Yes, I saw him today.'

My grandmother's eyes twinkle, her expression acknowledges the joke. She would be glad to share it if only someone would let her in on it. She turns to my mother. 'Did he really see him today?'

'Yes,' my mother says mechanically, tired of the subject. My grandmother covers her face and starts to work her jaw. 'Tell us about your work,' my mother says to me.

My narrative is brief, the same circumscribed report made to parents by every child away from home in a big city. 'What have you been reading?' my father asks.

'I checked *Ulysses* out of the library this week.'

'Odysseus?' he asks, leaning toward me.

'No. *Ulysses* by James Joyce.'

'You remember Padraic and Molly Colum talked about James Joyce,' my mother reminds him. He nods and picks up some crumbs of gingerbread from the plate. 'Oh, I didn't tell you what happened at the school post office the other day,' and she commences another of her inventions that transforms the event into the evening's entertainment.

'That's the stuff,' my father responds at one point in her story, as if she were a heroine in a play outwitting some evil circumstance.

In fact, she put together a stock company for his diversion every evening, using the old techniques and devices remembered from when she toured *Cappy Ricks,* stepping into all the parts in that book-jammed living room with the same expression of delight she must have worn when she stepped off the train into the one-night stands of those small Western towns, a look that already celebrated the pleasure her part would bring.

I would help her clean up after supper, doing the dishes and washing the pots and pans in the bathtub and small sink. My father would move into a large easy chair and fall to reading. My grandmother would fold herself into the corner of the daybed she would use that night, though I wondered if she ever slept at all, if I would find her lying in the moonlight, her face moving in hinged rhythm. As a child I had lain against her to ease a midnight cramp, gentle a nightmare.

My mother grades papers at the cherry table which, cleared of dinner, is returned to a usage that goes with the room. My father reads and smokes. He chooses an anthology of poetry or a collection of essays, perhaps a memoir, but never a long, sustained work. Never anything current. I take a book from the small library that is stacked on window ledges, chair seats, and all other available surface space, in addition to the two or three bookcases. It is a small library for a man of his years and profession, though it is a select one and one that has been concentrated, it might be said, by the existencies of his life's journey, by the many departures he has made since his first arrival in Chicago with that original small collection in his satchel.

As we sit for this last picture, each of us in this room has been similarly reduced, our lives slowly coming together, reduced to this peaceful essence layered by fragrant pipe smoke, this remedy of time that my mother's pen stroke seems to prescribe with each scratch upon a term paper. My travels are over.

There is no great distance now for me to cross between them. I look up from the book I read, my attention blinded by this revealing star, for to pass between them, if only in this inner space, is to separate them from me as I once held their separations together.

My father has lowered his book and holds the pipe in one hand as he looks at the portrait of himself done by Gordon Stevenson. It hangs on the wall behind my mother; on the bookcase shelf beneath it is a vase with spires of dried bittersweet. The painting is a good likeness, though the color is a little high, and the pose is the same natural position he has unconsciously taken in the armchair. There is a speculative look in his eyes as he studies his own image, almost a weight of recollection, and the portrait returns the same bemused regard, looking out from the canvas upon its own model, not to judge the prototype, but to observe some change in him. There has been little change since the picture was painted many years before; they are like twin brothers greeting each other after a long absence. In fact, I begin to wonder which of them will resume reading, will lift his book first.

But before that happens, my mother has also looked up from her school work, pulled away possibly by the silent alarm that had startled me. Her pen is poised over a student's essay but she marks my father's gaze, his expression and all his features. Her expression is bland, the deep circles beneath her eyes more pronounced, but a light in those eyes surpasses the intensity that travels between him and the face in the painting. Her look explores him. It explores her history with him. It explores all that has happened to him and to her because of him and—like the portrait behind her, but for a different reason—makes no judgments.

Afterword

Even after three novels published—and one of these offered by the Book-of-the-Month Club as well as optioned for a film—it became apparent that my kind of writing was not going to support my family or even measurably contribute to its sustenance. Surveys conducted by the Authors Guild produced figures that confirmed this perception—the average annual income of its membership from writing amounted to a little more than $4,000. The idea had already been current in my wife's family. ("What does Hilary *do*?") And then one evening my wife said to me, "Get a job." And she said it once more.

So, in 1975 I accepted an invitation from Drake University in Des Moines, Iowa, to come be their visiting writer-in-residence, and this appointment was to initiate a ten-year itinerary that took me from one campus to another, the back seat of my car a clatter of pots and pans, a duffel of clothing, folders of manuscripts, and my Olympia standard typewriter. A lot of us were on the road and still are.

I left New York, and by the time I crossed the Mississippi at St. Louis, this enterprise had already begun to pull apart the very family unit I had hoped it would sustain, for at the end of this decade of apprenticeship in academia, we were no longer sharing the same rooms. I did not know this then as I crossed the great river and headed northwest on Route 40 toward Kansas City, my birthplace. Nor do I remember entertaining the too easy irony of the situation or any suspicion that this journey west, this travel back into the neighborhood of my past, would separate me in more ways than anticipated from wife and children. I do remember being grateful for the job and lifted by the sense that some people in Iowa valued my writing. And I am still grateful.

Next to the Olympia in the back seat of the Plymouth were some pages of reminiscence I had begun in New York. Tom Coyne, the grandfather in whose home in Kansas City I grew up, had entertained and thrilled my childhood with the stories of his days on the western frontier with the U.S. Cavalry and with accounts of his adventures as a soldier of fortune-turned-civil engineer in the jungles of Mexico, Central and South America, and on the construction of the Panama Canal. I had wanted to set down these tales of an immigrant finding his way in the New World for the benefit of my children. His struggle for identity was a story I wanted them to know and cherish, so that their own citizenship—so easily earned—might become meaningful to them, if not enhanced. But these grandfather stories, unique in their separate narratives, lacked a context that would grant them a harmonious assembly. Also, other figures had begun to crowd into the remembrance. My grandmother, my mother, and my father.

How to incorporate these four lives into a single structure began to challenge me as the musty, old Plymouth rolled on mile after mile across Pennsylvania, Ohio, Indiana, and Illinois. Their eccentric histories, their different time frames, would make a logistical nightmare of a straight narrative. The carpentry would be pedestrian and the design gawky. Somewhere along the road—and surely this point of epiphany should have a marker—it occurred to me that I was traveling essentially the same route between New York and Kansas City over which I had shuttled as a child—back and forth from grandparents to parents and then back again; year after year, summer after summer. It wasn't a straight line but one that looped and curved back onto itself, similar to the roads before the interstate highway system. Detours were frequent, and the Greyhound bus that often carried me would have to pull off onto a smaller road for a bit and then find its way back onto the main highway.

So why not route this anthology of four lives the same way? Why not make it a journey sustained by memory, where the sequential is not enforced and chronology has no hands on its clock? The past is always available to be rummaged through as we wish; we confer upon it whatever logic the quotidian seems to require. Or the story.

By the time I drove through Kansas City, in a torrential line squall, I remember, the rough geography of this chronicle had begun to appear before me. In my imagination I had begun to bring together once more the four characters of this disparate family. I walked them alive once more, into the same rooms where I had been their transient witness, and I had already determined to be only a witness. This exercise was going to be not about me, my growing up in various harrowing circumstances (fill in the blanks), but an attempt to put these four people into a fabric of history that would illuminate that history as it revealed their lives.

Once in Des Moines, I set up the Olympia in a corner of the bedroom of a small apartment across from the gymnasium on the Drake campus. I started typing. The words seemed to surface on the paper in the platen by themselves, and if I came to an obstruction, a hole in the facts or a psychological dead end, I would simply go around, making sure the reader would understand the deviation. I could hear the bus driver say, "Folks, the road up ahead is washed out, and we're just going down here through Coal Bluff and be back on the main road in no time."

Three years later, I finished the last page of the memoir in Worcester, Massachusetts, where Clark University had invited me to conduct a fiction-writing seminar. I had pounded the Olympia next to the stove in the kitchen of an unfurnished apartment that had no bed. I slept on the floor on top of my duffel bag and a blanket. It was the winter of the blizzard of 1978, and I cooked a lot of pasta. By now, the manuscript had a title, "Our Hearts Are Drawn to Stars."

My father often recited lines by his favorite poets, Keats, Shelley, and Goethe, and I had picked my title from the German I remember him quoting. "Our hearts are drawn to stars / That want us not." The words seemed to epitomize the longing of my four characters, their struggle for recognition, their yearning for affection. Goethe's words had a ring to them, and their resonance accompanied me through the maze of towering snowbanks that lined the city's streets and lay between my apartment on Benefit Street and the Clark campus. Their eloquent melancholy warmed me, and I also told myself that the metaphor would surely attract the attention of an editor, a publisher, in this era of space exploration. So I put the manuscript in order and entered some of its pages in a contest for new work sponsored by Houghton Mifflin of Boston. The response was positive, and they asked to see the rest of the manuscript. But then—regretfully—they rejected the book, saying the eccentric narrative gave them a problem.

Thus began an odyssey that is not unknown to many writers in America. In the next three years, every major publisher in New York and Boston—some more than once—would read the manuscript. Somewhere along the line, I acquired Felicia Eth, of Writers House, as my agent, and this good woman bore the brunt of the rejection letters that routinely responded to her tireless advocacy. They fill a thick folder in my file cabinet, and the majority seemed to agree that the odd structure of the narrative was too confusing. They didn't get it. These editors dismissed the very quality that critics such as Jonathan Yardley and Donald Hall were to admire later. Their letters, some more cursory than others, now offer a heady elixir for ailing days.

Earlier, I had been corresponding with Nikki Sklar, at David Godine of Boston, about a collection of short fiction that my agent was not interested in representing. Neither Sklar nor Godine was interested in the manuscript either (Stuart Wright was to publish the collection as *Hammertown Tales*), but, Sklar asked, did I have anything else? Of course, I did, and with my agent's knowledge I forwarded the memoir.

It turned out that Sklar was a young intern employed to paw through the slush pile at Godine, probably one of the more elegant dustbins in publishing. She liked the memoir and passed it on to Bill Goodman, a veteran of many years in publishing and now the executive editor of the Boston house. In our first phone call, he compared my work to several classics of the genre—his enthusiasm still embarrasses me—and, yes, they would publish the book. "But we have to change the title," he said. Strangely, I was relieved.

So, it was Goodman who came up with "Last Stands," and I supplied the afterthought "Notes from Memory." Sklar's patient and wise handling of the prose contributed a deft editing. But the manuscript had yet to be reviewed by the surviving member of the quartet—my mother. She had not read any of it and had only been vaguely aware of my project. Her approval was important for several reasons, foremost because she held the copyright on the several letters and poems written by my father that I had put into the story. To my complete dismay, her reaction to the manuscript was violently negative.

She felt I had been critical of my grandparents, that my picture of my father's last days was incorrect and disrespectful, that I had misinterpreted their marriage—yes, there had been a separation, but it had been to further each of their careers—no, the whole thing would not do. No, no, no. She would not give me permission to quote the copyright material.

It was a crushing interview, though the trauma of it was not unfamiliar in the record of our relationship. I remember thinking of the three years of work, of the three years getting the manuscript accepted, and all of it coming to nothing. Of course, I could rewrite portions of the book to remove the actual excerpts from letters and poems, but the flavor they added to those sections was important, and they could not be paraphrased, I argued. Their exact references authenticated the narrative and, not so incidentally, gave dimension to one of the characters—the father figure, her husband. My mother saw none of this, nor did she seem to understand how important this book and its publication might be for me. That morning in my living room, she became for me what the Irish know as "the sow that eats her own farrow."

The next morning in our kitchen, my wife, Polly, denounced her as they had breakfast—my mother was always at her most vulnerable at table. I was not present, and it must have been quite a speech, for my wife's words shamed her, and she reluctantly granted me permission to use my father's material. When the reviews began to appear, she learned that many critics saw her as the important figure in the memoir, and that the same grit and intelligence by which she had kept that earlier family together also energized the narrative. Somehow, reading the manuscript on her own, she had not seen herself in that role.

Nor had that been my intention. Her appearance and eventual command of the narrative forcibly came about as it had in real life. Nor had it been my intention to make my father the central figure, nor is he. As I said earlier, I had hoped to make the grandfather the dominant figure.

It was now the spring of 1982, and I had just finished an assignment at Denver University and was about to drive back east to Ohio University for another gig when the first reviews began to appear. Their favorable reception continued as I prepared to leave for Finland on the first of the year, to take up a residency at the University of Jyväskylä as a Fulbright lecturer. The notices in *Newsweek* and *Time* especially impressed my mother, not so much for the merit they awarded my work, but for the that fact that her son, pictures and all, would be browsed in waiting rooms across America. It was an achievement she couldn't shrug off.

So, some twenty years later, here comes this new edition from Southern Methodist University Press. All the participants moving and talking once again—facing their destinies. When the book opens, three of them have died, but by book's end my stitching and piecing—much like my grandmother's quilting—have brought them back to life, and it turns out that had been my real intention. All four have now fallen silent save in these pages. To preserve them thus is to preserve the love I bear them.

HILARY MASTERS
2004

SELF-PORTRAIT

HILARY MASTERS grew up in Kansas City, Missouri. He is the author of eight novels, two story collections, and a collection of essays. He's been a Fulbright lecturer to Finland and the recipient of Yaddo fellowships and an Award for Literature from the American Academy of Arts & Letters. His essays have been republished in *Best American Essays* and *Anchor Best Essays,* and his short fiction has been cited in *Best American Short Stories* and *Pushcart.* He is professor of English and creative writing at Carnegie Mellon University and lives in Pittsburgh, Pennsylvania.

An acclaimed essayist, film critic, novelist, and poet, PHILLIP LOPATE has written and edited more than a dozen books and contributed to many diverse publications, including *The Art of the Personal Essay* and *The Anchor Essay Annual.* His latest book is *Waterfront: A Journey Around Manhattan.*